EARLY
GARDENING CATALOGUES

A

Other Books by John Harvey:

HENRY YEVELE
GOTHIC ENGLAND
THE PLANTAGENETS
DUBLIN
TUDOR ARCHITECTURE
THE ENGLISH CATHEDRALS
THE GOTHIC WORLD
ENGLISH MEDIAEVAL ARCHITECTS
A PORTRAIT OF ENGLISH CATHEDRALS
THE CATHEDRALS OF SPAIN
THE MASTER BUILDERS

bibliographies:
ENGLISH CATHEDRALS — A READER'S GUIDE
CONSERVATION OF OLD BUILDINGS

revised:
Muirhead's Blue Guides —
NORTHERN SPAIN
SOUTHERN SPAIN

edited with translation:
WILLIAM WORCESTRE: ITINERARIES 1478-1480

The list of subscribers to Robert Furber's *Twelve Months of Flowers* (1730), headed by Frederick, Prince of Wales, the later founder of Kew Gardens.

EARLY

GARDENING CATALOGUES

with complete reprints of
lists and accounts of the
16th – 19th centuries

by

JOHN HARVEY

PHILLIMORE

London and Chichester

1972

Published by
PHILLIMORE & CO. LTD.
Shopwyke Hall, Chichester, Sussex

SBN 85033 021 1

Text set in 9 pt. Baskerville
Printed by Her Majesty's Printers,
Eyre & Spottiswoode Ltd., at Grosvenor Press, Portsmouth

CONTENTS

LIST OF ILLUSTRATIONS

THE ILLUSTRATIONS are reduced from the magnificent series designed by Pieter Casteels and engraved by Henry Fletcher for the famous *Twelve Months of Flowers* issued in 1730 by the great nurseryman Robert Furber of Kensington Gore, pioneer in this of the illustrated catalogue, as he had previously been of the printed catalogue of plants in book form.

The present study is merely a preliminary exploration of this almost uncharted field. It is the result of the accidental discovery that a copy of the priced catalogue of trees and shrubs sold by the famous firm of Telford of York survived in the British Museum. It is of 1775, and though by no means the earliest surviving nurseryman's catalogue, in manuscript or print, it is at least one of the very first to give prices. Even the later, and better arranged, catalogues of the great London firms, generally give no prices until after the opening of the 19th century. The interest of Telfords' catalogue is therefore manifold: it affords an unexpected glimpse into the economics of gardening two centuries ago; it concerns not a metropolitan but a provincial area and is thus genuinely representative of what was available for the ordinary Englishman, from squire to cottager; and it shows the remarkably wide range of woody plants, mostly hardy, which might be bought at surprisingly low prices.

By way of introduction I have brought together comparative material of earlier and contemporary dates, and sketched the main lines of development of the nurseryman's catalogue as a literary form, if it may be dignified by such a description. No attempt has been made to search for parallels abroad[1], though it is to be supposed that important survivals of the same sort must exist in foreign countries and in particular in Holland, where so large a proportion of the early trade in plants and bulbs was concentrated. It is probable that other early price-lists exist in private hands and in local libraries and record repositories, but in view of the difficulty of compiling an exhaustive list of such scattered items it seems permissible to publish this rudimentary survey, hoping to draw attention to a neglected subject.

In the search for catalogues and relevant information I have received help from a great many libraries and institutions, too many to list in full. Notable assistance has been given by several bodies in America, and particularly by the Massachusetts Horticultural Society (through Mr. Henry G. Wendler), the L.H. Bailey Hortorium of Cornell University (Mr. Peter A. Hyypio) and Colonial Williamsburg (Mr. Alden R. Eaton). In Britain I have to thank especially the following libraries and institutions: Bodleian Library, Oxford; Borthwick Institute, York; British Museum; Business Archives Council; Chelsea Physic Garden; the County Record Offices of Essex, Northumberland, Wiltshire, the East and North Ridings of Yorkshire, and the Lincolnshire Archives Office; Garden History Society; Gateshead Borough Libraries; Greater London Record Office; Guildhall Library, London; Historical Manuscripts Commission and National Register of Archives; John Rylands Library, Manchester; Leeds and Liverpool City Libraries; Linnaean Society; London Library; Norwich Central Library; Royal Botanic Gardens, Kew; Royal Horticultural Society (Lindley Library); the Royal Library, Windsor Castle; University Botanic Garden, Cambridge; Victoria and Albert Museum Library; York Minster Library, and the York City Library with its remarkable index to early Newspapers. Several firms of nurserymen and seedsmen have provided valuable

[1] Miss Alice M. Coats has pointed out to me that there are printed catalogues of 1621, 1651 and later, issued by the Paris nurserymen René and Pierre Morin.

A LARGE PROPORTION of all literature meant for reference has always consisted of lists: bibliographies, dictionaries, encyclopaedias are generalized examples of this. Every imaginable subject tends to produce an inventorial literature of its own, and this will fall under two main headings: the scholarly, scientific and permanent on the one hand, and on the other the commercial, empiric and ephemeral. Because of its 'serious' value, items in the first class are carefully preserved from century to century, to form part of the growing corpus of human knowledge. It is quite otherwise with matter in the second category, which has a limited period of obvious utility and is then discarded wholesale. This is intelligible, but unfortunate; for a great deal more of everyday life, human interest, and social history is contained in this great body of ever-changing and continually destroyed writings and printings than might at first sight be supposed.

In certain fields this has, of course, long been recognised. Museum curators have always been aware of the immense value of outdated catalogues, for instance the illustrated catalogue of the Great Exhibition of 1851; railwayacs have never been oblivious of the interest of old timetables, and historians of architecture and art devote a great deal of study to the copy-books which diffused styles in design and, when they happen to have been preserved, price-lists of fittings. Comparatively little attention has so far been paid to another wide field of publications of the same kind, concerned with the raw material for agriculture, forestry and gardening, namely the lists issued by seedsmen, florists and nurserymen.

For the last two centuries the number of firms in Britain concerned with this trade has been very large, and many of them have, for at any rate the last 100 years, distributed large editions of their catalogues every year, or at intervals of a few years. Economy in costs of printing has been and is achieved by several devices: the issue of an unpriced catalogue at fairly long intervals supplemented by annual priced lists; the printing (in former times) of unpriced lists which could be marked up with current prices by hand as required; in recent years by the use of letter-codes for a range of prices, and the issue annually of a fresh key to the actual prices indicated by the letters. Nearly every one of these thousands upon thousands of catalogues, lists, leaflets and code-cards, pouring out year by year, is destroyed. Fortunately a few libraries and societies have made collections, both in Britain and in the United States, and there is at least a representative cross-section of this type of material available for the period since about 1800. This coincides with the great age of plant-exploration and will in due course enable the history of Anglo-Saxon horticulture in that period to be followed in detail. For all periods before the closing years of the 18th century the picture is very different: catalogues or lists recording the prices charged are extremely rare, and even unpriced lists of what was to be had in the trade are very few.

information: among them I would particularly acknowledge historical details received from Messrs. Caldwell & Sons Ltd. of Knutsford, Cheshire; and from Messrs. Finneys Seeds Ltd. of Newcastle-upon-Tyne a copy of their excellent facsimile (1925) of the Catalogue of William Falla & Co. issued in the 1820's. Separate Acknowledgments are given for permission to reproduce or to quote from copyright material.

Personally I wish to place on record my warm thanks to Dr. Keith Allison, Messrs. M.Y. Ashcroft, H.M.G. Baillie, C.B.L. Barr, Geoffrey Beard, F.B. Benger, Hugh Bilbrough, Gavin Bridson, William Brogden, T.S. Cardy, C.E.R. Clarabut, Miss Alice M. Coats, Messrs. J.M. Collinson, R.G.C. Desmond, Dr. F.G. Emmison, Messrs. J.S.L. Gilmour, Peter J. Gwyn, Norman Higson, Dr. Albert E.J. Hollaender, Messrs. John Hopkins, J.L. Howgego, T. Jaine, K. Lemmon, W.G. Mackenzie, R. Mackworth-Young, Miss M. Mauchline, Miss E.D. Mercer, Mr. D.J.H. Michelmore, Miss P. Minay, Mrs. Ann Rycraft, Mrs. K.N. Sanecki, Messrs. Colin Simms, Maurice Smith, K. Spelman, Dr. C. Thacker, Dr. Joan Thirsk, Mr. D.H. Varley, Mrs. Joan Varley, Mr. J.R. Whitehouse and Miss E.J. Willson.

A special debt is owed to Mr. Francis W. Steer (see Appendix VI); to my publishers for their care over the details of production; and to my wife for her help throughout.

John H. Harvey

Postscript This book had already been completed and delivered to the publishers before I learned of the work done by Miss Blanche Henrey on the subject of old gardening catalogues for her book, *A History and Bibliography of British Botanical and Horticultural Books up to 1800* (Oxford University Press, forthcoming). Miss Henrey kindly gives independent confirmation that the catalogues of 1727 issued by Robert Furber (p. 14) seem to be the earliest to survive as separate publications with their own title-pages; and that Northern nurseries were the first to mark prices in their lists of general stock (p. 36). Miss Henrey also points out that Furber's list of Roses (p. 14) was printed at the end of volume II of Miller's *Gardener's and Florist's Dictionary* of 1724; it may never have had independent existence in printed form.

In *The Garden History Society Newsletter*, No. 14, September 1971, p. 11, Mrs. Lesley Bannister quotes from the preface to the translation of La Quintinie's *The Complete Gardiner* (1701) by London and Wise a reference to 'Gentlemen coming to London . . . and observing often that bundles of Trees are standing at the Seeds-Men Shops, or at least meeting with some of their Printed Catalogues, in which they make large offers of . . . Fruit-trees, Flowering Shrubs and Roots . . .' This shows that there were by the end of the 17th century printed lists (probably broadsheets) issued by the London seedsmen (see Chapter II).

Miss R.J. Ensing has generously communicated to me her recent discovery that Robert Furber (see List of Illustrations and pp. 14-15) was buried at St. Mary Abbots, Kensington, on 1 September 1756, aged 82.

ACKNOWLEDGMENTS

ACKNOWLEDGMENT is here made of permissions to reproduce or to quote from copyright material:
Her Majesty the Queen for accounts relating to the stocking of Kew Gardens; His Grace the Duke of Norfolk for the list of F. Mackie; the Rt. Hon. the Lord Monson for the catalogues of Flanagan & Nutting and other material from the Monson archives deposited in the Lincolnshire Archives Office; the Trustees of the British Museum for the catalogues of Telford of York and Perfect of Pontefract; The East Riding Record office for the list of Stephen Garraway and other material from the Grimston papers; the Gateshead Borough Libraries for material from the Ellison Papers; the late Captain R. Hyde Linaker and Liverpool University for Willoughby Aston's letter; the Rev. A.L. Drinkwater for the catalogue of William Lucas; Leeds City Libraries for documents concerning Temple Newsam; the North Riding Record Office for material from the Cholmeley archives; the Northumberland Record Office for items from the Blackett and Delaval archives; Commander Clare Vyner for the Studley Royal accounts; the Borthwick Institute, York, for the garden accounts for Kirkby Overblows Rectory; and the Yorkshire Archaeological Society for various documents in its collections. For permission to include extracts from the account of Edward Fuller of 1697-98 quoted in Appendix II (pp. 63-4) I am indebted to Colonel W. Chandos-Pole, as well as to Mr. Francis Fisher the transcriber and Mr. R.A. Storey of the National Register of Archives, who brought this important document to my notice.

The illustrations have been reproduced from Robert Furber, *Twelve Months of Flowers* (1730), by permission of the Trustees of the British Museum (Natural History).

INTRODUCTION

AT THE START of any discussion it is as well to define the terms used. What is a gardening catalogue? The answer may seem obvious, but any attempt to trace the genus back beyond the quite modern period shows that the precise definition shades off into a limbo of obscurity. Even at the present day there are catalogues issued by commercial firms of nurserymen which, because of rapidly changing prices, do not include any financial terms. In such cases, separate price-lists are issued, generally at yearly intervals. So we find that what is commonly a single item — list with prices — may in fact comprise two quite separate issues, to be used in conjunction with one another. It is usual for the catalogue in such cases — and often otherwise — to contain a great deal of useful information on the plants named. Outstanding examples may give up-to-date botanical nomenclature, a brief description, colour of flowers and fruit, size, and special particulars such as awards from the Royal Horticultural Society. In some way, whether by the use of reference to notes, or by classification, the degree of hardiness is likely to be indicated. Something may be said as to cultivation if individual plants are 'particular', e.g. in requiring lime-free soil, a position in sun or shade; or in objecting to town atmosphere, the drip of trees, or wet or dry root-run. In the case of catalogues of seeds and bulbs the best time to sow or plant will be stated, and probably further information also.

In spite of the many differences between the various kinds of catalogue, all are alike in being based upon a list of species or varieties of plants. The list may, in any given case, be a single unit, or a group of lists classified for a particular purpose. A large firm of general nurserymen may, for example, issue separate catalogues of Fruit Trees, of Ornamental Trees and Shrubs, of Herbaceous Plants, Alpine Plants, Plants for Greenhouse and Conservatory, and Bulbs. A general seedsman may issue a list in a single alphabetical order, or more frequently divided into two parts comprising Flower Seeds and Vegetable Seeds; or very often subdivided into categories of Annuals, Biennials and Perennials, with or without cross-division as Hardy, Half-Hardy, and Tender. Specialist firms may produce catalogues and lists for a small field only, but even within that field, e.g. Clematis, there may be a classification such as that between large-flowered and small-flowered varieties.

Many features of this highly complex modern classification are refinements produced by competition between different dealers, aware of their catalogues as valuable advertisement for their products. It is not intended here to follow out the details of this modern phase of competitive development (for outline, see Appendix VII), but it will be seen that even two centuries ago several important modern tendencies already existed in embryo. The factor of classification goes back very much earlier still and would obviously have arisen as soon as any single business became large enough to deal with a range of seeds or plants wider than a small specialisation. An interesting outcome of research into the background of such lists is the revelation that relatively large businesses in this field already existed well back into the seventeenth century. Since the first of the great waves of plant introductions — from Turkey and southern Europe — took place only during the reign of Elizabeth I, this means that a major industry had come to maturity in well under a hundred years.

There certainly had been seedsmen and nurserymen even before the great enlargement of the number of species cultivated in this country, but they must have operated on a small and local scale. In only a very few large towns can there have been a sufficient demand for stocks of seed and plants to produce firms of dealers. Throughout the Middle Ages, and until the latter part of the 16th century, seeds of vegetables and herbs must have been part of the produce that changed hands in markets and fairs all over the country, while slips and grafts must have been bought from neighbours, exchanged, or possibly in some cases had from the orchards and gardens of monasteries and hospitals. There was at least one important exception to this general rule: as early as the thirteenth century the interest in good varieties of fruit trees, especially pears and apples, had produced an international trade engaged in the import of continental varieties. Nicholas the Fruiterer, who supplied King Edward I with different sorts of fruit, probably had his own orchards, and very likely was concerned in the importation of trees, grafts and seeds. The spread of medieval business in this field is indicated by the appearance in York of Gerard 'le fruter' who took up the freedom to trade in the city in 1322, while Philip 'le fruter de London' became a freeman of York in 1336. The first recorded gardener to be a freeman of York was Gilbert de Ilkley in 1334.

The origins of commercial horticulture in England are then apparent in London by the late 13th century, and in the second city, York, within the next 50 years. This must have been based upon an adequate technical knowledge of that side of gardening we now know as plantsmanship. Independently of the few scientists of the period, mainly physicians, who concerned themselves with botanical studies in any form, the professional gardeners of the later Middle Ages were building up a body of craft information by trial and error, as did the practitioners of all the other medieval crafts and misteries. In the same way too, these practical gardeners achieved a more advanced knowledge (i.e. 'science') of plants than theoretical students of botany were to reach for several hundred years. This was parallel to the way in which lay minstrels expert in the playing of their instruments came to be far ahead, in the development of harmony, of the academic students of Music as a university subject, and to the effective advances in applied geometry made by architects and surveyors, long before an underlying theory had been supplied by professors.

Even though skilled professional gardeners, and an organised trade in plants and seeds, existed by the 14th century, it is not likely that any trade lists as such were produced until long afterwards. Business was no doubt mainly conducted on a basis of the open market and direct supply and demand. Moreover, the total number of field crops and of plants and herbs in normal cultivation, was extremely small. Even in the orchard, there was a manageable quantity of named varieties of apples and pears, and of kinds of grapevines, cherries and other fruits. Yet, although there were as yet no catalogues for strictly business purposes, lists of plants were already being made. These lists came from two different sources, though there was some degree of what, to use an appropriate metaphor, may be called cross-fertilisation.

First there was the main stream of botanical listing which had maintained a continuous, even if tenuous, existence from the period of classical antiquity. Food-plants and medicinal herbs, what may be described as 'plants in the service of man', had been studied by Theophrastus, the 'Father of Botany', in the fourth century B.C., by Dioscorides, an army doctor, in the first century A.D., and by other Greek and Roman naturalists. From them, and from Arabian commentators whose work reached the west in the 12th century, the Middle Ages derived a considerable if rather static knowledge of plants and their uses. Catalogues of plants were drawn up mainly to enumerate their particular virtues, for dietetic and medicinal purposes. Problems of nomenclature arose and were answered by the production of word-lists arranging the names of plants alphabetically in Latin, and setting against each the French and English equivalents. In this connection it must be remembered that while Latin was the international language of learned men, French was the speech of courts, and in England also the language of schools until 1350 and of the courts of law until 1362. The best of the plant lists produced in England was that of Master John Bray (died 1381), physician to Edward III. His list is not merely of medicinal herbs grown in England, but includes plants imported as drugs.

At an earlier date there had been an offshoot from the tradition of medical lists, in the catalogue of herbs which the Emperor Charlemagne included in his Capitulary on towns. These herbs, beginning with the (Madonna) Lily and Roses, were to be grown in a garden in each town throughout his dominions. It is not known how far this regulation was obeyed, but it had at any rate the notional effect of raising a plant catalogue to the level of an imperial decree. It is obvious that the main intention of this law was to make the equivalent of a health service available without being dependent upon uncertain imports. The historical links between Charlemagne and Caliph Harun al-Rashid at Bagdad make it at least possible that this unusual enterprise was promoted by the arrival at Aachen of fresh medical and botanical information from oriental sources. Though outside the Empire, England must have acquired indirect benefits from such legislation through diplomatic and commercial contacts with the Low Countries and the Rhineland. This is in fact demonstrated in the case of the Mediterranean plant Rosemary, sent to England along with a treatise on its virtues by the Countess of Hainault in 1338. Her daughter Philippa, queen of Edward III, frequently crossed the Channel, and her son Lionel was born in Antwerp, and John 'of Gaunt' in Ghent.

It is through this instance of Rosemary that the development of horticultural method in England can best be proved. English translations of the treatise were soon made, and many copies survive. Some of them contain a long appendix on the plant's culture, showing that within the two or three generations after 1338 there had been continuous practical experiments in keeping this tender shrub alive in the open air. It is possible that the gardeners concerned were monks or friars tending infirmary herb-plots, but the extremely practical suggestions on shelter, planting, watering, taking cuttings and general treatment indicate the rise of a quite professional approach. About the same period, the end of the 14th or beginning of the 15th century, a practical guide or 'do-it-yourself' for gardeners was compiled, perhaps originally in Latin. The full text seems to be lost, but the purport survives as *'The Feat of Gardening'*, a handbook in verse by Master John Gardener. This includes both a classificatory approach and a long list of herbs, and exemplifies a thoroughly practical attitude, though it was no doubt influenced by the medical lists from 'scientific' sources. *The Feat of Gardening* represents the second tradition of plant lists in England, directly responsible for the later emergence of the nurseryman's catalogue.

Master John's classification is simple: starting with Trees and their grafting, followed by Vines, it then moves to the Vegetable Garden and takes in the Onion tribe including leek and garlic, then 'Worts' (Cabbages and Kale), and a separate section on Parsley, followed by a long list of Herbs, and with a final treatise on the culture of Saffron. The herbs include not only plants of chiefly medicinal use but also salads such as Lettuce and Cress, and a number of flowering plants which were probably being grown to please the eye rather than for strictly material reasons. The items which we should now regard as essentially belonging to the Flower Garden included: Cowslip, Daffodil, Hollyhock, Honeysuckle, Lavender, Lily, Paeony, Periwinkle, Primrose, Red and White Roses, Scabious, Tutsan (Hypericum androsaemum), Valerian, Violet, Waterlily, and two Ferns, hartstongue and polypody. Several more, undoubtedly grown for use, were also highly decorative, such as Borage, Clary, Foxglove, 'Gladyn' (an Iris, either I. foetidissima or I. pseudacorus), Hyssop, Liverwort (Hepatica), Sage and Southernwood.

Finally, at the close of the Middle Ages, we reach a classified list which at any rate in form is the ancestor of the lists made for commercial purposes by nurserymen and seedsmen (see Appendix I). This list was entered in blank leaves of a manuscript cookery book which seems to have belonged to Thomas Fromond of Carshalton in Surrey, who died in 1543. The list may be slightly earlier than his time, but not before c. 1500. First comes a general list of 'Herbs necessary for a garden by letter', that is to say arranged alphabetically. The same herbs, with a few added afterthoughts, are then arranged in the following classes: for Pottage, for Sauce, for the Cup, for a Salad, to Still (i.e. distil), for Savour and Beauty, Roots for a Garden, and lastly 'also for an Herber (Arbour)'. The total number of kinds of plant listed is 138 against only 97 mentioned in the *Feat of Gardening* of about a century earlier, but not everything is repeated, so that the total number of plants in regular cultivation was even greater. Inclusive of trees that were deliberately planted there must have been quite 200 species available by the reign of Henry VIII.

As far back as the 13th century there are records of prices paid for trees, occasionally plants, and seeds of such crops as corn, peas, beans, onions and the like, but these give hardly any indication of the cost of stocking a garden with herbs, flowering plants, shrubs and climbers or bulbs. Most of the documentary sources that have so far thrown any light on the economics of ornamental gardening in the Middle Ages date from its last phase, in the first half of the 16th century. There are no catalogues or price-lists, but a few accounts of works for Cardinal Wolsey and for Henry VIII show payments for plants and seeds that indicate the existence of established nurserymen and seedsmen around London. In 1515 Wolsey paid 13s. 2d. for 40 Hyssop and Germander plants for the great garden at York Place, Westminster, indicating

1. Pellitory with daisy flowers
2. Winter Aconite.
3. Great early Snow drop.
4. Single Snow drop.
5. White edged Polyanthos.
6. Dou. Peach colour Hepatica.
7. Double blew Violet.
8. Winter blew Hyacinth.

9. Lesser black Hellebor.
10. Dwarf white King Spear.
11. Flex leav'd Jasmine.
12. Red Spring Cyclamen.
13. Acacia or sweet button tree.
14. White Cyclamen.
15. Creeping Borage or buglos.
16. Strip'd Spurge.

17. Lisbon Lemmon tree.
18. Canary Campanula.
19. Dwarf Sichymall.
20. Double Stock.
21. Filberd tree in flower.
22. True Venetian Vetch.
23. Seville Orange.
24. Grey Aloe.

25. Winter white Hyacinth.
26. Spotted Aloe.
27. Narrow curld leav'd Bay.
28. Tree Savory.
29. Triangle Yellow Ficoides.
30. Strip'd Orange.
31. Strip'd candy tuft.
32. Tree Sedum.
33. Single blew Anemone.

JANUARY

Designd by P. Casteels.

From the Collection of Rob.t Furber Gardiner at Kensington 1730.

Engravd by H. Fletcher.

FEBRUARY

From the Collection of Rob.t Furber Gardner at Kensington. 1730.

Drawn by P.t Casteels.

Engrav'd by H. Fletcher.

1 Royal Yellow Auricula	19 White flowering Almond	19 Large leav'd Norway Maple	27 Monument Anemone
2 Dwarf white starry Hyacinth	11 Dwarf blew starry Hyacinth	20 Double pulchra Hyacinth	28 Red flowering Larch tree
3 White Italian Narciss	12 American flowering Maple	21 Queen of France Narciss	29 Blew passe-flower
4 High Admiral Anemone	13 Goldfinch Polyanthos	22 White starr'd flame Tulip	30 Rose Jonker Anemone
5 Rhyven Narciss	14 Larger blew starry Hyacinth	23 Blew Oriental Hyacinth	31 White flowering Larch tree
6 White passe-flower	15 Virginian flowering Maple	24 Single bloody Wall	32 Purple strip'd Anemone
7 White grape flower	16 Narciss of Naples	25 Admiral blew Anemone	33 The Velvet Iris
8 The lesser black Hellebore	17 East Claremont Tulip	26 Bell Hyspice Anemone	34 Jerusalem Cowslip
9 Panac Auricula	18 The checker'd Fritillaria		

MARCH

Designed by P.t Casteels.   From the Collection of Rob.t Furber Gardiner at Kensington 1730   Engrav'd by H. Fletcher

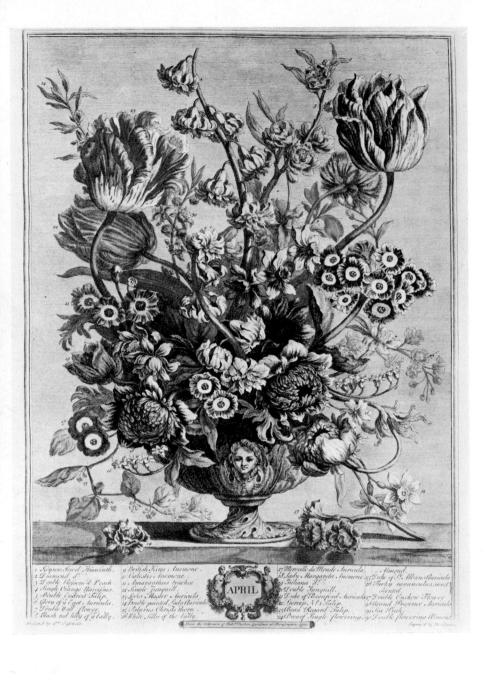

APRIL

a price of 4d. each less a slight discount, and the Master Gardener John Chapman accounted for 4d. spent on Lavender, 1s. 6d. for Thyme and Hyssop (no numbers stated), 4d. for a basket with 'pincrose' (presumably pinks[1]), and several vegetable seeds. Onion seed cost 1s. 8d. a pound, Leek seed 1s. a pound, Sage seed 6d. for (probably) ½ lb., while 3s. covered divers other seeds for the kitchen garden, unspecified.

In the 1530's the detailed accounts for Hampton Court give a much clearer picture of the range of prices, which was very wide. Even allowing for the difference in the value of money, the commoner trees were extremely cheap: quicksets for hedges were bought at 13s. 8d. for 3,000 from Lawrence Vyncent and John Gaddisby of Kingston-upon-Thames, while 6d. each was paid for 67 apple trees supplied by William Gardener, described as a merchant of London. Matthew Garrett, another gardener of Kingston, was paid at the rate of 3d. a day for setting strawberry roots and violet and primrose plants gathered for the gardens. It is not made clear whether the payment covered his work alone, or included the collection of wild strawberry, violet and primrose roots. The latter arrangement would have implied sweated labour, for another man, John Hutton, took 4d. a day for making, levelling and raking beds in the gardens in 1530. Young trees of Oak and Elm cost 12s. 6d. a hundred, but Service trees were 1s 2d. each, and Holly trees 3d. each; but surprisingly enough, trees of Yew, Cypress, Juniper and Bay could be had for 2d., and Cherry trees at 6d. a hundred, though Pear trees were 6d. each. Roses, which may have been small seedlings or slips, cost only 4d. a hundred, and plants of 'sweet flowers' such as violets and pinks were 3d. a bushel. It is quite impossible to say what these prices really mean in terms of present-day money, but some clue can be obtained by multiplying by a factor of about 80 for the latter part of the reign of Henry VIII. On this basis a good apple or pear tree would have cost the equivalent of £2, but a Service tree would be between £4 and £5, and a Holly £1; on the other hand a gardener would be paid only £6 to £8 for the whole week. The Head Gardener, John Chapman, had a regular stipend of £12 a year, quite a handsome amount for the time, but on the suggested basis worth less than £1,000 nowadays.

From the death of Henry VIII less than 50 years elapsed before the publication, in 1596, of John Gerard's catalogue of the contents of his own garden in the Holborn area of London. In it he lists over 1,000 different trees, shrubs and plants as being grown by himself. Many of these were admittedly native to Britain, and some doubt has been thrown on Gerard's reliability, but in outline at least his catalogue stands as giving an overall picture of what could be grown in one garden by one exceptionally enterprising skilled gardener. It has to be remembered that Gerard was not only a practising surgeon, but was for more than 20 years also chief gardener to Lord Burghley, the Queen's great minister, at London and at Theobalds in Hertfordshire. He must have acquired a great deal of skill which put him into the category of professional gardeners rather than amateurs. Although his personal catalogue was not that of a nurseryman (but see below, pp. 16-17), it did represent more or less what a leading nurseryman would have liked to be able to supply. Originally giving Latin names only, the revision of 1599 added English names, and this foreshadows the bilingual aspect of so many

[1] 'Pink' was not then used as an adjective of colour.

6

later catalogues and lists. Gerard's shortcomings as a scientist and as a man have been sternly criticised, but it was his enterprise that gave us the first serious catalogue of growing plants. It is his catalogue that deserves fame as the ancestor of all the later works of the kind with which we have to deal.

I

THE FIRST TRADE LISTS

THE CATALOGUE of Gerard's garden provided a master prototype for later plant-lists, but was itself composed in the simplest form, as a single alphabetical list. Every sort of plant was included, without any form of classification, and forest and ornamental trees jostle bulbous and herbaceous plants. Though this has always been the model for a small proportion of later catalogues, convenience and specialisation have usually imposed the use of classified and subdivided lists, or of lists of certain classes. Since few of the English nurserymen of the 17th century were in a very large way of business, it is not surprising to find that the earliest surviving examples are either partial lists of single classes of plants, or else general catalogues with many subdivisions. This latter type seems to have been based almost exactly upon a literary tradition descended from, or cognate with, the 'Fromond' manuscript list of Herbs for a Garden, of c. 1500. As we shall see, classified lists in the same line continued until the 19th century, when something more like the modern forms of classification was adopted.

There do not seem to be any strictly trade catalogues of the first half of the 17th century. There are lists of plants grown in several gardens, mostly those of scientific or amateur botanists. John Tradescant the elder (died 1638), who was a professional gardener as well as a traveller, plant collector and much else, formed an important garden at Lambeth, of which a list of 1634 survives. Under his son, John Tradescant junior (1608-1662), the garden was kept up, and a second list of 1656 formed part of the published catalogue Museum Tradescantianum. The total number of effectively available plants was growing rapidly, so that the catalogue of the Oxford Botanic Garden in 1648 included about 1,600 species and varieties. The period of the Civil War and the Commonwealth cannot have been conducive to the development of the gardening trade, though retirement from politics encouraged the practice of gardening in the country by several enthusiasts, notably the Parliament-arian generals Fairfax and Lambert. The Royalist Sir Thomas Hanmer, bart., whose important garden book of 1659 was only rediscovered and published in 1933, was probably the most distinguished of all these horticultural recluses. But it is only among his notes made after the Restoration that copies of nurserymen's price-lists are found. There is good reason for thinking that the Restoration, as in so many other departments of life, provided a fresh starting-point for the plant trade.

It is in the memorable year 1666 that we get a direct clue to the operations of the nurserymen. John Rose (1629-1677), Gardener to Charles II, in that year published the first edition of his book *The English Vineyard Vindicated*. The work was addressed to the King with the courtly phrase: 'Sir, I dedicate the Prince of Plants to the Prince of Planters, Your Majesty'; and later on Rose shows that he was not only the royal gardener, but was at the same time

in business as a nurseryman. 'Those who have a desire to store their Ground,
may receive them (Sets and Plants of all those Sorts which I chiefly
recommend) of me at very reasonable Rates.' The book besides dealing with
the grape-vine, rather mysteriously includes a table of the contents of a set of
treatises comprising over 294 pages, apparently never published. If these
actually existed in manuscript, as must be presumed, they would have formed
the first real gardener's encyclopaedia in English. Section VII, Of Trees and
Shrubs, was said to contain 'Pears, Apple-trees, Plum, Abricots, Peaches,
Cherries, Figs, Mulberries, Oranges, Limons. Shrubs — Granads, Jassemine,
Musk-Rose, Myrtles, Laurels, Philyroa, Alaternus, Althaea frutex, Arbor
Judae, Lilac. — Diseases'.

  Rose's lost treatises were evidently based upon a classified list, and
fortunately a very detailed list of this kind was soon afterwards included by
Leonard Meager (c. 1620 - c. 1700) in his book *The English Gardener*.
Meager's list may well be that of his friend Captain Leonard Garrle or Gurle,
who at any rate supplied the Catalogue of Fruit. This, Meager says, 'I had of
my very loving friend Captain Garrle, dwelling at the great Nursery between
Spittle-fields and White-Chappel, a very Eminent and Ingenious Nursery-man,
who can furnish any that desireth, with any of the sorts hereafter mentioned;
as also with divers other rare and choice Plants'. The list gives many different
varieties of each of Cherries, Plums, Apricocks, Nectorins, Peaches, Grapes,
Figs, Apples, Pears; it was as a grower of Nectarines that Gurle achieved
lasting fame, by naming a new variety with his own surname spelt backwards:
Elrug. Smoothed into 'Elruge' the variety is still grown as the hardiest
Nectarine available.

  When Meager wrote his book, published in 1670, he had been 'above 30
years a Practitioner in the Art of Gardening'; in other words his career, very
likely as a gardener's apprentice, started before 1640 and thus in the palmy
days before the Civil War. It has been noted that his book is old-fashioned,
and to that extent it has a special value as representing the state of English
horticulture as it had been before the impact of Charles II and John Rose.
The catalogues of plants it contains are either the basic trade-lists issued by
Gurle, or by nurserymen in other lines who were on friendly terms with
Meager. Although they do not include prices they can be accepted as showing
what could be bought from nurseries in the London area by the middle of the
17th century: that is to say, things for which there was a substantial public
demand. The fact that there was as large a demand as this implies, even before
the new interest in gardens stimulated by Charles II, is striking, but it was the
outcome of more than 500 years of development. By 1180 William Fitz-
Stephen in his famous *Description of London* had mentioned that 'on all
sides, beyond the houses, lie the gardens of the citizens that dwell in the
suburbs, planted with trees, spacious and fair'. The number of different kinds
of trees had increased, and of other plants mightily, but the tradition of
gardening was already a very old one.

  The main categories of Meager's catalogue are those which continued to
form the basis of the tradesmen's price-lists for a long time, and which are
largely still with us: Trees; Fruit; Herbs and Roots (i.e. Vegetables); Herbs for
setting Knotts etc. (the Flower Garden); Flowers (i.e. Florists' Flowers);
Flowering Trees, Evergreens, Tender Greens, plants to set about Arbors. This
last class includes both the Shrubbery and the Greenhouse, remembering that

the latter was still simply a shelter for wintering tub trees and shrubs that were set out throughout the milder months of the year. There was as yet no sign of the epoch of Stove and Conservatory.[1] Some of Meager's classes are subdivided, and the subdivisions conform to the mediaeval pattern of the Fromond list.

The first main class, of 'Trees fit to plant by Out-Walk sides, or otherwise', comprises Ash, Beech, Birch, Chestnut, Elm, Hornbeam, Lime, Oak, Poplars — both the 'Abeal' and the White Poplar[2], Service, Sycamore, Walnut, and Willow if near water; as well as the Fruit Trees Apple, Cherry, Black or Honey Cherry, Mulberry and Pear. At the end of the list are added, Fir-tree, wild Pine-Trees, &c., probably indicating the fairly new interest in planting conifers. What is of particular interest in this list of trees is its close resemblance to the list which can be inferred from Chaucer's reference to 'hoomly') (i.e. indigenous) trees in his version of The Romaunt of the Rose, and his other mentions of trees in *The Parlement of Foules* and *The Knightes Tale*. Chaucer's career not only included a period as Clerk of the King's Works, but also a term as Forester of North Petherton Park, and he evidently knew a great deal about trees and timber. Stripped of exotics Chaucer's familiar trees were: Alder, Apple, Ash, Aspen Poplar, Beech, Birch, Box, Bullace, Cherry, Chestnut, Cornel ('Whippeltree'), Elm, Fir, Hazel, Holly, Laurel (presumably Bay), Lime ('Lind'), Maple, Medlar, Oak, Peach, Pear, Pine, Plane, Plum, Poplar, Quince, Service, Thorn (i.e. Hawthorn), Willow and Yew.

Chaucer's trees raise several problems, especially his mentions of the conifers Fir and Pine, and of Laurel, Lime and Plane. It is not impossible that a few specimens of Norway Spruce may have been grown in England in the Middle Ages; Chaucer's references show that 'fir' was noted for making ships' masts, and trade relations with Norway were particularly close. Similarly a few Scots Pines, certainly native in Scotland, are quite likely to have been grown in the south. But the typical conifers, if they were known, were certainly far from common in England until about Meager's own time. The modern laurel was certainly not brought to the West until late in the 16th century, but the name had always been applied to the classical Laurel, now called the Bay. This was certainly used as a medicinal plant in the Middle Ages, and had presumably survived in cultivation from Roman times. The Lime known to Chaucer was probably the small-leaved species (Tilia cordata), which is accepted as native. The reference to the Plane presents quite a puzzle. Rightly or no, there is an old tradition that the Oriental Plane was brought back from the Crusades by the Templars, and though they must certainly have been most uncommon there seems little reason to doubt that a few specimens were known. On the other hand, Meager's 'Siccamores' probably were fairly recent introductions, though it is possible that he used the word (as in American English) to mean the Plane rather than the Great Maple.

Several of Chaucer's trees are included in Meager's lists of Fruit or Evergreens: Box, Holly, Peach, Plum and Yew, while 'White-bush' (i.e.

[1] In 1697 Meager published *The New Art of Gardening*, with 'Rules for the Conservatory, and Green-House.'
[2] See Appendix IV p. 79.

Hawthorn) was regarded as suitable for an Arbour. Meager does not include Alder, Bullace, Cornel, Maple (other than Sycamore), Medlar or Quince, the first four presumably scorned for gardens. The Medlar and the Quince, though long grown, never have been very popular fruit-trees in England. The modern additions to English arboriculture were surprisingly few: the Hornbeam was a native tree brought into polite usage; the rest were fruit-trees introduced about the time of Henry VIII and including the Apricot, Fig, Mulberry and Nectarine. These had become cherished playthings for the walled gardens of the gentry, and the sale of good varieties was undoubtedly an important source of profit to the nurserymen of Gurle's type. Among these was George Ricketts of 'Hogsden' (Hoxton), near London, whose price-list was fortunately sent to Sir Thomas Hanmer in 1667 and preserved. Ricketts offered four kinds of 'Nectorans' at 3s. each, and 18 varieties of Peaches, all at 2s. Of Cherries he offered ten sorts at 8d. a tree, with 34 Pears all at 1s. each and 17 Apples, all at 8d. except the 'Figg apple without a core' which cost 5s. a tree. Besides these fruit trees, Ricketts included a list of 23 varieties of Gilliflowers (Carnations), all at 1s. 6d. a root. In 1670 Hanmer noted the prices of several other kinds of flowers which he had sent from Ricketts: 11 roots of Anemones including '2 good rootes of Ricketts owne Violett Imperiall' at a cost of 8s., six kinds of Auriculas, one a double at 4s., the rest at 1s. each, which was also the standard price for Carnations, of which Hanmer had 10 different named varieties from Ricketts.

Leonard Gurle may have been rather senior to George Ricketts, but by 1665 John Rea described Ricketts as 'the best and most faithful florist now about London'. Though both men dealt in fruit-trees and in florists' flowers, Gurle was probably more a fruitist and Ricketts rather a florist, but he also specialised in tender Evergreens.[3] Also in competition as a general nurseryman was, as we have seen, the King's Gardener John Rose, who is said to have trained the two great gardeners, George London (died 1714) and Henry Wise (1653-1738). There were many other nurseries around London, but not many of them were extensive. An early specialist in forest trees was Moses Cook, who became chief gardener to Arthur Capel, Earl of Essex (1631-1683), at his estates of Cassiobury and Hadham. In 1675 Cook wrote, while at Cassiobury, *The Manner of Raising, Ordering and Improving Forest Trees*, published in the next year. Cook, with John Field (died 1687), chief gardener at Woburn Abbey, and George London in 1681 joined Roger Looker in a copartnership formed for several purposes. The four partners set themselves to regularize the correct names of varieties of Fruit Trees; undertook the design of gardens and carrying out of garden work; and founded the first really large nursery at Brompton Park. Looker (died 1685) was the prime mover and senior partner until his death. In 1687, two years after Looker, Field died and Henry Wise joined the firm; Cook retired in 1689. Thereafter the business of London & Wise, with the giant nursery at Brompton Park, became almost all-powerful and by 1705 the nursery was reckoned to contain about 10 million plants of all kinds.

Returning to Meager's catalogue we find that his class of 'ordinary Herbs and Roots' is subdivided, and it is largely in these sections that the influence

[3] Ricketts' catalogue (unpriced) of 'Housed Greens' etc. was printed in 1688 by J. Woolridge in *Systema Horti-culturae*, 3rd edition (pp. 268-70).

of the 'Fromond' list tradition can be seen. There is an alphabetical list under each heading, of Sweet Herbs, Physick Herbs, Pot-herbs or Chopping Herbs, Sallet herbs and Roots, Pease, Things . . . pickled for Sallets to use in the Winter, and things put with White-wine Vinegar and Sugar for Winter-Sallets. Later, in considering the complete Seedsman's Catalogue of William Lucas, of c. 1677, we shall see how the various sections tend to change position, though the general picture is very much the same. Some old headings disappear, as do the old lists of Herbs for Sauce and Herbs for the Cup; at least one very important new heading is introduced, Seeds to improve Land, which continued for a century or more to have a place in all general lists.

It was not only among the florists' flowers and fruit trees that there was a multiplicity of varieties. In 1670 Meager enumerates, for instance, the following categories of Pease: Hot-spurs-pease, Redding-pease, Sandwich-pease, Sugar pease, white and gray, Tuffted or Rose-pease, two sorts, Gray Windsor-pease, Great Maple-pease, Great Bowlins-pease, Great Blew-pease. In the Lucas list the classification of Peas is slightly different, into four main groups: Hotspur Peas along with Sandwich and Windsor varieties; Rouncivall Peas including Blue and Maple kinds; Sugar Peas; and Rose Peas grouped with Egg, Wing and Sickle Peas. The inclusion of Pease (in later lists Pease & Beans) gives the impression of being an afterthought. Peas and Beans are not given at all in the 'Fromond' list, nor are they mentioned by Master John Gardener. The reason appears to be that they were field-crops grown in ploughed land, and in mediaeval times not in gardens, and this gave them a different legal status. The law was that while great tithes from crops grown on ploughed land went to the Rector (whether clerical or lay), the Vicar took the small tithes which included those 'of all such small parcels of ground as are delved with a spade'. Incidentally this is also almost certainly the reason why Peas and Beans were, and still are, sold by dry measure (i.e. by the pint, quart etc.) like corn, all other seeds (and even shallots) in quantity being sold by the ounce and pound avoirdupois.

The Herbs for setting Knotts with, or to edge borders, were Dutch or French Box, Hyssop, sorts of Thyme, Germander (Teucrium chamaedrys) which Meager says 'was much used many years ago, it must have good keeping', Thrift, Gilded-Marjoram, Pot-Marjoram, Pinks, Violets double or single, Grass, Periwinkle, Lavender-Cotton, Herba-Grace (Rue, Ruta graveolens), Rosemary, Lavender, Sage, Primroses, Double-Dasies. With the list of Flowers grown we shall deal later in considering the seeds and roots sold by Lucas, but Meager's section on Flowering Trees and Evergreens is of great interest as showing the considerable importance already accorded to hardy shrubs and climbers as well as to the few tender 'greens' so greatly prized by the wealthy cognoscenti. The growing body of nurserymen must have been largely supported by a wide public demand for the commoner and cheaper plants in this group. The list begins with the flowering varieties 'with double Blossoms' of the fruit-trees Apple, Peach, Pear and Cherry. It continues with 'Melerion' (evidently a misprint for 'Meserion', i.e. Mezereon), Jassamines, Shrub-mallows (Hibiscus syriacus), Honey-Suckles or Wood-bines, Gilder-roses, Lelacks, Siringa (Philadelphus coronarius), Laburnum, Senas, two or three sorts (possibly the 'Bastard Sennas', Colutea arborescens, and species of Coronilla), Clematis, double and single (C. viticella and its double form), Prim or Prinet (i.e. Privet), Bladder-nut (Staphylea pinnata), Lawrus Tinus, and Pomgranat, double and single.

The 'Evergreen that are hardy' were: Allaternus, or ever-green Princt (Rhamnus alaternus), Arbutus . . . in a warm situation, Arborvita (Thuja occidentalis), Box, three sorts, Bayes ordinary, Cherry-bay or great Laurel, Lawrus Tinus, Cypress, Firr-tree, Holly, both red and yellow-berried, Piracantha, Perriwinckle, great and small, Pine-trees, two sorts (Pinus pinea, the Stone Pine, and P. sylvestris the Scots Pine), Yew-tree, and Evergreen Oak. To these might be added the 'tender or housed greens': Orange, Limon, Citron, Olianders, and Mirtles, four or five sorts. To the conservative Meager 'Plants for Arbors' were still a separate heading, which had lasted on from the Middle Ages. The 'Herber' or Arbour was from soon after the Norman Conquest until the 16th century the only part of the garden that was primarily for pleasure. Among the many herbs grown for medicinal purposes there were flowering plants of great beauty, but their practical value came first. In the arbour, however, there was an enclosed garden with turfed benches surrounded by climbers grown up trellis or trained to form arcaded walks, and with beds in the middle containing some choice flowers grown for show.

The late medieval 'Fromond' list puts the plants 'for an Herber' at the end, as if an afterthought; they form a curious collection which presents problems. First for the list itself in the original spelling, identifying where necessary: Vynes (i.e. grape-vines), Rosers (Rose bushes and probably climbing Roses), Lyles (Lilium candidum), Thewberies (Dewberry, Rubus caesius), Almondez, Baytrees, Gourdes, Date Trese, Peche trese, Pyne Appull (certainly not Ananas; Pine Apple was the older name for a pine-cone, so doubtless Pinus sylvestris is meant), Pyany Roman (presumably Paeonia officinalis), Rose campy (Campion, probably Melandrium album, M. rubrum), Cartabus, Selyan, Columbyn gentyle (i.e. domesticated as opposed to wild, Aquilegia vulgaris, cultivated forms), Elabre (Hellebore, either the native Helleborus viridis or H. niger). 'Cartabus' may be a corruption of Carthamus, or of Carduus, for some Thistle; Selyan or (in the alphabetical list) Selian seems unidentifiable. Almond, Bay and Peach had been mentioned by Chaucer and they had all presumably been introduced, even if they were uncommon. The real difficulty is over 'Date trese', which can hardly be either Date Palms or the Date Plum (Diospyros lotus). The fruit of the date as a dried import was very well known in England throughout the Middle Ages, and it is not inconceivable that seedlings were raised from time to time, as the stones will readily germinate in the open; but it is difficult to imagine that in medieval conditions any of them survived to become trees. Possibly a type of Plum, known as a 'Date', was meant.

In Meager's time 'Plants for Arbors' were: Sweet-bryer, Honey-suckles, Clematis, Jessamine, Scorpion-Sena (Coronilla emerus), Prime or Prinet, Tamarisk, Roses, white Frankford &c., White bush (Whitethorn or Hawthorn), Plum-trees; 'but if you would have it always green then' the following were recommended: Cypris, very good, Piracantas, Filaree, none better (Phillyrea), Allaturnus, Holly, Lawrels, &c. Of these plants those that were not native had mostly been introduced before Gerard's time, though Pyracantha coccinea and Rhamnus Alaternus had only come in shortly before Parkinson wrote in 1629. 'Jessamine' probably covers both the common white Jasminum officinale and the old yellow J. fruticans. It is evident that by Meager's time the word Arbour had come to have more or less its modern sense, whereas it had formerly meant the whole of the private pleasure-garden including the flower-beds within it. Hence the change of emphasis in the plants listed by 'Fromond' and by Meager, who mentions only the trees, shrubs and climbers used to form the arbour proper.

The flowers grown in the middle of 'knotts' or patterned beds, and in the beds inside the medieval herbers and later arbours, are well known from the various gardening books of the 17th century. A good list for the 'Summer Garden' was given in 1617 by William Lawson in his little book, *The Country House-wifes Garden:* Roses . . ., Rosemary, Lavender, Bee-flowers, Isop, Sage, Time, Cowslips, Piony, Daises, Clove-Gilliflowers, Pinks, Southern-wood, Lillies. This was compiled in Yorkshire and was meant to be representative of the simplest kind of garden, so that it needs expansion to reconstitute a contemporary seedsman's list. No such list has so far come to light,[4] but there is a manuscript list of flowers sown in 1639, probably the memorandum of a nurseryman or florist. In the same manuscript appear named Tulips for sale and notes of Auriculas and Tulips sold and exchanged. On 6 April 1639 the unknown writer listed 'Seedes of severall kindes sowed in my garden. From Mr Manneringe: Snapdragons of divers collours; Lupins blew, lupins yellow, Spanish lupins. Turkie starre (probably Scilla amoena). Prince's feather. Rose Rubic. Serpentarius (? Aristolochia serpentaria). Nigella Romana. The greate African marigold. Pionii 'vcorig' (?). Primrose flower. Stockes purple & white. Dubble Collumbines, Red, white & blewe. Tuft of Candie. Balsum foemina (Impatiens balsamina). Thorne Apple. Doubble gilliflowers. Palma Christi (Ricinus communis). The knotted marigold. Goe to bed at noone (Goatsbeard; Tragopogon pratensis). French honisuckles (Hedysarum coronarium). Honesti. Pease flower (Lathyrus latifolius). Viper flower'. This was the sophisticated selection of a professional gardener, giving some idea of the resources of seedsmen in the reign of Charles I.

[4] Miss Alice M. Coats tells me of a list of nearly 60 kinds of seeds, mostly herbs, with the prices per ounce, sent in 1631 to New England from Robert Hill 'gr.' (? gardener) of the 'Three Angells in Lumber Streete' (Anne Leighton, *Early English Gardens in New England,* 1970, p. 190).

II

THE CATALOGUE OF WILLIAM LUCAS

SERIOUS INTEREST in the history of gardening began over two centuries ago, and it is fortunate that a great deal of bibliographical work was done by Richard Weston (1733-1806) before 1769, and in the early years of the 19th century by Henry Phillips, John C. Loudon, and George W. Johnson. Some of the printed catalogues and pamphlets recorded by these pioneers have since disappeared, but we have at least their titles and dates. More recent research continuing down to the present day has served to emphasise the fact that printed catalogues of plants and seeds were extremely rare, even in London, before the middle of the 18th century. In spite of the losses of some recorded items, it is now possible to carry the story back a little further than was done by early bibliographers. On the authority of Johnson it has repeatedly been stated that a catalogue of trees and shrubs for sale by Christopher Gray (c. 1694-1764), dated 1740, was the first printed list issued by a nurseryman. Nobody since Johnson's time seems to have seen this catalogue,[1] though an edition of 1755 is in the Lindley Library of the Royal Horticultural Society. In any case, even 1740 is bettered by 1727, the date of *A Catalogue of English and Foreign Trees* and *A Catalogue of Fruit-Trees*, sold by Robert Furber at his Nursery over-against the Park Gate at Kensington. Copies of these survive both in the British Museum and Bodleian Libraries. The lists run alphabetically in English, that of Fruit giving names of varieties from Apples to Wallnuts. Furber had been one of two enterprising nurserymen, the other being Christopher Gray, who had bought rare plants from the Fulham Palace grounds after the death of Bishop Henry Compton in 1713. Furber had probably issued catalogues even before 1727, for a writer in the *Floricultural Cabinet* for 1838 says of the Moss Rose that 'by Furber's catalogue it appears that it was cultivated here in 1724.'[2]

It may well have been Furber who originated the nurseryman's catalogue in the modern sense, for besides these specialised lists of Trees and of Fruit, and presumably of Roses, he was to produce in 1730 what has been called the first lavishly illustrated nurseryman's catalogue: *Twelve Months of Flowers*, a handsome folio with 13 hand-coloured engravings after paintings by Pieter Casteels, a Fleming. The plants listed are mainly florists' flowers, the Auricula, Anemone, Hyacinth and Rose, but there are also 25 American

[1] In the John Johnson Collection of Ephemera in the Bodleian Library, Oxford, there is an undated sheet entitled *A Catalogue of American Trees and Shrubs that will endure the climate of England*, quite possibly issued by Gray; but it can hardly be identical with *A Catalogue of Trees and Shrubs which are prepared for sale by Christopher Gray, Nurseryman at Fulham*, dated 1740 — the title given by Loudon and Johnson.
[2] See postscript of Preface, p. xi.

plants. Three years later Furber brought together 'several useful Catalogues of Fruit and Flowers' in his book *A Short Introduction to Gardening*, 'or, a guide . . . in furnishing . . . gardens'. None of these printed lists includes any prices, and there may be some truth in the suggestion, often made, that this would have been too blatantly vulgar for the aristocratic clients at whose pockets Furber was aiming. Certainly his *Short Introduction* of 1733 flew high, the subscribers' list starting with an engraved page with a cartouche containing the names of H.R.H. Prince William Duke of Cumberland (then only 12 years old), H.R.H. Princess Mary, and H.R.H. Princess Louisa. Cumberland was later to achieve a sad fame as the merciless victor of Culloden, Mary became landgravine of Hesse-Cassel, and Louisa queen of Denmark. The rest of the names are historically valuable as a trade guide to six nurserymen (including Gray), five seedsmen and 49 gardeners of the period.

Provisionally we can put the introduction of the printed catalogue in pamphlet form to the 1720's — it may well have been preceded by printed broadsheets — and attribute it, along with the first illustrated list, to Robert Furber. The position of his nursery and his exalted subscribers suggest that during the period when Charles Bridgeman was enlarging and improving Kensington Gardens for Queen Caroline, the mantle of leading nurseryman had fallen on Furber. George London had died a few months after Bishop Compton, which may well be the reason why Brompton Park did not snap up the rarities of Fulham; Henry Wise was in retirement. London and Wise had, in their English version of *The Retir'd Gard'ner* published in 1706, included in print a transcript of the standard seedsman's catalogue of the time. They remarked of the original French list: 'The List of Seeds the author of Le Jardinier Solitaire has in this place given us, is very imperfect, and in no wise proper to be made use of in England. In lieu of it, take the following Catalogue of all the Seeds we sow in Kitchen-Gardens . . . ' There follow groups of Vegetable and Herb seeds, and then Flowers Annual and Perennial, Edgings, and Florists' Flowers.

The list printed by London and Wise differs only slightly from the complete text of the standard trade-list of the leading English seedsmen, printed by J. Woolridge (or Worlidge) as an appendix to the 1688 and later editions of his *Systema Horti-culturae, or The Art of Gardening*. This is stated to represent what was sold by Edward Fuller 'at the Three Crowns and Naked Boy at Strand-Bridge near the May-Pole'; by Theophilus Stacy 'at the Rose and Crown without Bishopsgate'; and by Charles Blackwell 'at the King's Head near Fetter-Lane end in Holborn'. Both the Strand and Holborn shops had a long history under successive proprietors, and this 1688 catalogue in fact follows almost exactly that of Fuller's predecessor in business, preserved in the form of a manuscript copy. The transcript, apparently complete, was made by a Surrey clergyman in his commonplace book: it is entitled 'A Catalogue of Seeds, Plants, &c. sold by William Lucas at the Naked Boy near Strand Bridg, London'.

Next to nothing is so far known of William Lucas, but it can at any rate be substantiated that his shop was at the sign of The Naked Boy, also known as The Three Naked Boys, in 1677. By 1683 the shop, then called The Three Crowns and Naked Boy, near the May Pole in Strand, was already in the hands of Edward Fuller, who there sold trefoil and hop clover seeds for

improvers. As we have seen, Fuller's complete list, printed in 1688 by
Woolridge, was essentially that of Lucas. Edward Fuller 'of Strand Bridge' is
also known as the principal seedsman patronised by William Russell
(1613-1700), fifth Earl and first Duke of Bedford, whose London mansion
was in the Strand and who was the landlord of Covent Garden Market. In the
Spectator of 11 August 1712 we learn that the water-stairs of Strand Bridge
were the 'market-port' for Covent Garden, where boats laden with apricots,
melons, and market-garden produce docked. The shop in this strategic
position, successively occupied by Lucas, Fuller, Edward Clarke and (c. 1750)
Arabella Morris, gave its name to Naked Boy Court, named on Rocque's map
of London published in 1746.[3] The courtyard lay between the top of
Strand Lane, which still exists, and Aldwych Underground Station, and in
1677 it is shown on Ogilby and Morgan's map as having a back exit onto the
elbow of the lane just above the well known 'Roman Bath'. The court and the
houses around it can be seen in Hollar's large bird's-eye view of West Central
London.

The date of the copy of Lucas's catalogue can be fixed almost as precisely
as the position of his shop. As we have just seen, Lucas is identified with the
shop in 1677, and this is the first year in which the copy could have been
made. William Walker, M.A., was instituted to the vicarage of Effingham on
26 February 1676/7, and copied the seedsman's list in the back of a small
note-book in which his main entries were notes of compositions with all his
parishioners for cash payments in lieu of tithes. These notes and accounts are
dated from 1677 to 1679; by 1680 probably and by 1683 certainly, Edward
Fuller had taken over the seed business. It is likely that Mr. Walker would be
concerned with stocking the vicarage garden as soon as he reached his parish,
so that a date of 1677 is by far the most likely for his visit to London. A
point of some interest is that, among the tithe notes but in another hand than
Walker's own, is a list of 18 herbs, vegetables and flowers: Hysop, Hollyhock,
Basill, Starflower (Aster), Chervill, French Marigold, Summer Savory, Virgins
bower (Clematis flammula), Buglosse, Love Apple (Tomato), Dill, Bellflower,
Leekes, Columbines, Collyflower, Poppey, Rockett, Flower of yè sun. Was
this Lucas's special collection for a country vicarage garden?

Before passing on to a consideration of the list, there is one further
problem to dispose of concerning the site of the seedsman's business. There is
no reason to think that the firm was new in 1677, and if as seems probable it
was the most important shop of its kind at the time, it may very well have
been long established. This might provide an explanation for the remarkable
coincidence — if mere coincidence it be — that the piece of garden ground on
the opposite side of Strand Lane, running from the bank of the Thames up to
the backs of the houses along the Strand, and stretching in width from the
lane to the east wall of Somerset House, had in August 1604 been granted by
the Queen (Anne of Denmark) to John Gerard. The grant was for a nominal
fine of 5s. and a yearly rent of 4d and, if lawfully required, 'at the due and
proper seasons of the yeare a convenient proportion and quantitie of herbes
flowers or fruite renewing or growing within the said Garden plott . . .' The
draft for the grant was drawn up at Theobalds and was evidently due to

[3] John Rocque the cartographer was brother of Bartholomew Rocque,
nurseryman at Fulham and writer on agriculture and gardening.

Robert Cecil, son of the great Lord Burleigh who had been Gerard's patron
for over 20 years. The grant was in consideration of Gerard's 'singular and
approved art skill and industrie in planting nursing and preserving plants
hearbes flowers and fruits of all kindes'. Seeing that, from the time of Queen
Elizabeth until 1775, Somerset House and its adjacent gardens continued to
be settled upon successive queens, and that in 1681 Roger Looker was
'Gardener to Her Matie.' (Catherine of Braganza), it seems possible that there
was a continuous tradition associating this garden with a succession of noted
gardeners, and with the central London trade in plants. While this would
increase the prestige and authority of nurserymen and seedsmen in this key
position, there is in any case no doubt that the firm of Lucas was, in the
middle of the reign of Charles II, completely representative of the highest
level in the trade.

The catalogue (for the full text see Appendix II) consists of 11 sections,
the first nine of seeds and the two last of Flower Roots, and Trees and Plants,
respectively. For the relationship of this classification to those of earlier and
later lists it is possible to draw up a chart (see pp. 18-19) which shows more
clearly than a lengthy description the continuous development from the
beginning of the 16th to the middle of the 19th century. The separate
headings are: Seeds of Roots, Sallad Seeds (including what we should call
Greens), Potherb Seeds, Sweet Herb Seeds, Physicall (i.e. medicinal) Seeds,
Flower Seeds, Seeds of Evergreen & Flowering Trees (including Shrubs), Sorts
of Pease, Beans &c., Seeds to improve Land, Flower Roots, and Sorts of
choice Trees & Plants. At the end is a tailpiece referring to garden tools and
requisites, Fruit Trees, Evergreens, and several types of Vegetable plants such
as Artichoke, Collyflower, Cabbage and Tarragon. The roots of Flowers
include herbaceous as well as tuberous and bulbous species, so that the
business in fact covered the whole of the horticultural field.

Like almost all the early catalogues, even until a century later, this omits
prices, except that opposite the first item (Seeds of five kinds of Onion) Mr.
Walker has written '8 d.' This may be the price per ounce, but if so it was
extremely high, since in 1695 the best Onion seed cost 5s. a pound, and by
1730 it was down to 3s. It is possible that the note was simply a
memorandum of the price paid for the quantity bought, perhaps two ounces,
but this is mere speculation. No other price appears and very likely none was
marked upon the original at Lucas's shop. Prices would vary according to
market conditions, rather than be fixed for the whole season, and this is
probably the main reason why a statement of prices for seeds and plants is so
rarely found except in the bills for what was actually supplied. In connection
with prices it may be worth noting that in the early 18th century, for which
several lengthy bills for vegetable seeds survive (see Appendix III), Onions,
Carrots, Parsnips, Turnips and Radishes seem to have been grown on a large
scale. A big estate, when ordering most seeds in quantities of half-ounces and
ounces, would buy one or more pounds of these seeds. This gives a possible
indication of the diet in the servants' hall.

The seeds of root-crops stocked by Lucas were Onion (5 kinds), Leek (2),
Carrot (3), Parsnip, Swelling Parsnip, Turnip (3 kinds), Skirret, Scorzonera,
'Sassify', Potato, Shallots, Rocambole and Garlic. Skirret and Rocambole are
not now in normal cultivation. The Salad seeds are Radish (4 kinds), Lettuce
(8), Spinach (2), as well as Berry-bearing Orach, Beet (3 kinds), Curled

COMPARATIVE CHART OF PLANT LISTS AND SEEDSMEN'S AND NURSERYMEN'S CATALOGUES

'Fromond' c. 1500	*Meager* 1670	*Lucas* 1677	*London & Wise* 1706	*Borthwick* 1759	*Garraway* c. 1770
7. Roots for a Garden	4B. Roots	1. Roots	1. Esculent Roots	1. Roots	2. Roots
2. Herbs for Sauce					
3. Herbs for the Cup					
4. Herbs for a Salad	4A. Salad Herbs	2. Salad (including Greens)	2. Salad	2. Salad 3. Greens	3. Salad
1. Herbs for Pottage	3. Pot Herbs or Chopping Herbs	3. Potherbs	3. Sweet & Pot Herbs	4. Potherbs	5. Pot & Sweet Herbs
6. Herbs for Savour and Beauty	1. Sweet Herbs	4. Sweet Herbs			
	6. Pickled for Salads				
	7. in Vinegar &c Winter Salads				
5. Herbs to Distil	2. Physic Herbs	5. Physical	4. Other useful Herbs		6. Physical
	8. Herbs for Knotts	6. Flowers	5. Flowers, Annual	6. Flowers	4. Flowers
	9. Flowers		6. Perennials		
8. For an Arbour	10. Flowering Trees, Evergreens, Tender Greens, Arbours	7. Evergreen & Flowering Trees		8. Trees & Flowering Shrubs	8. Evergreen & Flowering Shrubs
	5. Pease	8. Pease, Beans		5. Pease & Beans	1A. Peas 1B. Beans 1C. Kidney Beans
		9. To improve Land		9. To improve Land	7. To improve Land
		10. Flower Roots		7. Flower Roots	9. Bulbous & Fibrous rooted Flrs.
		11. Trees & Plants			10. Trees, Flowerg. Shrubs & Greenhouse Plants
					11. Fruit Trees

The prefixed numbers indicate the order of sections in each catalogue.

Malcolm 1771, 1778	Telford & Perfect 1775, 1793	Clarke (1833)	Flanagan & Nutting 1835	Mackie 1833
6. Esculent Roots	4. ('All Sorts of Seeds') 7. Seeds of Roots	5. Roots &c. (V. 271-286)	4. Roots, &c.	
4. Esculents & Salad Herbs	8. Sallad	2. Vegetables (V. 58-222) 3. Sundries (V. 223-243)	2. Garden Seeds (Vegetables)	
8. Sweet & Pot Herbs	9. Pot & Sweet Herb Seeds	4. Sweet & Pot Herbs (V. 244-270)	3. Sweet & Pot Herbs	
11. Physical*	10. Physical		-----	
7. Flowers: Annuals/ Tender/Hardy 9. Biennials 3. Trees & Shrubs	14. Flower 11. Trees & Shrubs	7. Flowers: Annual (F. 1-464) 8. Hardy Biennial & Perennial (F. 465-743)	6. Flowers: Hardy/ Half-Hardy/Tender Bien./Perennial 7. Hardy Trees & Shrubs	
5. Pease & Beans	16. Peas & Beans	1. Beans, Peas (V. 1-57)	1. Garden Seeds (Pease, Beans, Kidney Beans)	
10. Improvement of Land	12. To improve Land 13. Bird Seeds	6. Grass & other Agricultural (V. 287-328)	5. Grass & other Agricultural	
2. Bulbous & Fibrous Flower Roots	15. (Perennial Flower Roots) 6. (Bulbous Flowers)	9. (Bulbous Flower Roots)	8. (Dutch Bulbs & other Flower Roots)	
1. Fruit & Forest Trees, Flowering Shrubs	1. Forest Trees 17. Fruit Trees 3. Evergreen & Flowering Shrubs			1. Seedling Forest Trees 2. Transplanted Forest Trees 3. Ornamental Trees & Shrubs 4. Evergreens 5. American Plants 6. Fruit Trees

*omitted in 1778

Endive, Italian Celery, Finocchio, Samphire, Rocket and Spanish Rocket, Rampion, Hartshorn, Tarragon, Sorrel (2 sorts), Cardoon, four Cresses, described as Indian (? Tropaeolum), Garden, Broadleaved (? Watercress), and Curled; Chervil, Sweet Chervil, Purslane, Golden Purslane, Parsley and Curled Parsley, Alexanders, Corn Salad, Asparagus (2 kinds). The great variety of salads, many now quite obsolete, is remarkable. Green Vegetables, included under Salad seeds, comprise four varieties of Cabbage, two of Colewort, 'Broculus', 'French Choux', two sorts of Savoy and 'Coli Rapi.' At the end are three sorts each of Melon and Cucumber, 'Pompion' (Pumpkin), Gourd and 'Mekin'. As a dialect word 'Mekkin' or 'Makin' can mean the yellow flag, ferns, or water-milfoil, but none of these is likely. The London & Wise list of 1706 has the word in the same position, and it ought logically to stand for the Vegetable Marrow. This is made probable by a bill of 1729 for seeds supplied by Henry Woodman of Strand-on-the-Green, where 1 oz. of 'Gourd & Meckin' together cost 1s.

There are still separate sections devoted to Potherbs and Sweet Herbs. Potherbs included Endive, Succory (Chicory), Burnet, Sorrel, Marigold and French Mallow, as might be expected; but Clary, Columbine, 'Nepp' (Catmint), and Bugloss have long been banished from the repertory of the most conservative or eccentric cooks. It is remarkable that out of the 49 'Herbes for Potage' included in the 'Fromond' list, not less than 24 survived in the Lucas catalogue some 200 years later, nine in the list of Potherbs and 15 in other parts of the list. The decline in the number of kinds of vegetables in regular use has been continuous, in spite of the introduction of a few important ones since the Middle Ages: Potato and Tomato, along with the less common Capsicums, Egg Plant and Sweet Corn. Out of some 120 vegetables and herbs listed c. 1500 only about one-third appear in general seedsmen's catalogues of the present day. In 1677 the surviving proportion of the medieval list was about half, and included such things as Alexanders, Columbine, Elecampane, Fenugreek, Gromwell, Marigold, 'Langdebeefe' (Echium vulgare), Lovage (Ligusticum scoticum), Mallows, Nepp (Nepeta cataria), Orach (Atriplex hortensis), Rocket (Hesperis matronalis and Eruca sativa), Rue and Tansy, few of which are normally eaten now in any form.

The Sweet Herbs of Lucas's catalogue are mostly those still grown: Thyme, Hyssop, Savory, Marjoram, Basil, Rosemary, Lavender and Balm; only Sweet Maudlin (Achillea ageratum) has dropped out. Not many of the 'Physicall Seeds' are grown, since professional medicine has displaced home-grown herbal remedies, but some plants are still grown for different reasons, notably Angelica, Anise, Caraway, Coriander, Cumin, Dill, Flax, Rhubarb, Rue, Tobacco and Wormwood. Leaving to a later stage the seeds for the Flower Garden and Shrubbery, the Peas and Beans have already been mentioned; that category also included Lentils, now only rarely grown here. The group of 'Seeds to improve land', which in later catalogues was to become an extensive series of 'Grass and other Agricultural Seeds', already comprised Clover, Hop Clover, Sainfoin, 'La Lucer' (Lucerne), Rye Grass, French 'Furs' (Furze or Gorse) and 'Dantzick Flax'. The improvement of land by cropping with clover, sainfoin, lucerne and flax had come in soon after the middle of the 17th century as a major development in English agriculture. This is demonstrated by the interval of only three years between the two versions of Walter Blith's textbook, *The English Improver* published in 1649, and *The*

English Improver Improved of 1652. These new crops, and others such as weld, woad, madder, hops, liquorice and hemp, were advocated only in the second edition. William Lucas and his successor Edward Fuller could supply these new seeds to improving gentry and farmers.

Interesting as are the developments shown in the lists of vegetable and agricultural seeds, they are less striking than the extraordinary changes mirrored in the seeds and roots of Flowering Plants, Trees, and Flowering and Evergreen Shrubs. Instead of the mediaeval dual use of the practical herb garden for aesthetic and recreational purposes, the pleasure garden has come to take equivalent importance in its own right, occupying a full half of the whole catalogue. Of this half, about three-fifths is taken up with seeds, and two-fifths by plants: herbaceous, bulbous and tuberous; tender greens, flowering trees and shrubs. Seeds of some forest and avenue trees were offered, but not plants; this was before the great period of planting, and that was only to get under way on a grand scale after the founding of the Brompton Park Nursery in 1681.

The difficulties of equating the old English nomenclature to modern scientific usage are considerable. In most cases there is no doubt as to the genus of the plant, but the species is not always easy to determine and in several instances a good deal of doubt persists as to what plant was really being cultivated at the time. Matters are not helped by the total lack of alphabetical order, or of any other form of classification. Where several plants are brought together under one English name it is probable that this will prove a false friend. For example, the first seeds are those of Gilliflowers: the Double July Flower is the Carnation, (Dianthus caryophyllus), very properly given pride of place; but next to it is the Stockgilliflower which here (since the Wall Flower is mentioned separately) must stand for the Stock (Matthiola incana); then comes the Queen's Gilliflower which we know as the Rocket (Hesperis matronalis). The Wall Flower (Cheiranthus cheiri) is not under suspicion; but what was the White Wallflower? It sounds like a form of single Stock, though it is generally stated that these were grown only to produce seed yielding doubles.

The problem of the White Wallflower also provides an example of the interlinking of one problem with another. Although Gilliflowers might belong to different natural orders, there is a fairly strong likelihood that a 'White Wallflower' named immediately after the Wallflower would bear some resemblance to its flower — that is, it would be a crucifer; or else that it would be grown on walls. The most probable plant to fulfil both conditions is the White Wall Cress (Arabis albida), now always called Arabis, but at first sight there would seem to be difficulties. What Gerard named Arabis in Latin was 'Candie Mustard' in English, and has been identified as Candytuft (Iberis umbellata). This could be a candidate for 'White Wallflower' but that in Lucas's list the 'Candy Tuft' appears a few lines lower down. This leaves Arabis as the best bet, more particularly as its now disused name of Wall Cress comes into the equation.

The Larksheels are what we call Larkspurs, and were certainly annual species of Delphinium. The Double Larksheel was no doubt the double form of D. consolida; but was the Upright Larksheel D. ajacis? Was the Rose Larksheel named from its colour or was the flower thought to look like a rose? Except for the Rose Campion, the word 'rose' does not otherwise

c

appear in the catalogue. Next we get a pair of splendid examples of the misnomer that sticks for ever: African and French Marigold are still called just that, in spite of their introduction from Mexico. 80 years before Lucas the names were used by Gerard, but were undoubtedly common still earlier — according to Gerard the plants were brought back from Tunis by the Emperor Charles 'the first' (i.e. of Spain; Charles V as Emperor), after his conquest of 1535. It is easy to believe that seeds were brought back to Spain by the conquistadors after taking Mexico in 1520, but why the plants should have attained their main Old World distribution along the North African coast within 15 years is still unexplained.

The Sweet Scabious (Scabiosa atropurpurea) is well attested, but what was the Spanish Scabious? Gerard's flower of this name was identified by B.D. Jackson as S. stellata, but the date of introduction of this has been put as late as 1823; experts disagree and we must leave it at that. A long series of Lucas's flowers is identifiable without difficulty, but it is worth a reminder that 'French Honysuckle', then as now, was neither French nor a Honeysuckle but Hedysarum coronarium, and 'Narturtium indicum' was the Indian Cress or Tropaeolum minus, which Gerard received 'from my loving friend Iohn (Jean) Robin of Paris', and which, with T. majus and hybrids, has been the Nasturtium of flower gardens ever since. Both Red and White Valerian are forms of Centranthus ruber, but Greek Valerian, bracketed with them by Lucas on the ground of its English name, is better known to us as Jacob's Ladder (Polemonium caeruleum) and strangely enough is a native British plant. It is possible that 'Fox Taill' was the Fox-tail Grass, Alopecurus pratensis, still grown, but by no means certain. The Love Apple is simply the Tomato, grown in 1677 as an ornamental plant. 'Bottles' were species of Centaurea, notably the Cornflower (C. cyanus), and had been developed in several colour variations before the time of Parkinson. The Lupins grown in earlier centuries are identifiable, but are not the plants we now think of when seeing the name. They were all annuals, the Common or White Lupin having been introduced as a medicinal plant in the Middle Ages and figuring in the splendid series of ink drawings of plants in the early 15th-century manuscript of John Arderne's works in the British Museum.

To us the Scarlet Runner belongs firmly in the Kitchen Garden, but as 'Scarlett Beans' had an honoured place as one of the most notable introductions from the New World. The mysterious 'Snaills & Caterpillars' and 'Horns & Hedghoggs' were two species of Calvary Clover, with seed-vessels of intricate forms: Medicago scutellata and M. intertexta. After a little group of noted Florists' Flowers there come two other oddities at the end of the list, the formerly popular Sensible (i.e. Sensitive) Plant (Mimosa sensitiva) and the Humble Plant (M. pudica). The Florists' Flowers call for little comment, except that the sale of Tulip seed implies that there was already a widening circle of raisers prepared to wait for new forms. The interesting point is the inclusion of Polyanthus, supported in the later section of Flower Roots by the entry 'Polyanthus all sorts'. They were already a commonplace, though it is usually said that they were first mentioned by Rea in 1665 and even that the garden strain was only developed in the 1670's. But Sir Thomas Hanmer in his manuscript book of 1659 had already referred to Cowslips of various colours as 'Polyanthes', and they had evidently become a completely normal plant before 1677.

The seeds of evergreen and flowering trees offered by Lucas are of considerable interest. First come the Cypress and five firs and pines, showing that the vogue for conifers had already begun; lower down come berries of a number of trees and shrubs including Cedar, Juniper and Yew — the Cedar being the 'Bermuda Cedar' (Juniperus bermudiana). The evergreens grown from seed included Phillyrea, Alaternus, Pyracantha, Arbutus, Laurustinus and the Evergreen Oak, as well as Holly, Laurel, Bay and Myrtle. Amomum Plinii, so frequently mentioned in the older literature of gardening, was Solanum pseudocapsicum (Winter or Jerusalem Cherry), grown mostly as an annual for its scarlet fruits. Among the 'Flowering Trees' so far mentioned, only the Arbutus and the Myrtle would now be thought of as noted for their flowers; the beginnings of the flowering shrubbery come with Mezereon (Daphne mezereum), Senna (Colutea arborescens), Althea (Hibiscus syriacus) — now an unfairly neglected plant — two kinds of Laburnum (L. alpinum and L. anagyroides), and Spanish Broom (Spartium junceum). The seeds of ornamental trees conclude with Chestnuts and Almonds.

Trees and shrubs could be obtained as plants, besides those sold as seeds. Omitting duplications, roots could be had of the tender Citrus fruits, the Pomegranate, six kinds of Myrtles, Red and White Oleander (Nerium), the Olive, Cedar of Lebanon, Agnus Castus (Vitex agnus-castus), Arbor Judae (Cercis siliquastrum) — another undeservedly neglected tree in modern times — at least four kinds of Jasmine, 'all sorts' of Cistus, and variegated Nightshades and Woodbines. Oddities comprised: Marum Syriacum (Origanum syriacum), then a popular pot-plant, Geranium noctu olens (Pelargonium triste), introduced by Tradescant in 1632 and loved for its fragrance, and 'Jucca Peruana', presumably meaning the Yucca gloriosa which had grown hardily for Gerard and flowered in Essex for William Coys in 1604. Forest and specimen Trees included both Oriental and American Planes (Platanus orientalis and P. occidentalis), the Horse Chestnut, and the conifers and other items that could be grown from seed, including the Cork Oak, the Lime and Sweet Chestnut.

We return to the Flower Roots, notably consisting of all the Florists' Flowers in 'all sorts', which would have required very long and frequently changing special lists: Ranunculus, Anemone, Tulip, Carnation, Auricula, Polyanthus, Narcissus, Jonquil, Hyacinth. The Primrose is added, its 'sorts' referring to the wide range of colour variations still obtainable and to kinds such as 'hose-in-hose' virtually extinct. Other distinguished plants were Lilies, Crocus, Colchicum, Paeonies and Fraxinellas purple and white, i.e. the Burning Bush (Dictamnus albus). There were all sorts of Fritillaria, but of the Crown Imperial only the yellow, but both double (now unknown) and single. The impression left by Lucas's catalogue as a whole is that the 17th-century gardeners had already worked wonders with relatively small resources. What they lacked in species available they made up by intensive experiment with bulbs and several other types of flowering plants and shrubs. Variegation of leaves and diversity of colour in flowers had already been successfully achieved after 100 years of relentless enthusiasm.

III

THE AGE OF PLANTING

THE HISTORY OF GARDENING, like that of many other activities, shows a continuous development, but the speed of change varied greatly at different times. Certain dates stand out as marks which divide, even if somewhat artificially, the separate ages which together form the whole story. In western Europe the issue of Charlemagne's list of plants that should be grown, about 812, marks the beginning of real history as opposed to vague deduction. In English plantsmanship another era, that of learning about half-hardy and tender plants, opened in 1338 with the arrival of plants of Rosemary sent to Queen Philippa from the continent. Oddly enough, we even have a scrap of evidence as to precisely how such transfers of plants were effected. The famous treatise on Domestic Economy by a citizen of Paris, compiled for his young wife about 1393 ('Le Ménagier de Paris') and translated into English by Eileen Power as *The Goodman of Paris*, contains a section on Rosemary which notes that it will not grow from seed in (northern) France, but can be propagated by cuttings. 'And if you would send them far away, you must wrap the aforesaid branches in waxed cloth and sew them up and then smear the parcel outside with honey, and then powder with wheaten flour, and you may send them wheresover you will.' So the course of the 14th century had seen a vogue for growing the plant rosemary, famed for its virtues, and had found means to spread it by specially wrapped parcels of cuttings.

The experience gained with the tricky shrub rosemary and a few later importations enabled English gardeners to cope with the much faster influx of new exotics in the 16th century. Probably a good many of the best medieval gardeners had been attached to monastic gardens, either those of infirmaries concerned with the raw material of the pharmacopoeia, or the pleasure and fruit gardens of abbots and priors. At the period of the Dissolution in 1536-40 it is known that important plants were removed from some monastic gardens, while in other cases the new owners of monastic lands kept up the gardens for their own enjoyment. Many gardeners must have been out of work, however, and this provided a force of skilled labour ready to accept any challenge. This came within a generation in the shape of a host of new plants from two chief sources. The Spanish conquests in America brought a completely strange flora from the New World; and the Turkish conquest of the Balkans and Hungary brought to the threshold of the West all the treasures of Persian and Turkish horticulture, along with a number of plants transmitted even from China and India. All this was happening at the same time as the onset of the Reformation and in England the Dissolution of the monasteries. The generation of 1520-1550 saw all this happen and began to tackle new problems.

Though the introductions from America might be the more startling, and certainly in the cases of tobacco, the potato and the tomato had results of enormous economic importance to the future, it was the fresh contacts with Turkey that brought about the new gardening in western Europe and in Britain. The crucial date is that of the return from Constantinople in 1562 of the Imperial ambassador Ogier Ghiselin de Busbecq. Although a few of the fashionable Turkish plants — notably the Tulip and the Hyacinth — had come some years earlier, and others like Lilium chalcedonicum and L. martagon, with Iris susiana, Nigella damascena and Ranunculus asiaticus were not to arrive until rather later, the coming of both the Lilac (Syringa vulgaris) and the Mock Orange (Philadelphus coronarius) in Busbecq's baggage was the turning point. From Vienna the plants soon moved to Paris, the rich towns of Flanders, and to London. From Gerard's catalogue we know how much had reached England, and was well established here, before 1600.

This first age of plant introductions lasted for a century and gave rise to the intense activity of botanists and of florists — in the sense of raisers of fresh varieties of fashionable flowers from seed, and their competitive improvement. The hundred years from the accession of Elizabeth I to the Restoration of Charles II was dominated by this phase of introductions from Turkey, along with something of the Turkish attitude of flower mania. For it was very largely due to the example of Turkish princes, Timurid as well as Ottoman, that the intensive cultivation of flowering plants in many varieties was due. The great Babur, later conqueror of India, wrote in his journal about 1505 of a district near Kabul: 'Tulips of many colours cover these foot-hills; I once counted them up; it came out at 32 or 33 different sorts. We named one the Rose-scented, because its perfume was a little like that of the red rose; it grows by itself on Shaikh's-plain, here and nowhere else.' A couple of years later Babur again mentioned these tulips, this time reckoning the number of kinds at 34, and quoting verses written in praise of the verdure and blossom of Kabul in spring. The Ottoman Sultan Selim II (1566-1574) started the first great tulipomania, sending orders to remote parts of Turkey for as many as 50,000 bulbs 'for my royal gardens' at one time; this was probably the cause of the extinction of the parent species in the wild. (The second mania was the well known Dutch episode of 1634-37; the third was once more in Turkey under Ahmed III whose reign, 1703-1730, is historically known as the Lâle Devri or Tulip Period).

The great age of planting which in England opened soon after the Restoration undoubtedly owes much to the remote oriental precedents of the 'paradises' of trees and water formed for eastern rulers since ancient times. Here again the outstanding patron of the formed and planted garden was Babur, who on the threshold of the modern world both in time and place was causing splendid gardens to be formed wherever his armies had set foot. It was he who joined together the horticultural traditions of Central Asia, Persia and Iraq and carried them eastwards to Afghanistan and into India, setting up a standard of landscaping, planting and waterwork that has probably never been equalled. The reason why these distant prototypes had such surprising repercussions in England is to be found in the sudden vogue for oriental studies in the time of Charles I and particularly the embassy to Persia of which Sir Thomas Herbert (1606-1682) was a member. The opening of English factories in India and the acquisition of Bombay as part of the dowry of Catherine of Braganza were important contributory factors.

The essence of the great eastern gardens was their combination of long-lived trees with water and with terraces from which fine views of the landscape could be obtained. England already had the vestiges of a much earlier tradition of the same kind, brought by the Normans from Sicily in the · 11th and 12th centuries and reaching its climax in Woodstock Park, formed by Henry I and improved by Henry II. Chaucer's knowledge of trees and forestry, already mentioned, indicates that as late as the 14th century there were still re-echoes from this old usage. After 1660 there was to be an extraordinary revival, in which every large estate and most small properties were profoundly influenced and the whole of the English countryside transformed. The making of fenced and walled parks, not for hunting but for pleasure, became a national hobby and at times a mania. The cost of the digging of lakes and canals, of growing, transporting and planting thousands of trees, was — on this scale and pervading the whole country — unprecedented. The buying out of whole villages of peasant proprietors to form parks may be an historical scandal, and the gigantic trade in plants be regarded as almost a parasitic growth upon society; yet the results are, in many cases, so magnificent and so lasting as to compel our admiration and applause.

The new vogue and the consequent demand for young trees in a number of varieties set in quite suddenly and only towards the end of Charles II's reign. It was largely to meet this new and profitable demand that Looker and his partners formed the Brompton Park Nursery in 1681, and the fortunes of the firm were improved by an accident of history. George London, senior partner by 1688, was also head gardener to Henry Compton, the horticultural bishop of London. The bishop was not only a keen gardener and botanist, but an active Protestant and opponent of James II. At the outbreak of the Revolution of 1688 it was Bishop Compton who secretly got Princess Anne away from London to Nottingham, to prevent her falling into the hands of her Catholic father and stepmother; and the bishop's chief agent in the melodramatic escape was his gardener George London. So the nursery was doubly recommended to William III who was himself a keen gardener and brought in Dutch fashions of gardening. The king and the nobility sent to Holland for trees and plants if they could not get them in England, and Dutch influence was paramount until after the turn of the century.

As an example of the mechanics of getting trees sent to the remoter parts of the country we may quote a letter to Sir Willoughby Aston, Bart., of Aston Hall in Cheshire, written by his son Willoughby from London on 9 November 1700. The reference to taking boat to Putney suggests the nursery of the Hunt family, perhaps founded by the Francis Hunt who died in 1662.

Honoured Father,
  In Wensday last the Lime trees were taken out of ye Ground, & on Thursday morning they were ship'd. I went the Wensday before to choose them, and mark them, which I did. I cou'd have wish'd for a fresh Nussery to have chosen them from, but that was not to be had, however I believe they are the finest trees in Cheshire. On Wensday last I went to see them taken up that I might be sure of the same Trees which I had mark'd, and to see them taken up with good Roots, then I saw them pack'd up, they are in 20 Bundles, ten of which have 8 trees, and ten 7. The Roots are coverd with straw and then bound in a Matt, and another matt about the bodies of ye trees, the heads are all cut as they must be, (and are never to be cut again either when they are sett, or afterwards, severall assuring me that it checks the growth and very much prejudices a Lime tree which naturally will have a spreading head) only some of the small twigs which are not cut must be cut proportionable to the rest

when they are set. The reason of leaving them uncutt was, I thought they might be usefull in lying betwixt the larger branches to prevent their galling. One thing the Gardiner told me as a Mistery in planting tho it may be none to you concerning the cutting of ye Roots, viz. the long large Roots, or any that are broken which must be cutt, when they are planted, are to be cutt sloaping, and the side sloap'd off must be downwards that the fibers may shoot downwards, this he pretends is of great use, and practis'd by few. All the shagg or hair like fibers which are of the greatest use to a tree new planted must only have the ends snip'd off, if they happen to be long at sea so that the Roots are very dry, and it be a dry season two (sic), then it will do well to let the Roots lye 4 or 5 hours in Water before they are planted. They must not be planted deep, 6 or 7 Inches above ye Root is enough, and there shou'd be Farn (fern) or litter lay'd about the Roots to keep off Frost. If it be dry in the Spring when they shou'd draw root once watering then is better than ten times in the Summer. And the next winter the earth shou'd be open'd just att the Top and some dung laid in. I have giv'n you all the Instructions I receiv'd which you it may be knew before.

They are all near one size, the bodies betwixt 7 and 8 Foot high and att Breast high betwixt 6, 7, & 8 Inches about. The Carriage of them I left to my brother to agree for, an account of wch I have receiv'd from him this Morning. The usual rate is 20s. a Tun either by the weight or Bulk; I told him I thought they weigh'd a Tun, but he sends me word they weigh almost 3 Tuns and are five Tunns in Bulk. He has agreed for ye freight at 3 pounds 10 shillings, and the master tells him no two Waggons in England can carry them as they are pack'd; all this I very much doubt for I saw one Cart carry em from the Nussery to the Barge by which they went down to ye ship. And as for the weight one of ye bundles with 8 after it was matted I threw it upon my shoulder with a great deal of ease, wch I cou'd scarce do 300 weight. But he will give you an account of the freight by this post, and I Care not to say any more of it, for I have offended him by thinking him too negligent, and he in return thinks I have bin unnecessarily troublesome, I cou'd not help resenting his management a little, when I had a note sent me on Thursday from the Wharfinger to come below the Bridge to take out a Sufferance or else the trees he said wou'd not be clear'd, and when I came it was a sixpenny business. However if they come safe betwixt us both I grudge not my pains. The Ship's name is ye Providence the Master's Ralph Higginson of Leverpoole, they will be deliver'd to you there or at Nessen within 3 miles of Frodsham Bridge which you please. I only desire you will let me know what one of ye Bundles weighs, whether it be not nearer one hunderd than three. They wou'd sail he said Yesterday.

Yesterday the fruit trees went by Knowles. I did not see them but Coll. Standley's gardener gave me an account of their delivery; he got them for me, and was likewise with me the two days before about the trees, for which I gave him ten shillings.

I am Your dutifull & obedient son

(signed) W. Aston

	L	S	D
Limes 150	7	00	0
Matts	0	15	9
Wharfage	0	03	4
Sufferance	0	00	6
2 Wateridge to Putney	0	07	6
To ye Gardiner	0	10	0
7 Peaches	0	14	0
2 Vines	0	01	6
1 double Matt	0	00	6
In all	9	13	1

It will be seen that the Lime trees, already some 2 inches in diameter of trunk, cost less than 1s. each, a Peach tree 2s. and a Grapevine 9d. The cost of transport, of which £3 10s. for shipping was merely the largest single item, would altogether amount to nearly 50% of the net cost of the plants.

The amount of trouble taken to obtain trees and plants was remarkable. When Sir Edward Blackett, Bart., was laying out the gardens of Newby Hall near Ripon he engaged as his chief gardener Peter Aram, who had trained at Fulham Palace under George London. Aram, who was something of a botanist (and father of the brilliant if notorious Eugene Aram), got the then handsome salary of £16 a year, probably starting in 1693. Trees were mostly brought up from the Brompton Park nursery, and Blackett dealt personally with Henry Wise. This later on led to a family romance, for Wise's daughter Patience was to marry John Blackett, and the Wise family moved up into the country gentry themselves. Aram was sent on journeys to find plants, notably in 1695 when he went to Holland to get trees and seeds. He was paid a total of nearly £20 for the costs of his journey and of seeds bought, apart from heavy expenditure on trees: £66 in addition to £15 customs duty paid at Hull, and £3 13s. for the transport costs from Hull to York by water and from York to Newby. No particulars of these accounts survive, but prices are given in a later statement of trees and seeds bought in London in 1714:

2000 Elms 1000 Beech at 5s. per 100	07. 10. 00
1000 less (i.e. smaller) Beech at 2s. 6d. per 100	01. 05. 00
27 Fruit Trees	01. 11. 08
30 lb. Clover Seed	00. 12. 06
Garden Seeds & Walnuts	01. 02. 07
Charges of these things	00. 16. 08
Charges of Boxes &c. from New &c.	00. 07. 04

Seeds were commonly bought from John Turner of London, whose firm, at 'the Orange-Tree, over against the Duke of Bedford's House, in the Strand', lasted a long time. He was still in business in 1733 and by 1760 Minier & Co. were seedsmen at the same address, which became No. 60, Strand. Like Lucas, Fuller and several others in the trade, Turner made a speciality of seeds for Improvement, and issued a pamphlet of four pages on Trefoyle, Ray-Grass, La Lucerne, Clover-Grass, St. Foyn and Spurry-Seeds, concluding with the large-type manifesto: 'You may likewise be Furnished with Right-Riga, or Dantzick Flax-Seeds'. Turner's bill for seeds sent to Newby in 1695-96 was £2 4s. 10d. and in 1697-98 a total of £5 16s. 0d. One detailed note of seeds survives from 1694-95, and gives an idea of what was bought and of current prices:

By paid for Strasburg Onions	1½ li.	00.	07.	06
London Raddish	2½	00.	08.	00
Black & White Spa(nish) Rad(dish)	4 ozs.	00.	04.	00
Bees (? Best) Collyflower	½ dr.	00.	02.	06
Ital(ian) Sallary	½ oz.	00.	00.	06
Sweet Marjoram	1	00.	01.	0
Golden Purslan	3	00.	03.	0
Kidney Beans	3 qts.	00.	03.	0
Double Afr(ican) Mar(igold)		00.	01.	0
Fr(ench) Marrigold		00.	01.	6

Belvidear	½ oz.	00.	01.	6
Hysop	2	00.	00.	8
Capsicum Indicum all Sorts		00.	02.	6
By paid for Silver fir	2 ozs.			
Salsify	3			
Scorzoneray	3 / 8 at 2s.	0.	16.	0
Amomum Plinij	0½	0.	01.	0
Sensitive Plans (sic)		0.	01.	0
porter			01.	

Most of these plants have been met before, but it is interesting to note the inclusion of Silver Fir seeds along with vegetables, herbs and flowers. Belvidere was the old name for Summer Cypress (Kochia scoparia), still praised in late Victorian times by William Robinson and holding its place in the catalogues even today. Prices for flower seeds seldom state the amount, being still sold by 'the packet', but a few accounts of the early 18th century mention ounces or half-ounces. In 1729 Henry Ellison of Gateshead Park bought from William Lowther of London a long list of seeds including French and African Marigold both at 8d. an ounce, Marvel of Peru at 1s., and 'Purple Stock Jullyflower' at 6d.; while in the same year Henry Woodman of Strand-on-the-Green supplied 2 ozs. of 'Sweet Sented pease' at 1s. an ounce, 'Venice' (Venus') Looking glass (Specularia speculum) at 1s. 6d., Scarlet Lupins at 6d., and Double Lark Spur at 2s. Woodman in 1733 was sending seeds of French and African 'Marygould' to Gateshead, 2 ozs. of each at 1s. an ounce. Since there is evidence that Woodman, a tree and shrub nurseryman, got his seeds from Moses James of Stangate, Lambeth, the high price was not neccessarily due to inflation since 1729. On the other hand, Stephen Switzer in 1734 charged only 6d. an ounce for Annual Sunflower, Red Candytuft and Prince's Feather, and 4d. an ounce for French Marigold.

Fruit trees were still a preoccupation of the country gentry at the end of the 17th century, and the prices current are well shown by some bills for plants supplied to Lord Irwin at Temple Newsam near Leeds in Yorkshire in 1692-95 through the gardener Thomas Cooke. Peaches and Nectarines were from 2s. to 3s. 6d. each, Pear 1s. each, Apple, Cherry, Plum, Quince and Vine only 6d. each. Two dozen 'Douch Gousbere and Courrent plantes' cost 2s. 6d., and two 'orring Aprecox' (Orange Apricots) 1s. each. Considerable numbers of trees were planted: in the season 1692-93 alone 129 Apples, 45 Cherries, 14 Peaches and Nectarines and 20 Pears, besides other things in small quantity. Forest trees were planted rather later: they were still coming from London & Wise at Brompton in 1701, but the next wave of large-scale planting in 1728 and onwards depended upon the firm of John Perfect of Pontefract. The great turning-point in the history of the British nursery-trade was reached about 1700, when the earliest of the great provincial firms were launched, characteristically in Yorkshire.

Apart from the famous florist John Rea (c. 1605-1681), whose nursery was in the remote village of Kinlet in the south of Shropshire, all the early nurserymen of note were based in the London area. In the provinces generally there is little sign of serious activity before the middle of the 18th century, though William Lucombe is said to have started his famous nursery at Exeter in 1720. The first great nursery in Scotland was founded at Hassendeanburn near Hawick in 1729 by Robert Dickson. In the city of York, however, there was an ancient nursery which had existed since 1665 if not earlier and which had been taken over in 1695 by George Telford. George's son John Telford (1689-1771), who took over the firm from his widowed mother in 1714, had in the next 20 years made a great name for himself, as we shall shortly see. When subscriptions were invited for *The Practical Husbandman and Planter* in 1733 a total of 350 (as well as six subscribers outside England and Wales) was obtained. This total includes 39 professional gardeners, mostly head gardeners to big estates, three London seedsmen, and only two nurserymen, both in Yorkshire. These were John Telford and John Perfect of Pontefract. The Pontefract nursery, like that at York, went back at least to the previous generation, for the first John Perfect (died 1722) had by 1717 been able to supply Elms and Limes for the great planting at Studley Royal near Ripon.

The Perfects must have had influential backing from the start and secured a large share of the trade in the North and North Midlands: by 1769 their (manuscript) catalogue reached Savernake in Wiltshire. For four generations the family flourished exceedingly (though accused of over-charging), then turned to banking and sold the plant business about 1811. It was, however, John Telford who first won fame. Francis Drake published *Eboracum*, his folio history of York, in 1736. In describing the site of the former Dominican Friary, Drake thought it worth while to say that it was 'at present occupied by Mr. Tilford, a worthy citizen, and whose knowledge in the mystery of gardening renders him of credit to his profession; being one of the first that brought our northern gentry into the method of planting and raising all kinds of forest trees, for use and ornament'. The Friars' Gardens at York had almost certainly been occupied as a trade nursery from 1665, and may have had a much earlier tradition of horticulture going back to monastic times. They were occupied by Matthew Wharton until his death in 1695, when George Telford took them over, founding the famous firm which lasted under the next three generations of his own family until 1816, and then in the hands of the botanical family of Backhouse until 1955.

The great age of planting in the North of England began in earnest at Studley Royal soon after 1710, when John Aislabie undertook his grand and unsurpassed design. Aislabie, a leading politician and Chancellor of the Exchequer from 1718 until his disgrace two years later in the South Sea Bubble, was well served. His head gardener, William Fisher, was a good deal more than that, acting as clerk of the works and surveyor for his master's buildings as well as for the great changes in the grounds and gardens. Fisher, like Peter Aram at Newby, had a salary of £16 a year, but was also paid board at 4s. a week. His son, Richard Fisher, was a noted sculptor and produced carved work for the house and ornaments for the gardens. Major work was certainly under way by 1716 and in 1717 John Perfect was paid £16 13s. 4d. for Limes and Elms, in 1721 over £32 for trees, and in 1724 £15 10s. for 300 Elms. By 1729 works were in progress around the lake formed from the River Skell, when a letter from William Fisher to Aislabie shows that an estate nursery for trees had been formed and that a new nursery was being made. Aislabie clearly disliked spending money in the furtherance of his great project; Fisher wrote: (18 February 1728/9)

'We have froast every Night but are making readey for planting; we have made the Grownd at the head of the great Dam fit for planting . . . . . we have Trenched the pece of grownd next to the Lane in Lay garrs for a Nursery to move the trees that we leave in the old Nursery . . . . . . I am verey sorry that your honor thinks i am Extravegent in Gardin Seeds, I sent for no More then was absolutely Nesearey . . . . . Seeds £2 15s. 4d.' (with another £1 8s. 6d. for two spades, hoes, mats, etc.).

A Green House was built at Studley by William Etty, the well known carpenter-architect of York (c. 1675-1734), at a cost of over £43, but the bill was not paid until four years after the work was done and three after William Etty's death. Nicholas Terry, a nurseryman not otherwise known, supplied 124 Yews in 1737 for £4 10s., and in the same year John Telford obtained payment for a long account for seeds supplied in 1729-33 as well as for several ornamental trees, including two Larches:

1737 Nov.15	Bot. of Jno. Telford		
2 Larix	0	2	0
1 Benjamin Tree (Lindera benzoin)	0	2	6
1 Cassina (Maurocenia capensis)	0	2	6
1 Paliurus (Paliurus spina-Christi)	0	2	6
1 Nettle Tree (Celtis occidentalis)	0	1	0
1 Double Flowering Allmond	0	1	0
	0	11	6

Aislabie was still getting some plants and seeds from Perfects, and in 1738 paid them for 60 English Elm trees (£2 5s.), 6 Variegated Nightshade (1s. 6d.), 3 Phillyrea vera (1s. 6d.) and 3 Double blossom'd Thorns (1s.), as well as seeds to the value of £4. In the following year Perfects provided a few seeds and some fruit trees and stocks: 8 Dwarf Morrello Cherry trees (6s.), 50 small Peach trees for stocks and 10 Breda Apricots ditto at 4d. each (£1), 50 Muskle Plum stocks, 40 St. Julian Plum stocks and 50 Pear stocks, all at 1d. each (11s. 8d.). A 'dwarf' fruit tree was what is known nowadays as a bush tree, in contradistinction to a standard. The provision of fruit stocks suggests that John Hossack, who had succeeded William Fisher as head gardener in 1733, was an orchardman and proposed to undertake a campaign of grafting.

The detailed accounts for vegetable seeds supplied by John Telford in 1729-33 state amounts as well as itemised costs, so that they form a good substitute for a price-list of the period (see Appendix III, p. 75). Prices per ounce varied very greatly. For instance, seven kinds of Lettuce seed were bought for the Studley gardens, Cabbage Lettuce at 3d. an ounce, Brown Dutch and Capuchin at 6d., White and Green Cos both costing 1s., while Imperial and Silesia varieties were as much as 1s. 3d. an ounce. Most kinds of Peas were 6s. a peck, but Long Hotspur cost only 3s. 6d. Dutch Savoy seed was 6d. an ounce, Early and Red Cabbage 1s. each, Best Cauliflower 4s. an ounce. In general seeds of herbs cost 4d. an ounce, but Sweet Marjoram only 2½d.; very cheap seeds, at only 2d. an ounce, were Red Beet, Corn Salad, and Yellow Turnip. (For full text of accounts see Appendix)

The existence of the two great nurseries at York and Pontefract gave estate planting in Yorkshire a flying start. It was not until a generation later that Tyneside, for example, was able to buy locally instead of importing by ship from London. This is well shown by the detailed accounts preserved for Gateshead Park, where vast numbers of trees, shrubs and plants were bought from Henry Woodman in 1729-33 at prices which led to recrimination, and difficulties over shipment. To us the prices seem modest enough, for a thousand mixed flowering shrubs were sent for £12 10s., a standard price of 3d. each. The planter, Henry Ellison, was in his own way a pioneer, for he had 'no great Veneration for greens' and 'wou'd have of the Flowering evergreens Nothing but Laurestynes & of them but 50'. This notable order consisted of 100 'Satisus' (Cytisus), 100 St. John's Wort, 100 Scorpion Senna, 10 Bladder Senna, 100 Spanish Broom, 100 'Lealocks', 100 'Saringas', 50 Yellow Jesamins, 40 Cornelian Cherries, 30 Althaea Frutex, 100 Spiraea Frutex, 50 Gelder Roses, 50 Roses several sorts, 20 Sumachs, and the 50 'Laurestyness'. Besides these there were four White Jasmines, 16 Laburnams, and 16 Woodbines, all at 4d. each. By 1751 Mr. Ellison was dealing with Perfects at Pontefract, but at about that time Gateshead was itself becoming one of the centres of the plant trade. About 1734 George Dale of Hebburn Quay founded a nursery which, after his death in 1781, was taken over by William Falla and made into one of the most flourishing in the North; and the rival firm of William Joyce in Gateshead was by 1754 advertising fruit trees, shrubs and seeds 'as cheap as in London'; in 1757 his stock was very large.

In contrast to the large-scale operations of great estates, we can look at the stocking of a rectory garden at Kirkby Overblows, about 5 miles south of Harrogate, for the Rev. Thomas Metcalfe in 1763-66. The rector spread his custom between three nurserymen, the first, Richard Simpson, being apparently a local gardener who undertook planting as well as supplying the plants. His account runs:

March ye 14th 1763 the Revd. Mr. Medcafe to Richard Simpson	
4 Men one day	6. 0
and one Boy a Day	1. 0
2 Qurt of Early Chorlton peas	1. 4
2 Qurt of Marrow pease	1. 4
(various other vegetable seeds)	
4 Score Cabege plants	1. 0
2 Score of Califlower plants	2. 0
6 Score Lettus plants	1. 6
2 Peach and 2 Nectron trees sorts	6. 0
4 Dwarfe appletrees of sorts	4. 0
21st (March) Tow Men one Day each	3. 0
100 of Garding Nails	0. 4
June 27th My Man 2 Days	2. 0
Ohortchocks (Artichokes)	0. 9
Sept. ye 6th 2 Men tow Days each	4. 6
October ye 4th thyme Sage Sweet Margrom and Mint	0. 7

Simpson receipted for the total, £2 16s., on 26 January 1764

In the autumn of 1764 Mr. Metcalfe ordered more fruit trees and some

ornamental shrubs and flowers from Telford of York, whose account has a
short letter appended to it:

York the 12th Decembr. 1764		Bought of John Telford Sr.
2 Nonparells		
2 Ribston Pippins	5 Dwarf Apples on Dutch Stocks	3. 4
1 Piles Russet		
4 Dwarf Codling Apples on Crab Stocks		2.
1 Magdalen Peach		1. 6
1 Roman Nectarine		1. 6
1 Orange Apricot		1.
2 Syringas (Philadelphus coronarius)		6
1 Cytissus		3
1 Persian Jasmine (Syringa persica)		4
2 Mezereons (Daphne mezereum)		8
1 Hypericum Frutex (Spiraea hypericifolia)		3
1 Gelderose (Viburnum opulus)		3
1 Purple & 1 White Lilacs (Syringa vulgaris)		6
2 Double flowering Thorns		1.
Double Violet Roots		
A mat		8

£   13. 9

The Trees you gave me orders for the last week, I have now sent by John Wharton
the Skipton Carrier, & hope all may be agreeable.

I am Sr. your Most Obt. hble Servt. (Signed) John Telford Junr.

P.S. I saw Mr. Ewbank yesterday who was very well and desir'd his Comp(limen)ts.

Two years later a third nurseryman, Christopher Thompson (died 1782) of
Pickhill near Thirsk, appears on the scene and with an 8s. order for fruit trees
threw in free no fewer than 31 ornamental shrubs. His covering note gives
further information on the local transport of plants:

To The Revd. Mr. Metcalfe at Kirkby Over Blow near Harwood Bridge

Pickhill 21st Nov. 1766

Sir/   Agreable to the orders you were so kind as favour me with have this day sent
you as per Contra. They are sent by Pickersgill's Waggon pack'd up in one Matted
Bundle directed as usual to be left at Harwood Bridge, & I hope they'll come safe &
to your approbation. Your Orders & Interest at all times will greatly Oblige, Revd. Sir

Your most Obedt. Servant

(signed) Christr. Thompson

The Revd. Mr. Metcalfe		Of Christr. Thompson
1766 Novr. 21st		
1 Drap d'Or		1. 6
1 Le Roche Courbon	Plums Dwf	
1 Nobless Peach		1. 6
1 Black old Newington Nectarine		1. 6
2 Dwarf Nonpariel on Paradise stock		2. —
1 Bass Mat 10d. Carrg. paid to Harwood		1. 6

£0. 8. 0

3 Elders of sorts
4 Bladder Senas
4 Spanish Brooms
4 Goosberry leav'd Currans
3 Female Dogwoods   gratis
4 Rhamnoides's
4 Viburnums
2 Strip'd Sycamores
3 Aria Theophrastes

At the prices in Telford's catalogue of 1775, this collection of shrubs was worth about 9s. 6d. or well over the total value of the order it accompanied. It may be that Thompson's nursery was a fairly new one and that this bonus represented an advertisement that might help to win further custom.

Throughout the 18th century and on into the 19th this intense interest in planting pervaded the country. In some cases timber trees were grown as an ultimate source of profit, in others they were lavished to improve the aesthetics of home park and garden or to enrich the scenery of great estates such as Studley and Stourhead. Elsewhere it was the modest garden and shrubbery surrounding a small house that was the object of care. In all, the demand for trees and shrubs rose to fantastic heights, and before 1800 nurseries were springing up everywhere. That it was possible to fulfil the many thousands of orders was due to a wonderful development of enterprise and skill, building upon the foundations of a few pioneers: Roger Looker and his associates of 1681, and the two Yorkshire nurseries operating within the next generation under the Perfects of Pontefract and the Telfords of York.

IV

THE FIRST PRINTED LISTS WITH PRICES

AT THE START of this book it was remarked that even at the present day very few indeed of the many thousands of nurserymen's and seedsmen's lists and catalogues issued yearly are preserved. The survivors from former times are hardly to be numbered in dozens, and the available scatter from before 1800 — even before 1840 — is not conceivably representative. In such conditions it is impossible to prove whether or no there were any detailed printed catalogues including prices before 1775. Obviously there must have been manuscript lists marked with current prices, at the shop or nursery if nowhere else, but to judge from those early printed lists that have survived, it was extremely rare for prices to be set up in type. From an interesting group of catalogues of the 1830's preserved among the muniments of the Lords Monson and, perhaps, more truly representative than any body of earlier material, it is clear that right up to Victorian times it was customary for the general lists of seedsmen to be current for several years and to bear no date and carry no prices; or else to be dated (but possibly issued once in several years) but still to be unpriced. Every year, at that period, a separate list with all prices was issued of the imported Dutch bulbs and flower roots of the season. There are precedents for this in the priced lists of such bulbs printed by Richard Weston in the fourth volume (1777) of his remarkable work *The Universal Botanist and Nurseryman.* Most of Weston's lists are dated to 1777, but some go back to 1769: all of these priced catalogues refer to bulbs and to Florists' Flowers except for one catalogue of named varieties of Gooseberry 'Trees', raised from seed in Lancashire to 1780, 320 sorts in all. These Gooseberries, like the bulbs for which prices were given by Weston, were sold by James Maddock or Maddox, an enterprising florist of Walworth near London. What may well be significant is that Maddock was a Quaker of Warrington, Lancs., where he had trained before coming to London.

The connection of a Lancashire nurseryman in London with Gooseberries raised in Lancashire is obvious, but his northern background may imply a good deal more. Any customer living in the London area, and members of the nobility and landed classes who had agents in the metropolis, could easily find out the fair market prices of plants, seeds and bulbs. It was easy to go direct to the main nurseries, to inspect large stocks of bulbs, to see them in flower at such establishments as that of Maddock in Walworth. This worked well for those who could afford to pay high prices for newly imported exotics, or newly raised named varieties of Florists' Flowers and other choice plants. It was not helpful to those who rarely if ever visited London, had slender means, and needed to be able to buy from stocks held regionally. It is notorious that in the North of England a penny has always been looked at several times before being spent. Furthermore, it was mainly in the North that there was a widespread cult of growing and raising Florists' Flowers among the poorer classes of society. There was then in the North a much wider demand for plants of all kinds, from a greater number of individuals drawn from a broader spectrum of incomes; yet the number of suppliers was extremely low. Until the last quarter of the 18th century there were, as has been said, very few provincial nurseries of any standing; so that those that did exist had to serve a large region as well as a greater number of potential growers to the square mile.

There is thus a prima facie case for regarding the issue of lists with prices as in the first instance a phenomenon of the North of England, where there were many more would-be customers, but of far lower average incomes than elsewhere. If James Maddock was already used to priced catalogues in the Warrington area before he moved to London, it would account for his being, to all appearance, the first of the London firms to issue statements of prices. In the case of trees and shrubs the same factors applied to the two great nurseries serving the region, and it may well be no mere accident of survival that the first catalogues in print to give prices throughout should be those of John and George Telford of York, issued in 1775, and of William and John Perfect (see Appendix IV).

Two points need to be made. Firstly, that in referring to prices as being given throughout, allowance must be made for a few left blank and filled in in ink in the surviving copy of 'Telford'. These were few in number, and were obviously prices exceptionally liable to fluctuation. Secondly, it is necessary to discuss the dating of Perfects' catalogue, which bears the printed figures 17 and a blank; this is filled in on a copy in the John Rylands Library, Manchester, as 1776; and in the copy in the British Museum as 1777. So far as surviving copies yet known are concerned, it is in any case correct to describe the Telford catalogue as the earlier. It is all the same desirable to know whether the Telford catalogue might not in fact have been plagiarized from a catalogue of Perfects already in print.

Comparison between the two lists, so extremely similar to one another, is in any case interesting and instructive. Both were printed in York, that of Telford by Ann Ward, and that of Perfect by C. Etherington. Each consists of 18 pages, and their basic arrangement is identical, but the paging is different. The Telford catalogue of 1775 has its title-page as the front cover, blank on the back, followed by the text printed on pages numbered up to 18. The Perfect Catalogue has a printed outer cover with half-title, backed blank, then the title page, backed by the first page of printed text, continued on pages numbered to 16. There are thus 16 pages of text in Telfords' list, but only 15 in that of the Perfects; yet the latter has a greater total number of entries. This is secured by printing the Pontefract catalogue in smaller type and having smaller margins at top and bottom. In arrangement the Perfects' catalogue is more accurately alphabetized, suggesting that its compiler was able to profit from the imperfections of a predecessor; it is far more difficult to imagine a plagiarist deliberately moving entries out of their correct order. The larger number of entries also indicates a determination on the part of Perfect to 'go one better' than Telfords. Finally, there are prices filled in in ink in the Telford list which are printed in the other. All factors agree in suggesting that it was Telfords who produced the pioneer list, and that Perfect made haste to copy and improve upon it.

Since the arrangement, and most of the details, of the two lists are

1. Double Nasturtium.	9. White Lilly strip'd with purple.	17. Princess picote July flower	25. Double white throat wort.
2. Double white Maudlin.	10. Spanish Broom.	18. Geranium noctu olens.	26. French Marigold.
3. Prince picote July flower	11. Carolina kidney bean tree.	19. White Valerian.	27. Double scarlet Lychnis.
4. True Caper.	12. Double strip'd female balsam.	20. Hop Horn beam.	28. Double blew Larkspur.
5. Virginian yellow Jessimine.	13. True Olive tree.	21. Indian or china pink.	29. Hungarian Glamer.
6. Painted Lady Carnation.	14. Red Oleander.	22. Double Pomegranate.	30. Double Stock.
7. Double blew throat-wort.	15. Painted Lady pink.	23. Double mouse ear.	31. Bean Caper.
8. Scarlet Martagon.	16. White Lupin.	24. Virginian scarlet honeysuckle	32. White Oleander.

JULY

Drawn by P. Casteels.

From the Collection of Rob. Furber Gardiner at Kensington. 1730.

Engrav'd by H. Fletcher.

1	Purple Althæa frutex.	9	Purple Coxcomb Amaranthus.		17	Egyptian scarlet holly hock.	26	Zisole from Genoa.
2	Ivy leav'd. Jasmine.	10	Shrub St Johns wort.		18	Yellow stript. marvel of peru.	27	Double spanish Jasmine.
3	Iris Uvaria.	11	Penas blew Throatwort.		19	Stript. Monthly rose.	28	White. Eternal.
4	Purple Sultan.	12	Palma Christi.		20	Double æther flos.	29	True bearing Palium flower.
5	Purple toad flax.	13	Purple Convolvulus.		21	Semper Augustus Auricula.	30	Scarlet. Althæa.
6	Purple Amaranthoides.	14	Polyanthos.		22	Dwarf. Convolvulus.	31	Canary shrub fox glove.
7	Double Arabian Jasmine.	15	Indian yellow Jasmine.		23	Willow leav'd. Apocynum.	32	Long blowing honey suckle.
8	Yellow Ketmia.	16	Double flowering Myrtle.		24	Ipios of America.	33	Double purple Virgin bower.
					25	Virginian flowering Raspberry.	34	Virginian scarlet Martagon.

AUGUST

From the Collection of Robt Furber Gardiner at Kensington 1730.

Design'd by P. Casteels.

Engrav'd by H. Fletcher.

identical, and it may safely be assumed that it was the Telford list which was the original, its description will serve for both. The title calls it a catalogue of Forest-Trees, Fruit-Trees, Ever-Green and Flowering-Shrubs; and that is exactly what it is. Forest Trees occupy six pages; Fruit Trees one page only; Shrubs the remaining nine pages. Evidently it was felt that no sufficient purpose would be served by listing the varieties of fruit trees, and in Perfects' catalogue a note is added to the list: 'N.B. On Application, written Catalogues will be delivered, containing the particular Sorts of the Fruit-Trees propagated in these Nurseries.' One of these lists, of 1769, went to Savernake and survives in the Wiltshire Record Office. The printed lists were therefore not intended as a complete guide, but were supplemented by manuscript lists of which only a few copies were required. While on the subject of the lists of fruit it may be said that, apart from the more precise alphabetical order of Perfects' list, there is no difference between the two, except that Telfords grew English standard Medlars as well as Dutch, the latter being the only kind stocked at Pontefract. The English type was regarded as superior, since it was priced at 1s. 6d. against 1s. 4d. for Dutch.

The prices charged for fruit trees may be compared with those of Ricketts' lists of 1667 and the more recent accounts already quoted. In a little over a century, Peaches and Nectarines had been stabilized at 2s. 6d., instead of 2s. for the one and 3s. for the other. Apples, which had been 8d., now cost the same as dwarfs on Crab stocks, but were 1s. on Paradise, and the same for standards. Cherries, which also had been 8d. from Ricketts, had risen to 1s. for a dwarf and 1s. 4d. for a standard; dwarf Pears could still be had for 1s. as before, but standards were up to 1s. 4d. Set against the general background of prices in the period, which showed some rise after 1667, later compensated by a fall towards 1700 and a relatively stable value of money until after 1760, followed by an inflation of some 10% – 20%, we can see that the general average cost of fruit trees had risen along with the inflation. The drop in the price of Nectarines must therefore have meant that they were much more commonly grown than previously. This in turn reflects both the popularity of gardening and the formation of many more walled gardens to maintain a domestic supply of fruit for the table.

The fact that a wave of inflation had begun about 1760 or so is interestingly confirmed by comparison with the prices charged earlier in the 18th century. We saw that in 1738 Perfects supplied dwarf Cherries for 9d. each, against the 1s. of 1775-76; Telfords themselves had charged only 8d. each for dwarf Apples on Dutch stocks in 1764, and 6d. each for Codlings on Crab stocks. A Peach or a Nectarine had then been 1s. 6d. (against that price for dwarfs or 2s. 6d. for standards), and an Orange Apricot 1s. as it had been in the 1690's at Temple Newsam; dwarf Apricots were now up to 1s. 6d. and standards to 2s., a big and sudden rise. Dwarf Plums, 9d. each in 1766, had nine years later gone up to 1s., and though many prices had not yet risen, the upward tendency had shown itself and had in fact come to stay. Taking published price indexes from 1775 at every five years, there was a continuous rise up to 1800, when the cost of living had doubled. After the end of the Napoleonic wars there came a downward tendency, so that by the mid 1830's costs stood at only some 20% above the general level of the first 60 years of the 18th century. Bearing these facts in mind, it is possible to regard the catalogues as still representative of prices during

D

the great age of planting, though just starting to show the upward tendency of their time.

The lists of Forest Trees show the very great difficulties which beset any attempt to compare quoted prices. Many kinds of trees were priced by the thousand, the prices being given for a number of different sizes. Taking Beech trees as an instance, the cost per thousand for one-year seedlings, 6 inches high, was 10s.; for two-year seedlings, 15s.; for transplanted trees one foot high the price went up to £2 a thousand; thereafter the prices are given per hundred: 6s. at 1½ feet, 7s. 6d. for 2 feet, 15s. for 3 feet, and £1 for 4 feet trees. Perfects, who specialised in even larger trees, charged 6d. each for 8-foot and 8d. each for 10-foot beeches. It is useless therefore to compare prices at all unless the precise state of the young trees, their size and whether transplanted or not, is clearly stated. The higher prices for larger trees were based not only upon the longer period of labour represented in tending and transplanting, but also on the greater area of ground occupied.

Taking the distances recommended in modern times, e.g. for growing oaks, acorns are sown three inches apart each way. If all came up, there would in theory be 696,960 seedlings to the acre; but when transplanted at one year old to a foot apart, only one-sixteenth as many trees, that is 43,560, would fill an acre of ground. On the other hand, from the point of view of the planter buying young stock to form an oak plantation at say three years old, permanent positions 20 feet apart each way will need only 108 trees to the acre planted. A larch plantation, spaced at only four feet apart, requires 2,722 trees. Consequently both the nurseryman and the planter are involved with the mathematical problem of how many trees, at what ages, of what particular kind, can be fitted into any given area of ground, and the answers differ enormously according to the conditions of each problem. Taking the prices of 1775 from Telfords', catalogue and the spacings quoted, one thousand English Oak seedlings, transplanted and a foot high, could have been bought for £1 10s., and put into permanent positions would need rather more than nine acres of land. In the case of larches, which should be planted out at two years old and four feet apart, the cost of a single acre of plantation would have been roughly 28 x 4s., the price per hundred, or £5 12s. To plant the nine acres or so available, but with larch instead of oak, would cost well over £50 for the young trees.

The sizes of nurseries have always varied very much, but in the 18th and early 19th centuries the really important nurseries around London varied from 30 up to 60 acres, and one was over 100 acres, namely Wilmot's of Lewisham. Lysons, who noted this, was 'told that there are some more extensive nursery grounds in Yorkshire, chiefly for forest trees'. At that time, soon after 1800, there were possibly three Yorkshire nurserymen operating on the grand scale: Telfords of York, Perfects of Pontefract, and William Pontey (died 1831), who had a large nursery for forest trees at Kirkheaton near Huddersfield. Much of his land was held by lease, and this seems also to have applied to Telfords and probably to Perfects. It is therefore not easy to discover just how much acreage was held, particularly as in some cases it was scattered out in several separate nurseries over a number of parishes. In the case of the Telfords it is known that they owned or leased some 20 acres in and around York in at least four different places, but they probably leased other large tracts of land not now identifiable. What sort of stock they held of each kind and size must have varied, but assuming on the average that they had 10,000 of everything sold by the thousand, and a thousand of everything quoted by the hundred, their stock of forest trees would have amounted to some 350,000; it may have been very much greater.

Some clue to the quantities sold is given by orders of Sir John Nelthorpe, Bart., of Scawby near Brigg, North Lincolnshire. In 1786 he had 7,000 Beech, 3 years old, at £1 10s. a thousand, as well as 2,000 Birch at 15s. a thousand; and next year he got another 6,000 Beech, 4 years old, but still charged at £1 10s. a thousand. Concerning this second order the nurseryman, David Watts of London, apologised for delay, 'large Beech being so scarce'. It was then quite difficult to fulfil an order for as many as 6,000 Beech at 4 years old. These London orders were sent by sea to Hull, and matting, packing, porterage and wharfage added some 4% or 5% in all to the cost of the trees. Transport across the Humber and by land to Scawby had of course also to be added. In spite of this, the reason for sending to London can be seen in the remarkably low price per thousand, only three-quarters of the 1775-76 price charged by Telfords and Perfects for the smallest size, 1 foot, of transplanted Beech. Presumably there were nurseries near London working on a scale which kept their overheads down to a minimum and enabled them to compete on favourable terms even when long-distance transport had to be added to the selling price.

This impression is borne out by a number of other prices quoted by Watts in 1786. His two-year old Larch, 'good plants', cost £1 a thousand, against £2 per thousand at York in 1775. Walnuts, also two years old, were 8s. a hundred, 'Filbards' 5s.; Mountain Ash at 3 years 10s. Four kinds of Poplars, viz, Large Balsam, Hardy Carolina, Berry Bearing, and Black Italian, 5 feet high, were all £1 5s. a hundred; Telfords charged 2s. 6d. each for Balsam and Berry Bearing Poplar, 1s. each for Carolina, 10s. per hundred for Black Poplar or Abele, 3 feet, and 15s. for Italian or Lombardy, 6 feet high. The Lombardy Poplar had been introduced as recently as 1758, and it is one of the few striking differences between the Telford and Perfect lists that, while the York nursery was able to offer both 3-feet and 6-feet specimens, Perfects of Pontefract had only 2 feet and 3 feet sizes, at 6s. and 10s. per hundred respectively. In conifers Watts had Balm of Gilead Firs and American Spruce, both at 6s. a hundred; in 1775 the smallest size of the former, 6 inches high, had cost £1 5s., and White American Spruce, 1 foot high, 9d. each. No doubt these very big reductions in price, as in the case of the Lombardy Poplar, meant that the species were becoming much commoner in Britain.

There was another method open to the owners of large estates prepared to wait for results: sowing seed in their own nurseries. This seems to have been the way in which stock was raised on the Delaval estates in Northumberland. The Seaton Delaval papers include a series of letters from London seedsmen in regard to tree seeds, covering the period 1776 to 1784. The main supplier was James Shiells of Parliament Street, who was able to provide seeds of Scotch Fir and Crab, but when asked for Birch seed in 1781 replied that the crop had failed. Shiells could, however, supply young Birch plants at 10s. a thousand in quantity up to 200,000 or 300,000; he pointed out that each acre would need 4,840 plants at 3 feet apart in each direction. Unfortunately there is no real basis for comparing this with Yorkshire prices, as neither Telfords nor Perfects supplied Birch except after transplanting, at 7s. 6d. per hundred 2 feet high.

Though of less economic importance than the forest trees, and with less impact on the landscape, the Evergreen and Flowering Shrubs are intrinsically the most interesting section of the catalogue. It is here too that the technique of printing could be used to particular advantage. Telfords, or Ann Ward, used the marginal asterisk to indicate plants 'tender, and fit only for the Greenhouse or Stove'; and Perfects, or their printer Etherington, carried this a stage further by employing the obelus also to show which plants were evergreens. Both lists are in English only, and make no pretences of a literary or scientific kind. Perfects, improving upon Telfords' catalogue, were able to go a little further in description: for example, where the York list enters 'Cistus, Willow-leav'd, with spotted Flowers', Perfects spread the entry onto two lines as 'Cistus, with Willow Leaves and White Flowers Spotted with Purple'; both nurseries charged 1s. for the plant. It is worth emphasising that these were straightforward trade price-lists for the model already existed for a more pretentious approach based on the Latin names of the genera, in Richard Weston's Catalogue of Trees and Shrubs published in 1770 in volume I of the *Universal Botanist,* which had been printed for three London Booksellers and also for C. Etherington at York. William Malcolm, a nurseryman and seedsman near Kennington in Surrey, had in 1771 produced an admirable general catalogue classified in the Lucas tradition (see chart, pages 18-19), and had in places employed Latin binomial names and English names as well, and the same method was employed by Gordon, Dermer & Co., who were in business before 1779, in an undated catalogue of about this time. The famous nursery of Loddiges of Hackney, in a catalogue of 1777, listed the plants in Latin and gave both German and English names.

As might be expected, each of the two firms, Telfords and Perfects, had certain plants which the other had not. Perfects were at great pains to expand their list as much as possible, and in some places where Telfords had simply said that they had 'sorts' (i.e. varieties) of a plant, Perfects listed theirs separately; in some cases they did have important species which could not be found in York, notably the Fruit-bearing and Purple-flowering Passion Flowers (? Passiflora quadrangularis and P. incarnata), in addition to the Common species (Passiflora caerulea). Only the Purple kind was marked as tender, which must indicate that P. caerulea (introduced 1699) and a fruiting species were being grown outdoors in the North, presumably against walls and matted in winter. It was, however, with Telfords that the advantage mainly lay. They had in stock several hardy exotics that were not at Pontefract, notably two Kalmias (K. latifolia and K. angustifolia), three Magnolias (M. tripetala, M. grandiflora, and ? M. virginiana), the only Rhododendron 'or Rose-Bay' (R. maximum), and the Evergreen Spindle Tree (Euonymus americana). Except for the last, priced at 2s. 6d., these were very expensive plants, costing either 7s. 6d. or 15s.

The Greenhouse and Stove specialities which only Telfords stocked included Cassine capensis ('Cape Philerea') and C. maurocenia (Hottentot Cherry), the Azorian Jasmine (Jasminum azoricum), the Golden-Rod Tree (Bosea yervamora), Royena lucida, and the white variety of the Oleander. Except for the last, these plants would cause little excitement now, yet the two Cassines were priced 5s. each, and the Royena at 4s. On the whole both lists lay a heavy emphasis on hardiness, and it is precisely in this that a great deal of their interest lies. They bear witness to the fact that, before the age of tropical importations for the stove, there had been a period when the shrubbery must have excited as keen an interest as it does again, now that scarce fuel and high labour costs have almost put an end to hothouse cultivation. From the great estates down to the cottage gardens, at any rate in the northern counties of England, the 18th century was an age of stocking up with very many different hardy trees, shrubs and climbers. Only a very widely based demand could have brought prices down to the amazingly low figures shown for the commoner plants. Bearing in mind that, as regards the general cost of living, we must multiply the money of 1775 by a factor of 10 or 12 to yield a very rough idea of present-day purchasing power, we can see with a few examples just how well off plant-buyers were two centuries ago. Flowering Almond bushes, or four varieties of Althea frutex (Hibiscus syriacus), or a Bay Tree, could be bought for 6d. (say 5s. or 6s.); a Spanish Broom (Spartium junceum), Guelder Rose, a White or Yellow Jasmine (Jasminum officinale or J. fruticans), a bush Laburnum, a Laurustinus, a Lilac (in one of three colours), a Pyracantha, a Philadelphus ('Common Syringa') or a Traveller's Joy for 3d. apiece (say 2s. 6d. or 3s.); while for 2d. (about 1s. 9d. or 2s.) it was possible to get one of six kinds of Honeysuckle or one of three sorts of Periwinkle, a Privet, a Sweet Briar or a Spreading Tutsan. The rich flora of northern cottage and village gardens is easily explained. Inclusive of all the items which could be bought for not over 1s. each, Telfords offered more than 200 varieties of shrubs and 37 different Roses.

By good fortune an independent check survives, showing exactly what was most propagated at this period by the York Nursery. The Grimston family of Kilnwick, some 8 miles north of Beverley, were planting extensively, and dealt with Telfords. In 1778 they had obtained a French catalogue of fruit trees: Apricots, Peaches, Pears, Plums and Vines, which they lent to the brothers Telford. The Telfords copied the list and returned it with comments, noting that most of the French varieties were such as 'we esteem here chiefly for Hotwalls'. In regard to Plums, 'the Reine Claude de Tours, wch he calls "La Meilleure d'l'Europe" is our Green Gage, the Damask Noir, Royale, Violet Perdrigon, Drap D'or, & some others We propagate here, but in general the better sorts of Plumbs bear badly in this part of the World, which makes Variety in them less sought after; We propagate about Thirty sorts in our Nurseries but chiefly under different Names to those in this Catalogue, though most likely some of them are the same'.

Four years later, on 12 January 1782, Telfords wrote to Mr. William Pontey, evidently chief gardener at Kilnwick, and very probably identical with the later nurseryman and expert on forest trees. The letter refers to plants already sent, which they hoped 'are all securely disposed of as the Weather is now set in Frosty'; and continues, referring to a List of Shrubs on the other side. The list is of those 'which we are most particularly well stock'd with, we also abound in most other Articles mentiond in the Catalogue' . . . 'We have a large Stock of Beech, Fir, Larch, Elm & other Forest [Trees]'. The list includes well over 100 of the species and varieties of the 1775 catalogue, mostly the cheaper kinds, and also half a dozen things not in the catalogue, two of which – the Manna Ash and the Striped Nightshade – had appeared in Perfects' list of 1776. The other new items were the Entire-leaved Ash, the Weeping Ash, the White Broom (Cytisus albus), the Pennsylvanian Crab, and the Large American Azarole. In the reproduction of the 1775 Catalogue (see Appendix IV), the sorts noted as heavily stocked in 1782 have been marked.

Also among the Grimston estate archives is a broadsheet seedsman's catalogue issued by Stephen Garraway, Seedsman and Net-Maker, of the Rose, near the Globe Tavern, Fleet Street in London. This is of outstanding interest as a surviving example of the type of printed list directly based upon the Lucas model. Although considerably expanded and re-arranged, this list continues most of the traditional classes of seeds and plants and demonstrates the long continuance of the bare series of names, without description or further information. The only concession made is the use of an asterisk to mark Annuals, which are interspersed in the same lists with the Biennials and Perennials. Though undated,[1] Garraway's catalogue probably belongs to the same period of gardening at Kilnwick as the correspondence with Telfords. The mention of 'Double Nastursian' probably implies a date not earlier than 1770.

Though we cannot be certain that Telfords' catalogue of 1775 was the first printed catalogue to quote prices for general stock, or that it was the first printed catalogue issued in the provinces, it is likely that it was among the first in both respects. As we saw, Perfects were sending out catalogues in manuscript in 1769, and there is nothing to suggest that they had ever gone into print before they followed Telfords' lead in 1776. It is suggestive that the few years following 1775 produced a crop of provincial catalogues of which copies have survived. In 1776 William Middlewood of Manchester issued his catalogue of seeds and flower roots 'with the times of sowing and planting, calculated for this Part of the Country'. The idea of combining the trade-list with a calendar of garden operations came from London, where John Webb in 1760 had issued a list 'with instructions for sowing and planting', of which at least three copies are in existence. Johnson assigns to 1753 a catalogue with the same title, put out by W. Webb, presumably John's father or predecessor, but this does not now appear to be in any of the main collections. Also missing is an important catalogue printed in 1779 for James Clarke, Seedsman of Houghton-le-Spring, co. Durham. Fortunately this was described in detail in 1917 by its possessor, William Roberts, in an article in the *Gardeners Chronicle*. Clarke sold 'Kitchen-Garden, Flower, Grass, Forest Tree Seeds and Flower Roots' and his list, running to 52 pages octavo, gave 'their season of Sowing etc. Chiefly adapted to the Northern Climates', on the model of Middlewood's Manchester pamphlet (only 24 pages) of three years before.

Clarke did not mark prices for seeds and plants, but did price the Fruit Trees on his last page. Standard Apples were 1s., dwarfs on Paradise stock 10d., on Crab 8d.; Apricots from 1s. 4d. to 2s. and dwarfs 1s. to 1s. 6d.; Currants, Filberts and Gooseberries were 2d. each; Pears 1s. 2d. for standards and 1s. for dwarfs; Plums 1s. 2d. and 1s., Nectarines and Peaches 2s. and 1s. 6d., and Quinces 8d. Although many of these prices are the same as those charged by Telfords in 1775, a few are cheaper, notably standards on which from 2d. to 6d. a tree might be saved. Quinces were only two-thirds the price,

[1] Stephen Garraway was in business in 1766, as Dr. Albert Hollaender informs me (London Guildhall Department of Prints, collection of Trade Cards and Billheads), and he appears in directories until 1774.

1s., charged at York or at Pontefract. It looks as though Clarke's enterprise marks the beginning of a phase in which small local firms could win custom away from the great undertakings by marginal undercutting. The evidence, however, is slight, since almost all the surviving catalogues come from firms of sufficient standing to maintain the general level of prices.

Among the very few provincial lists to survive is one of 1777 'botanically arranged according to the system of Linnaeus', of plants 'most of which are cultivated and sold by John Brunton & Co.' of Birmingham, a substantial book of nearly 100 pages. Later catalogues of Trees by the same firm were issued in 1782 and 1787. Another substantial octavo book of 100 pages was that printed at Norwich for John Mackie (died 1797) who had founded the Lakenham nursery about 1773. This catalogue, probably to be dated in or soon after 1787, essentially follows the London model and includes forest trees, fruit trees, evergreen and flowering shrubs, hot-house, green-house and herbaceous plants, and seeds. On the old broadsheet pattern, but expanded to four pages, was a general catalogue of Peter Lauder of Bristol, undated but probably of the 1790's. This gives the names of varieties of Fruit Trees, 100 Apples and 32 Cyder Apples, 8 Apricots, 2 Almonds, 3 Barberrys, 20 Cherries, 5 Currants, 6 Figs, 2 Filberts, 67 Gooseberries 'with many other common Sorts', 30 Grapes, 4 Medlars, 3 Mulberries, 18 Nectarines, 43 Peaches, 68 Pears, 34 Plums, 5 Raspberries, 3 Services (Fruit-Bearing, Ash-leaf'd, Common), 6 Strawberries 'with all the Common Sorts', as well as the Sweet or Spanish Chesnut and the Portugal Quince. Herbaceous Plants (including bulbs) follow, then an extensive list of Forest Trees and shrubs, and finally short lists of Green-House Plants, Plants for a Dry Stove or Glass-Case, and Stove Plants. Seeds are mentioned but not listed.

By remarkable good fortune copies of the catalogues of the two great Yorkshire nurseries for 1793 have come down to us, as well as that of William Thompson of Pickhill, son of Christopher Thompson whom we have already met. The father died at the beginning of April 1782, and this list is probably not much later; as it bears the imprint of A(nn) Ward of York it must in any case be earlier than 1788, when she took into partnership her son-in-law George Peacock. The text is very closely based upon both the Telford list of 1775 and Perfects' improvement of the following year, so far as alphabetization is concerned, and the use of the asterisk for tender plants and the obelus to mark evergreens. Plants stocked by Telfords in 1775, but not by Perfects, are included though a few are unpriced and were probably not actually in stock at Pickhill when the catalogue went to press. Spelling has in some cases become less correct. Almost all prices have remained the same, but a very few of the expensive items have dropped a little: thus the Small or Swamp Magnolia cost only 10s. 6d., against 15s. in 1775. About a dozen new plants have appeared, including the single Camellia (still called the 'Althea or Japan Rose'), Arbutus andrachne (introduced in 1724), at 7s. 6d., the White Portugal Broom (in England since 1752), two kinds of Tree Germander, the Spanish with blue flowers (presumably Teucrium fruticans), and with Sulphur-coloured flowers, both at 1s. 6d., Halesia, costing 3s., the Madagascar Periwinkle with white flowers at 2s. 6d. and with purple flowers at 1s. 6d., and 'Veronica quadrata', at 2s. This last was V. elliptica, introduced about 1776 from the Falkland Islands, though it is surprising that it should so soon have reached the North Riding, and not be marked as tender. Still, it appears in Perfects' catalogue of 1788 at the same price as 'Shrubby Veronica' and in Brunton's of 1787 as 'Veronica, Falklands island, with beautiful white flowers' (tender, 2s. 6d.). The explanation lies in the fact that this plant was introduced by John Fothergill, the famous botanist, himself a Yorkshireman and one of the founders of the Quaker school set up in 1777 at Ackworth near Pontefract.

The catalogues of Telfords and Perfects, dated (in ink) to 1793, must both have been printed not earlier than 1790, for both are by George Peacock, who succeeded to the printery on Ann Ward's death in 1789; Perfects' title-page actually bears 179(.). Very few new plants are included beyond those already discussed in connection with Thompson's list. Among the few additions perhaps the most interesting is the Purple or Ponticum Rhododendron, priced at 7s. 6d., while R. maximum still stood at 15s. What is to us the 'ordinary' rhododendron, 'the commonest of exotic evergreens on lime-free soils' (R. H. S. *Dictionary*), had been introduced in 1763: from Gibraltar, as Miss Coats tells us, for it had been carried from Turkey to Andalusia. Until after 1800 it was still in the expensive class, but by the 1820's could be had from Falla of Gateshead from 1s. upwards. Possibly the most interesting feature of these catalogues, which they share with that of the Pickhill Nursery, is the fact that much larger sizes were stocked of some forest trees. Whereas in 1775 the largest Beech listed were 4 feet, in 1793 Telfords were offering up to 6 feet; the same applies to Horse Chestnuts; Ash, formerly 3 feet, could now be had up to 4 feet, and the same was true of Oaks. On the other hand, Walnuts of 4 feet were now the largest, but in 1775 had gone up to 8 and 9 feet. Perfects, however, had been advancing on all fronts, offering White Beam ('Area Theophrasti'), Birch, Elm, Poplars, Sycamore and Walnut up to 10 feet high.

One is left with the impression that Telfords had done little more than mark time, but that Perfects had put on a spurt; though Telfords still had a few items not stocked at Pontefract, it was on the whole with Perfects that the honours rested. Perhaps only by an accident of survival, Perfects' catalogue is accompanied by an unpriced catalogue of Seeds; it is of 12 pages, printed by Peacock, but does not bear a date. The interesting feature of this list is that it harks back to the early subdivisions: Seeds of Roots, Sallad Seeds, Pot and Sweet Herb Seeds, Physical Seeds, Seeds of Trees and Shrubs, Seeds to improve Land, Bird Seeds (Maw, Rape, Hemp, Canary), Flower Seeds (now a long list, but including most of the items already familiar more than a century earlier), the Flower Roots, Sorts of Peas and Beans, and a list of the main kinds of Fruit Trees.

All the surviving Yorkshire catalogues are relatively short, unlike those printed in Birmingham and Norwich. It was only after 1800 that the lengthy book-style list replaced the kind pioneered by Telfords in 1775. There are copies of the 2nd and 3rd 'editions' of the general catalogue produced by Thomas and James Backhouse after they had taken over the York nursery in 1816. That of 1821 is meticulously produced, with Latin and English names in double column, and fills 76 pages. The next issue, in 1827, had been expanded to 124 pages and included a detailed index. Though an enormous advance as works of botanical scholarship, these lists are disappointing in that they give no indication of prices. This lack is to some extent made up by the 64-page catalogue of William Falla & Co. of Gateshead, already mentioned, valid for the 1820's and reproduced in facsimile. Here ancient and modern meet: the forest trees in different sizes, still demanded by the planter; the wider choice available of evergreens and deciduous shrubs; plants for greenhouse and stove; and looking towards English flower borders of the future, an immense list of perennial herbaceous plants.

V

THE END OF AN OLD SONG

THE EARLIER CHAPTERS of this book have sketched in brief outline the history of nurserymen's and seedsmen's catalogues in England, from their roots in the classified lists of desirable plants compiled in the Middle Ages. We have seen that, so far as surviving documents are concerned, the gardening catalogue as a vehicle of trade began in earnest soon after the Restoration of 1660, and that a couple of generations later such lists began to appear in print. So far hardly any of the specimens preserved give an indication of prices. Then in 1775 there appeared the first known list of long-lived nursery stock, trees and shrubs, to be priced throughout. This was, it appears, the response of the enterprising and old established firm of Telford of York, and their innovation was at once followed by their main northern rivals, the Perfects of Pontefract. By the last quarter of the 18th century the trade had begun to broach a new public: the widening middle class who, it may be, could not afford to buy the latest exotics or to form major plantations, but who could in mass absorb a very large output of the cheaper lines of well-known plants. A good and clearly priced catalogue of what was to be had would no doubt have circulated widely and done much to stimulate demand.

Something remains to be said of the later developments of the older tradition of unpriced catalogues, largely or wholly of seeds, of which the best example is the list at the shop of William Lucas in the Strand about 1677. As has been said, this was very closely followed by the standard list of seeds inserted by Woolridge in his *Art of Gardening* and by London and Wise in 1706 in their translation of *The Retir'd Gard'ner;* in internal arrangement as well as in general classification the resemblance is much too close for chance coincidence. It is quite plain that Lucas's catalogue, itself compiled along the lines suggested by much earlier classifications of herbs, was drawn upon as the main source of later trade lists. It is not unlikely that the list was handed down to Lucas's successors in the same business and if that was the most influential firm of its kind in central London, it would be natural for Woolridge and for London and Wise to quote it almost verbatim. No plagiarism would in that case be involved. It is otherwise with the Catalogue of Seeds, Roots, &c. which were to be had 50 years later from Mr. William Borthwick, seedsman in Lawnmercat, Edinburgh. Borthwick's list, with the correct months for sowing added in parallel column, was printed by James Justice in his book the *British Gardener's Calendar* of 1759. Though a good deal of addition and shuffling about has taken place, the descent of Borthwick from Lucas is evident. In the intervening 80 years there were more varieties to insert, and some logical changes had taken place: Radishes had simply been moved up into Roots from beneath the cross-heading 'Sallad Seeds'; Pease and Beans came at the end of the Vegetable seeds instead of being an afterthought after seeds of flowers and trees. Borthwick had also added a new class at the end, of American Tree Seeds.

This final section of Borthwick's catalogue is prefaced by a note of considerable interest: 'N.B. The North-American tree and shrub seeds for the most part arrive here in Winter, or early in the Spring; and all of them must be sown in the Spring. I shall mark with the letter H. those which require hot-beds; with the letter B. those which require boxes or pots to have their seeds sown in; and shall add the mark Op. to those which may be sown in the open ground.' The list comprises about a hundred varieties of seeds, which are in addition to the normal list of Seeds of Trees and Flowering Shrubs. Apart from the section on American seeds it is safe to conclude that the catalogue had been produced with scissors. and paste. The same process can be seen earlier in a manuscript list issued in 1681 by Henry Ferguson of Edinburgh, virtually an abbreviation of Lucas. The appearance of this form of list in Scotland proves the dependence of Edinburgh upon London in the trade; and this has indeed been shown independently by Mr. Tom Donnelly's study of the Edinburgh seedsman, Arthur Clephane, whose business records for the period 1706-30 have survived.

As has been mentioned, the catalogue of William Malcolm issued in 1771 is again a reshuffle of the Lucas scheme, and it even retains the class of 'Physical Seeds' as does Perfects' seed-list of c. 1787; but Malcolm's later edition of 1778 omits this category, while preserving all the rest. Malcolm, like Borthwick, brought Pease & Beans up into a rational position at the end of the vegetable seeds. He subdivided Flower Seeds into Annuals, Tender and then Hardy, and after interpolating a section of Sweet and Pot Herb Seeds, went on to Biennials. A rather different line of development is suggested by the catalogue of the firm of Kennedy & Lee at the famous Vineyard Nursery, Hammersmith. This list, printed in 1774, starts with Hardy Trees and Shrubs, then continues with Herbaceous Plants, followed by Greenhouse Plants, Plants for a Dry Stove, Stove Plants, and Fruits. After this come Bulbous, Tuberous and Fibrous-rooted Flowers; then Kitchen-Garden Seeds, with the subdivisions: Legumes — Oleraceous — Esculent Roots — Pot Herbs. The seedsman's side of the business follows, again starting with seeds of Trees, classified as Evergreen Trees and Shrubs; Pines; Firs; Deciduous Trees and Shrubs; then seeds of Perennial Flowers; Annual Flowers, classified as Strong Hot Bed, Moderate Hot Bed, and Natural Ground; Biennial Flowers; and at the end, Seeds to improve Land, with the common-form notice: N.B. Matts, and all sorts of Garden Tools.

The magnificent trilingual catalogue of Conrad Loddiges of Hackney, published in 1777, has already been mentioned. A fine example of the improved arrangement of London catalogues from the leading firms is the list issued in 1783 by Luker & Smith, Nurserymen and Seedsmen in the City Road, also at their Shop in Covent Garden, London; and at their Nursery at Dalston. This is a substantial book containing 68 pages of lists, in seven main classes: I. Hardy Trees and Shrubs; II. Greenhouse and Stove Plants; III. Herbaceous Plants cultivated in the Open Ground; IV. Fruit Trees; V. Seeds and Plants for the Kitchen Garden; including sub-classes of Sweet Herbs and Pot Herbs, physical Seeds and Plants (re-appearing here), Seeds and Plants for improving of Land; VI. Flower Seeds, divided into Annual, Biennial and Perennial, and followed by Seeds of Timber-Trees, Flowering Shrubs, &c.; and VII. Bulbous-rooted Flowers, comprising Hyacinths, Tulips, Ranunculus, Anemones, Polyanthus, Narcissuses, Jonquils, Crocuses, Fritillaries, Snowdrops, Star of Bethlehem,

Irises, &c. It is tempting to wonder whether the senior partner of this firm, Warren Luker, seedsman and cornchandler of the parish of St. Luke Old Street, may have been descended from Roger Looker of a century before.

The recrudescence of Physical Seeds may have reflected the contemporary activities of William Curtis, the famous founder of *The Botanical Magazine*. In the same year as Luker & Smith's lengthy catalogue, 1783, he published a catalogue of the Medical, Culinary and Agricultural Plants that he cultivated. Its sections cover Medicinal Plants, Culinary Plants, Poisonous Plants, Plants useful in Agriculture, Plants Noxious in Agriculture, and British (native) Plants. This dealt with one very specialised group of plants of economic importance, but the general trend of the big nurseries was into the high-priced field of the new exotics. As a rather later sample of the kind of thing produced primarily to appeal to wealthy collectors and specialists, we turn to the 1827 Catalogue of Plants sold by James Colvill of King's Road, Chelsea, described as the 3rd edition and so doubtless representative of a rather earlier date. Colvill's father had been a leading London nurseryman since 1786, and the son was in business until he died in 1832. The catalogue consists of 49 pages and gives pride of place to Hothouse Climbers, followed by other Hothouse Plants; then Amaryllideae; Orchideae; Greenhouse Climbers; Greenhouse Plants; Geraniaceae; China Roses; Hardy Climbers; Hardy Flowering Shrubs requiring Peat Soil; Hardy Trees and Shrubs; and Hardy perennial herbaceous Plants. Herbaceous Plants occupied the last ten pages, and were at last forging ahead in popularity, but the connoisseur approach is marked not only by the emphasis on the Hothouse at the start, but by the 'throwaway' note at the end: 'N.B. A good Collection of choice Fruit Trees of all kinds. Kitchen Garden and Flower Seeds. Also Dutch Bulbs annually imported. Garden Mats, &c, &c.' As might be expected, no prices are disclosed.

The beginnings of the vogue for exotics as the very latest thing in new introductions went right back to the 16th century, with the first imports from America and Turkey, and after the Restoration had found encouragement from a few distinguished patrons, of whom Bishop Compton was probably the most influential. In the British Museum is a tiny pocket-book of his time which evidently recorded the arrival or sowing of seeds from abroad between 1685 and 1688. 'Severall seeds from Fort St. George' (i.e. Madras in South India) are mentioned under 7 April 1687, and 'Indian sedds from Mr. London' were received 3 May 1687. There is a note of things 'from Meur Tournfort', Joseph Pitton de Tournefort (1656-1708) the celebrated French botanist. On 24 March 1687/8 there is a record of 'severall mixt seeds from the Indies', and on 6 April 1688 'severall seeds from America'. Most of these seeds were of unidentified plants, new to western science, and for another century and more it was still possible for a few great amateurs to play this game with the help of friends and correspondents. We can see the same process still at work during the formation of Kew Gardens.

Kew Gardens, as the gardens of Kew Palace, owed their botanical importance very largely to the interest and enterprise of the Princess Dowager of Wales (Princess Augusta of Saxe-Gotha), mother of King George III. A number of bills for plants, preserved at Windsor, show that in 1768-69 she was buying from several different nurserymen new plants that had not, apparently, even been named. One account, from John Cree of Addlestone near Chertsey in Surrey, is of particular interest:

1768 Feb. 16 Her Royal Highness the Princess Dowager of Wales	Dr. John Cree
Three new Andromedas	£1 – 1 – 0
Nine plants unknown	0 – 18 – 0
Two Clematis crispa	0 – 5 – 0
One new Rudbeckia	0 – 2 – 6
Two new Helianthus's	0 – 5 – 0
One Hopea a new Genus	0 – 7 – 0
Two new laurel leav'd Olives	0 – 5 – 0
A new climbing plant	0 – 2 – 6
Two new Eupatoriums	0 – 4 – 0
Two new shrubby Vacciniums	0 – 5 – 0
Two new Asters	0 – 3 – 0
One perennial Convolvulus	0 – 2 – 6
Two new Agaves	0 – 5 – 0
Two new Carolina Smilaxes	0 – 5 – 0
A new Styrax tree	0 – 2 – 6
A new Toothach tree	0 – 3 – 0
Two new Hedysarums	0 – 4 – 0
One nearrow (sic) leavd Dhoon Holly	0 – 2 – 0
A new Sideroxyllon	0 – 3 – 0
A new Sassafras tree	0 – 5 – 0
One Tetragonotha (Tetragonotheca)	0 – 2 – 6
One Laurus astivalis	0 – 3 – 0
Two Hypericum Lasianthus	0 – 5 – 0
	£6 – 0 – 6

Received the above Contents of this bill for John Cree
pr. John Cree   Archibald Waterstone[1]

Other plants described as new were supplied by John Bush (i.e. Busch) of Hackney, who three years later disposed of his nursery to Conrad Loddiges; by Kennedy & Lee (receipted 'for self and Co.' by Lewis Kennedy); by William Malcolm, whose catalogues have been discussed; and by William Watson, who had a nursery at Islington and was mentioned several times by Curtis as introducing plants from Carolina. Watson was also the first to flower Azalea pontica (Rhododendron luteum) in this country, and his plant was used by Curtis for the beautiful plate in the *Botanical Magazine* (vol. 13, no. 433). The account from Kennedy & Lee is also of interest as it includes 25 Occidental Planes at 4d. each and 25 Carolina Poplars at 1s., besides two Magnolias costing £1 4s. the pair. Williamson & Co. supplied six pots of Burgundy Roses costing £2 5s., and hyacinth and narcissus bulbs were obtained from Edward Cross 'at ye Orange Tree, Fleet St.'. These more normal items could have been picked from catalogues, but the new and even unnamed exotics must surely have been sent under some general instruction, or chosen for Kew by the Princess's chief gardener, William Aiton.

In the last 30 years of the 18th century there were certainly many catalogues issued, but they came mostly from the London firms. One of the very few surviving exceptions is a list of 1793 cataloguing the flowers, plants, seeds etc. sold, 'at the very lowest prices' by Richard Clarke, florist of

[1] Royal Archives 55512, here reproduced by the gracious permission of Her Majesty the Queen.

Cambridge. In the far North of England the firm of William Falla & Son of Hebburn Quay, Gateshead, succeeding to an establishment of 1734, was issuing a whole range of catalogues by 1795-97, covering Trees, Bulbs, Seeds and Greenhouse Plants. Their later detailed catalogue has already been described. Yet it would seem that the London firms retained for a very long time a strong grip on even rather distant parts of the provinces. It is striking that Lord Monson, at Burton Hall close by Lincoln, seems to have dealt with several London seedsman, and even with John Smith, a nurseryman of Westerham in Kent, although in Lincoln the firm of Richard Pennell, founded in 1780, was of high standing; but there was another family seat at Gatton in Surrey.

The group of catalogues which, as already mentioned, were preserved in the Burton Hall archives, show the persistence of traditional features to quite a late date. Henry Clarke, of 315 Oxford Street, London, issued two catalogues, both printed on large broadsheets. His general list of Vegetable and Flower Seeds was not dated, and since it contained no prices it could serve for a number of years. Its categories correspond fairly closely to the Lucas tradition, but there are two innovations, not so far observed elsewhere at the period (c. 1833). One is the introduction of the modern system of giving every item a serial number; the two main divisions of seeds had separate numerations, with 328 entries for Vegetables, Herbs and Agricultural seeds, and 743 for Flowers, which are classified as Annual (1 — 464) and Hardy Biennial and Perennial (465 — 743). The Annuals are also marked by the second innovation — really a different application of Telfords' method of 1775 — an asterisk being placed against the Half-Hardy, and an obelus beside the Tender. The list refers to 'Bulbous Flower Roots of which a separate Catalogue is annually printed.' A copy of this separate list of 'Dutch Flower Roots' is dated 1833, and marks the items with prices.

There are also both general and bulb lists from the well known seedsmen Flanagan & Nutting, of 9 Mansion House Street, London. In 1833 they had been referred to in the *Floricultural Cabinet* as specialists in Hyacinth and Narcissus, and in 1835 issued a priced list of the best Hyacinths, costing from 1s. up to 5s. In the Monson papers are copies of the general list, in booklet form, for 1835 and 1839, and also an 1837 broadsheet of Flower Roots. Only this last gives prices. The general list of 1835 is a pamphlet of 20 pages, *A Catalogue of Seeds*, with a general advertisement on p. 2, Garden Seeds, alphabetically, followed by Sweet and Pot Herbs, Roots, etc., occupying pages 3 — 7, and Grass and other Agricultural Seeds going on to p.8, where Flower Seeds begin. Hardy Annuals, alphabetically (pp. 8 — 12) are followed by Half Hardy (pp. 12 — 14), Tender Annuals (pp. 14 — 15), Biennials and Perennials not Hardy (p. 15) and Hardy Biennial and Perennial Flower Seeds (pp. 15 — 18). Finally come Hardy Tree and Shrub Seeds on pages 18 — 20. There are notes on appropriate culture at the head of some classes. The 1839 edition had been reduced to 16 pages. The copy of the 1837 broadsheet which has been preserved, unlike the general lists, marks all prices, and corresponds to the note as to 'Dutch Bulbs and other Flower Roots Annually imported, of which a separate Catalogue is printed'. (see Appendix V)

Lord Monson also obtained broadsheet catalogues of 'Foreign Flower Roots' from George Batt, seedsman of 412 Strand, London, dated 1840; and of 'Bulbs and Flower Roots' from Theodore & Charles Lockhart, of 156

Cheapside, London, and Haarlem, Holland (not dated). Both these give prices throughout. The firm of Lockhart was mentioned in 1837 as successfully cultivating Ixias in the open air, but they were not exclusively bulb specialists, since in 1840 they were suppliers of the Carnation Poppy. Lastly there are two lists from Westerham, Kent, both broadsheets. The first, on paper watermarked 1820, is a Catalogue of Fruit and Forest Trees, Flowering Shrubs, Evergreens, American Plants, etc., sold by John Smith, nurseryman and seedsman. No prices are printed, but many have been entered in ink. The other list, likewise undated but on paper watermarked 1835, is a list of Flower Seeds sold by Joseph Smith, nurseryman, seedsman and florist, who had probably succeeded to the business of John Smith. It was presumably for Lord Monson's estate at Gatton in Surrey that plants were bought at Westerham, yet it must have been felt worth while to 'shop around' for plants, bulbs and seeds, even when the cost of transport was added. The lack of local lists may simply mean that many provincial firms did not find it worth while to have any printed. Existing firms of old standing seldom have any early catalogues: Messrs. Pennell of Lincoln, who have kept their business archives since 1830, have no catalogue earlier than 1846; Messrs. Caldwell & Sons of Knutsford, with records back to 1789, start with a catalogue of the 1850's.

From the opening of the reign of Victoria to the present day the surviving trade literature offers an immense field for future research. It would be premature to attempt to trace, in advance of thorough investigation, the various types of list issued by general and specialist firms. What can be seen on inspection is, that in the majority of the catalogues now published that are sectionally classified, there are still traces of the grouping imposed on plants in the Middle Ages. The short list of Herb seeds recalls the Pot Herbs and the Sweet Herbs of the 17th and even the 15th century. The groups of seeds of Shrubs and Trees sometimes found reflect the great ages of importation and the lists of William Lucas and William Borthwick. The British nurseryman's catalogue may fairly be described as a hardy tree, deeply rooted, in many varieties, but breeding true.

EPILOGUE

SOME PROBLEMS AND CONCLUSIONS

IN THE COURSE of this sketched development we have seen the English gardening catalogue take its rise in the lists of herbs which, for reasons of diet, health and medicine, were compiled during the Middle Ages. Like most, if not all, art forms, these lists were handed down by higher authority: in this case that of the Emperor Charlemagne. For some seven centuries the lists compiled were a series of variations upon a theme. New motives appeared rarely, when some plant praised for its virtues by the authors of classical antiquity, was sought out and introduced. This phenomenon is specifically recorded in the case of the valuable and beautiful aromatic shrub Rosemary, sent in 1338. Again the introduction is a matter of taste and initiative shown on the highest level, by the Countess of Hainault, Jeanne de Valois, a princess of the French Blood Royal, sister of Philip VI. Advised by her physicians of the remarkable virtues of the plant, she had a treatise compiled and sent a copy, with plants or cuttings, to her daughter Philippa, queen of Edward III. A pattern had been set, and it was followed in later centuries by the introductions for the royal gardens of Henry VIII, the economic botanizing of James I (who introduced the White Mulberry as the food-plant of the silkworm), the garden and park patronage of Charles II, and the founding of Kew Gardens.

Next to the activities of royalty came those of the notable peers and prelates who from time to time showed a keen interest in forming collections of living rarities brought from parts of the globe in course of exploration. New species, either as seeds or as living plants, were acquired by personal gift and exchange, and some time was likely to elapse before a rarity passed out from the garden of its proprietor into the general currency of trade. Yet from the time of Gerard a trickle of plants was reaching Britain through another channel, that of the enterprising professional gardener, not always acting under direct instructions from a patron. By the eighteenth century this trickle of commercial enterprise, parallel to the main stream of noble exploration by proxy, became a flood of increasing volume in its own right. Important plants from outstanding gardens were acquired by nurserymen, notably at the death of Bishop Compton by Robert Furber and Christopher Gray, who thus saved many of the rarities of Fulham. In course of time those trees, shrubs and plants which proved to have a horticultural value exceeding that of mere novelty, began to circulate.

A great deal has been written on the subject of plant introduction and plant exploration, and so far as the facts are on record it is likely that the greater part of this story has been told. At the top level, that is to say the date and means of the first known introduction of each species, not a great deal remains to be discovered, so far that is, as concerns the best and most significant kinds added to British gardens in the last 300 years. What has hitherto remained far less clear is the actual state of gardening generally, in regard to plants grown by keen plantsmen who were outside the charmed circle of royal and noble patrons and leading botanists. All that has been known has been derived from the lists of plants recommended by the authors of leading didactic works on horticulture. Each author wrote from his own experience, and probably himself knew most of the plants he mentioned. It does not follow that all of these plants had a wide general distribution. Most gardeners were far more strictly limited in their choice than might appear from the printed lists: they could only buy those plants which were offered for sale by the trade. Furthermore, remote provincial areas were unlikely to get those specialities only obtainable from the metropolitan firms, though there was a better prospect in the case of sorts which could be raised from seed and fairly quickly brought to maturity.

The problem of what was really being grown in the country at large can then be solved from the trade lists with much greater accuracy than is possible from published literature. As has been remarked earlier, provincial catalogues have especial value in this way. It is axiomatic that the great majority of the stock of any nurseryman consisted of plants for which a market existed or could be induced, by advertisement of any kind. The opportunities for advertising were extremely slight in most parts of England until the 18th century was well advanced. The rise of regular local newspapers offered a new medium for widening of commercial contact with the public, and almost at once advantage was taken of it by nurserymen. Thus Samuel Smith (c. 1695-1757), a leading York florist, twice advertised in the *York Courant* during April 1730 that at his 'Flower Garden without Michael-gate Bar, York, is to be seen a choice Collection of Ariculas, Animonies, Renunculos, Tulops, and other Flowers just coming into Bloom, where any Persons may be furnish'd with the best and newest Flowers, at reasonable Rates'.

The catalogues of Telfords and Perfects, in the mid 1770's, came 50 years after the effective start of a local Press in York, and indicate that the regional trade had become very highly developed. While the list of plants comes late enough to be extensive, a good deal of its interest is derived from the number of plants we take for granted, but which were not yet introduced, or had not yet reached the North. It is difficult to imagine English gardening before the arrival of what we know as the Chrysanthemum (in 1793, first effectively flowered in 1796); the Dahlia (1798-1804); the Pansy in our sense of the term, only developed from about 1812-16; or the brilliant Zinnia (Z. elegans), first here in 1796. In the domain of woody plants the absences seem still stranger: the first Buddleia (B. globosa) reached us only in 1774; the first double Camellia — it is said — in 1792; the first blue Ceanothus in 1818. There were no Japanese Quinces (Chaenomeles lagenaria) until 1796, no Forsythia before 1845; no Fuchsias until 1788-93. The 'great' Hydrangea (H. macrophylla) came only in 1789, the Tree Paeony (Paeonia suffruticosa) during the years 1789-1794, and the important Wisteria (W. sinensis) not until 1816.

This extreme modernity of whole genera or of the typical species now cultivated might seem to imply that earlier gardens, and still more shrubberies, were barren and poverty-stricken. It is a wholesome corrective to read and re-read the lengthy lists of the things that could be supplied, and

E

particularly what was so cheap, relatively speaking, as to mean that it must have been well spread over the North of England. It has been pointed out that in the cheaper categories there were more than 200 kinds of shrubs, without counting Roses, and about 50 were evergreens. It is true that a substantial proportion of these was made up of varieties with different types of variegation; but variegated foliage was then highly fashionable. Among the deciduous flowering trees and shrubs at low prices there were flowering Almonds, Cherries and Pears — the double-flowered Pear seems to have gone out of cultivation; — as well as Guelder Rose, Laburnums, Lilacs and 'Syringa'.

One problem is the extent to which the garden could be kept interesting throughout the year, and modern introductions have certainly given us immense advantages. Yet two centuries ago it was possible to extend the flowering season with several sorts of Honeysuckles and Jasmines, and to carry on into the autumn with the Tree Hollyhocks (Hibiscus syriacus) in white, red, purple, and 'Painted Lady' varieties. There were Dogwoods and Maples to give autumn colour, and Barberries, Hollies, Pyracantha, Thorns and Spindle-trees with berries of various colours. Still keeping to the cheaper plants only, winter blossom was possible with the Cornelian Cherry at 6d., Mezereons in three colours at 4d. and 6d. (oddly enough the common and now rather despised purple had the higher price), and the Laurustinus in five sorts ranging from 3d. to 1s. The answer is that the shrubbery certainly did not lack interest, and that the choice already available was an extremely wide one.

Problems of a different kind arise in connection with some of the more expensive plants, and especially those which have no printed price, but are marked in ink. These, no doubt the most recent introductions to the York nursery when Telfords went to press in 1775, include a number of very handsome trees and shrubs and are in some cases still in the connoisseur's category. To deal first with some species with high prices in print, forming the wider class of distinguished kinds for the gardens of the gentry, these may be divided into the two main groups of Hardy and Tender. Among species still commonly grown there are the Strawberry Tree (Arbutus unedo), the Rose Acacia (Robinia hispida), the Snowy Mespilus (Amelanchier canadensis), the 'Styrax' (Liquidambar styraciflua), Tulip Tree — all at 2s 6d., and the Catalpa at 2s. Of these the most recent introductions were the Snowy Mespilus (1746) and the Rose Acacia (1743); the Tulip Tree had been in England since 1663 and the Liquidambar since 1683.

Also priced at 2s. 6d. were the Tooth-Ache Tree (Zanthoxylum americanum), introduced in 1759, now replaced by a Chinese species; and a Clethra, probably Clethra tomentosa, for it is likely that the other common species of the period, C. alnifolia, is meant by the entry 'Pepper-Bush' — this last costing 2s. The Fringe Tree (Chionanthus virginicus), still grown but not very common, then cost 3s. (now 35s.). Except in the case of the Clethra there is no real doubt as to the species intended in any of these descriptions. It is less easy to be sure with some of the tender introductions. The 'Yellow Egyptian Acacia', costing 5s., was probably but not quite certainly Acacia farnesiana, for it seems impossible to reconcile some of the statements in the contemporary dictionary of Philip Miller with the scientific facts as known now. An even more fascinating problem is raised by the entry of the 'Double-flowering Althea, or Japan Rose', priced in print at 4s., marked as

Tender by both catalogues and as an evergreen by Perfects. The name Japan Rose is certainly that used at the time for the Camellia, and there is no possible doubt that only C. japonica can be meant. Yet it is received horticultural history that the first camellias grown by Lord Petre at Thorndon from 1739 were single red and single white only, and that double varieties arrived much later, in the period between 1792 and 1802. The 1786 edition of Chambers' *Cyclopaedia*, generally well informed on garden plants, gives a description without any reference to the plant being grown in this country, while Curtis in 1788 (*Botanical Magazine*, II, 42) says that the camellia 'was a stranger to our gardens in the time of Miller, or at least it is not noticed in the last edition of his Dictionary'. This must refer to the eighth edition of 1768. It seems an inescapable conclusion that at least one variety of double camellia had been in commerce for some time.

This conclusion leads to reconsideration of what is known of the introduction of the shrub to commerce by James Gordon (1708 ?-1780). Gordon had been chief gardener to Lord Petre, whose two camellias are said to have died under stove treatment. Yet it was Gordon who, after Petre's death in 1742, had a plant in his nursery at Mile End. Here we turn to a detailed account of the introduction given editorially by Joseph Harrison in his *Floricultural Cabinet* for 1 March 1843 (vol. XI, 49-53). Harrison's version of the story differs in several particulars from that usually recounted; he states: 'the Jesuit, George Joseph Kamel, visited Japan as a missionary in 1739, contrived to procure two plants of the single red, which he brought to Europe, and sold to Lord Petre for a considerable sum. His Lordship had them sent to the gardens at Thornden Hall in Essex, where, being kept in a hothouse temperature, they were killed. The gardener at Thornden, at that time, was a Mr. James Gordon, who in 1742, commenced a nursery at Mile End, near London. He, being somewhat aware of the value of so ornamental a plant as the Camellia, managed it so as soon to procure another plant, which he put out in the open border of a conservatory, where it continued to grow for ninety-four years, till the nursery was broken up to build upon in 1837: from it, it is supposed, many thousands of young plants had been raised as stools to bud, inarch, &c., the subsequent double kinds. It is generally understood that the Camellia was introduced into this country in 1792, but the above fact confirms the introduction from 1739 to 1742. Mr. Gordon died in 1780,[1] and he had not only obtained the single red, but the double white and red striped.'

Returning to the orthodox account as related by Miss Alice Coats, Collinson is quoted as stating that in August 1740 one of Lord Petre's two plants bore 'a most delightful crimsonish double flower of a Ketmia figure'; and Miss Coats adds that this was 'perhaps a bud-sport, since in this way many japonica varieties have originated'. This supposition makes sense of all the factors involved. Gordon, who started his own nursery in the year of Lord Petre's death, had presumably succeeded in propagating from the double sport, and may well have been allowed by his patron to have a young plant for himself. Double flowers were at the time so enormously more regarded than single ones that, regardless of whether or no Gordon also managed to perpetuate the red single, it would be this double form that was released to

[1] correct; commonly but mistakenly given as 1781.

the public. The description of the flower by Collinson as 'of a Ketmia figure' also makes sense, for Ketmia was a synonym for the Althea Frutex, or Syrian Mallow, that is the Tree Hollyhock (Hibiscus syriacus). This accounts for Telfords' trade description of the shrub as an Althea, surprising as it seems at first sight. Undoubtedly too the variety offered was a red or crimson, as it would otherwise have been called a white 'Japan Rose' to avoid misunderstanding. Finally, the reduction of the price to 4s., in contrast to the prices of from 7s. 6d. to 15s. for rarities, proves that the Camellia had reached York long enough before 1775 to have been extensively propagated.

A possible trade connection between Telfords and Gordon is also suggested by the fact that the York nursery could offer the Double Cape Jasmine (Gardenia jasminoides florida) which had been introduced in 1754 and distributed by Gordon from Mile End. The York price was 7s. 6d. (printed, not added in ink), so that we may imagine that the gardenia had been acquired at York later than the camellia, yet not very recently. It was Gordon again who was the great expert in raising Rhododendrons, Azaleas and Kalmias, which are among the biggest surprises in Telfords' catalogue. The Azalea (probably Rhododendron viscosum), at 7s. 6d., was also stocked by Perfects at Pontefract, but York had a northern monopoly of the two Kalmias, Broad-leav'd at 15s. and Olive-leav'd at 7s. 6d., as well as of the Rhododendron (R. maximum) or Rose-Bay, at 15s. Besides these, and very likely also originating from the Mile End nursery, Telfords could offer three Magnolias, two at 7s. 6d. (apparently M. tripetala and M. grandiflora) and one (M. virginiana) again costing 15s. All this group of plants have prices added in ink and were probably quite recent acquisitions at York. Another plant that may go with them, marked in ink at 7s. 6d., was Catesby's Alspice (Calycanthus floridus) that had been first introduced in 1726 but was very rare until fresh plants were imported by Peter Collinson in 1757. The Rhododendron had had a rather similar history in that, though it reached England in 1736, it did not flower until 20 years later. Similarly the Magnolia grandiflora arrived in 1737, but most young plants were killed in the dreadful winter of 1739, so that this also remained a scarce plant until the middle of the century.

From what has been said it will be seen that a rather vague time-scale can be deduced. Choice plants that had been introduced and effectively marketed before c. 1750, that is almost a generation before the date of Telford's catalogue, were no longer fetching the top prices. This seems to apply to the first Camellia, a double red almost certainly put on the market by James Gordon about 1745 and perhaps in the York nursery by 10 years later. The Azalea, long enough stocked to have been given a fixed price in printer's type, may have come north during the sixties; the group of the latest rarities, not likely to have been at all well known even in London until c. 1760, had probably not long been acquired by Telfords. A few other plants have prices marked in ink, but they were not all recent introductions. Orange and Lemon Trees were both marked at from 7s. 6d. to 10s. 6d., and Geraniums 'of Sorts', i.e. in variety, were from 1s. to 2s. 6d. The reason for marking these prices in ink may have been that there was great seasonal fluctuation from year to year, according to losses in severe winters. This would be particularly true of Pelargoniums in the days when real glasshouses mainly of glass were a dream of the future.

A puzzle of a different sort is set by the inclusion in the list of the Widow-Wail, marked as Tender and priced at 1s. This is duly identified by sound authorities as Cneorum tricoccum, and a plant under this name (and similarly identified by B.D. Jackson) was actually grown by Gerard in 1596. Yet Loudon, and the *Dictionary* of the Royal Horticultural Society, state that the plant was introduced as late as 1793. The *Oxford English Dictionary* implies, rather than clearly states, that early references to a plant under this name mean the Mezereon (Daphne mezereum), and this might be taken to support the late date of introduction. Yet the horticultural authorities must in this case be mistaken. The Garden Book of Sir Thomas Hanmer, of 1659, having already described the several varieties of the hardy and deciduous Mezereon, later inserts 'Widow Waile' among Evergreens and adds: 'Wee house this shrub in wynter'. In Perfects' catalogue, which indicates the evergreens with an obelus, the mark is present, completing the demonstration.

Enough has been said to indicate that a certain amount of new information can be derived from these old trade lists, or at least elicited by research into their difficulties and inconsistencies. Doubt as to particular identifications remains in some cases, but probably almost all the puzzles will be solved by further study. In general the catalogues, even as far back as that of Lucas in the time of Charles II, present an intelligible picture of what the ordinary man could go and buy, providing he had the money. Many plants remained expensive, and for this reason few but the nobility and gentry were able to enjoy them in their gardens or conservatories. But the lists also show that, in spite of fluctuation, prices had a tendency to fall, and the rarities of one age — provided only that they were really worth growing — became the commonplaces of the next. This process has continued over a longer period in Britain than anywhere else, and the total supply of different species of plants and plant seeds is doubtless greater than that ever available anywhere else. While the great age of plant introduction was just getting under way, on the 1st of August 1740, a masque was produced before the Prince of Wales, later the founder of Kew Gardens. In it the author, James Thomson, made a courtly reference to the fair sex in our country; but he might just as well have been thinking of our accommodating climate and future floral riches when he wrote the words: 'Blest isle, with matchless beauty crowned'.

APPENDIX I.

THE 'FROMOND' LIST OF PLANTS OF c. 15 00.

THIS LIST WAS printed, not quite completely, by A. Amherst in *A History of Gardening in England* (1895), 71-3, where it is described as of the 15th century. The manuscript in which it is preserved is a cookery book written in a hand of the late 15th or early 16th century (British Museum, Sloane MS. 1201). A number of names scribbled throughout the manuscript, 'Thomas Fourmond' or 'Thomas Formond of Carssalton in the Counte of Surr.' predominating, suggest that a former owner of the book was the Thomas Fromond who held estates in Carshalton and Cheam and died on 21 March 1542/3 (O. Manning & W. Bray, *The History . . . of Surrey*, 1804-14, II, 473, 513). The handwriting of the plant list is probably not very much earlier and may be put at c. 1500. The list must, however, be based upon an earlier original, for at least one striking mistake has crept in, 'Foothistell' appearing under the letter 'F' as well as 'Sowthistell' under 'S'. Several other names appear to be corrupt, and this implies that the basic manuscript copied was already of some age.

The date of the manuscript has an important bearing upon the list of plants, for it contains a number of exotics which are not generally supposed to have been cultivated in Britain until a decidedly later date. On the other hand, examination of other botanical and herbal literature of the later Middle Ages suggests that there may have been more plant introductions during the fourteenth and fifteenth centuries than has been admitted hitherto. The list is here printed as it stands in the manuscript, as an alphabet followed by classes of plants used for different purposes. An attempt is then made to identify the plants, giving a modern spelling or modern version of the English name whenever possible, with the scientific name as it stands in the *Dictionary of Gardening* of the Royal Horticultural Society (2nd edition, 1956). In a few instances other authorities have had to be used, and some names may therefore be botanically out-of-date. Where more than one identification is suggested, with a ?, the first scientific name given is regarded as the most probable, but it has to be realised that a few of the medieval English herb-names served for several botanically distinct plants, and certain identification is impossible. A few of the corrupt and dubious names call for special remark: 'Cartabus' should be Carthamus (Bastard Saffron or Safflower), a word which occurs in English glossaries of the 15th century (*Revised Medieval Latin Word-List*, ed. R.E. Latham, 1965, 74); the date of introduction was probably far earlier than the '1551' that is usually given. 'Cost' is generally identified with 'Costmary', though both are listed here; it is possible that some other plant or different species of Chrysanthemum is meant. The 'Date trese' of the list are unlikely to be Date Palms or Date Plums (Diospyros lotus); certain types of the common Plum were, however, formerly known as Dates. 'Ierlin' is almost certainly a scribal corruption of 'Ierlm', i.e. Jerusalem, in the original; it may stand as an abbreviation for 'Cowsloppus of Jerusalem' (Pulmonaria officinalis) found in the class of herbs for Savour and Beauty; another possibility is that it stands for 'Jerusalem Cross' (Lychnis chalcedonica) regarding which there is a strong tradition of introduction by returning crusaders or pilgrims not later than the thirteenth century. 'Lympons' is very likely a corruption for 'Lupins' as there is evidence for the cultivation of Lupinus albus as a medical herb in England in the 15th century. 'Palma Christi' should mean the Castor Oil plant (Ricinus communis), and there seems to be no reason why its seeds should not have been an early introduction by way of Egypt. 'Pyne Appull' can, of course, only mean Pine Cone, the original sense of the words, and presumably refers to the indigenous Scots Pine. The references to Almonds, Bay trees, Gourds and Peach trees, well known to English literature since the 14th century, probably indicate that they had been introduced well before 1500.

Herbys necessary for a gardyn by letter.

A. Alysaundre, Avence, Astralogia rotunda, Astralogia longa, Alleluia, Arcachaff, Artemesie mogwede, Annes, Archangel, (Almondez)[1]

B. Borage, Betes, Beteyn, Basilican, Bugle, Burnett, (Baytrees)

C. Cabage, Chervell, Carewey, Cyves, Columbyn, Clarey, Colyaundr', Colewort, Cartabus, Cressez, Cressez of Boleyn, Calamyntes, Camamyll, Ceterwort, (Cost, Costmary, Chykynwede, Cowsloppus of Jerusalem, Columbyn gentyle)

D. Daysez, Dyteyn, Daundelyon, Dragaunce, Dylle, (Date trese)

E. Elena campana, Eufras, Egremoyn, (Endyve, Ersesmert, Elabre)

F. Fenell, Foothistell, Fenecreke, (Fenell Red)

G. Gromell, Goldez, Gyllofr', Germaundr', (Gyllofr' gentyle, Seynt Mar' Garlek, Galyngale, Gourdes)

H. Hertez tonge, Horehound, Henbane

I. Isope, Ierlin, Iryngez, herbe Ive

K. Kykombre, yt. bereth apples, (Karett)

L. Longdebeff, Lekez, Letuse, Loveache, Lympons, Lylle, Longwortz

M. Mercury, Malowes, Myntes, Mageron, Mageron gentyle, Mandrake, Mylone, (Red Mynt, Mogwede)

N. Nept, Nettell rede, Nardus capiscola

O. Orage, Oculus Christi, Oynons

P. Persely, Pelytore, Pelytore of Spayn, Puliall royall, Pyper white, Pacyence, Popy whit', Prymerose, Purselane, Philipendula, (Palma Christi, Popyroyall, Persenepez, Peche trese, Pyany Roman, Pyne Appull)

Q. Qvyncez

R. Rapes, Radyche, Rampsons, Rapouncez, Rokettes, Rewe, (Rosemary, Rose red, Rose Campy)

S. Sauge, Saverey, Spynache, Sede-wale, Scalaceli, Smalache, Sauce alone, Selbestryue, Syves, Sorell, Sowthistell, Sothernwode, Skabiose, Selian, Stycadose, Stanmarch, (Saffron)

T. Tyme, Tansey, (Turnepez, Thewberies)

V. Vyolettes, Wermode, Wormesede, Verveyn, (Vynes)

[1] plants added in brackets occur in the manuscript only in the classified lists.

Of the same Herbes for Potage

Borage, Langdebefe, Vyolettes, Malowes, Marcury, Daundelyon, Avence, Myntes, Sauge, Percely, Goldes, Mageron, Fenell, Carawey, Rednettyll, Oculus Christi, Daysys, Chervell, Lekez, Colewortes, Rapez, Tyme, Cyves, Betes, Alysaundr', Letyse, Betayn, Columbyn, Alleluia, Astralogia rotunda, Astralogia longa, Basillican, Dylle, Deteyn, Egrymon, Hertestonge, Radiche, White pyper, Cabagez, Sedewale, Spynache, Coliaundr', Foothistyll, Orage, Cartabus, Lympons, Nepte, Clarey, Pacience

Of the same Herbes for Sauce

Hertes tonge, Sorell, Pelytory, Pelytory of Spayn, Deteyn, Vyolettes, Percely, Myntes

Also of the same Herbes for the copp

Cost, Costmary, Sauge, Isope, Rosemary, Gyllofr', Goldez, Clarey, Mageron, Rue

Also of the same Herbes for a Salade

Buddus of Stanmarche, Vyolette flourez, Percely, Redmyntes, Syves, Cresse of Boleyn, Purselan, Ramsons, Calamyntes, Prime Rose buddus, Dayses, Rapounses, Daundelyon, Rokette, Red nettell, Borage flourez, Croppus of Red Fenell, Selbestryune, Chykynwede

Also Herbez to Stylle

Endyve, Red Rose, Rosemary, Dragans, Skabiose, Ewfrace, Wermode, Mogwede, Beteyn, Wylde Tansey, Sauge, Isope, Ersesmart

Also Herbes for Savour and beaute

Gyllofr' gentyle, Mageron gentyle, Basyle, Palma Christi, Stycadose, Meloncez, Arcachaffe, Scalacely, Philyppendula, Popyroyall, Germaundr', Cowsloppus of Jerusalem, Verveyn, Dyll, Seynt Mar' Garlek

Also Rotys for a gardyn

Persenepez, Turnepez, Radyche, Karettes, Galyngale, Iryngez, Saffron

Also for an Herber

Vynes, Rosers, Lyles, Thewberies, Almondez, Baytrees, Gourdes, Date trese, Peche trese, Pyne Appull, Pyany Roman, Rose campy, Cartabus, Selyan, Columbyn gentyle, Elabre

THE LISTED PLANTS AND THEIR IDENTIFICATION

Where the modern name is printed in CAPITALS the plant also occurs in 'The Feat of Gardening' by Master John Gardener, of c. 1400.

Names in 'Fromond' list	Modern English Names	Scientific Names
Alysaundre	ALEXANDERS	Smyrnium olusatrum
Avence	AVENS	Geum urbanum
Astralogia rotunda	Round Birthwort	Aristolochia rotunda
Astralogia longa	Long Birthwort	Aristolochia longa
Alleluia	WOOD SORREL	Oxalis acetosella
Arcachaff(e)	(Globe) Artichoke	Cynara scolymus
Artemesie Mogwede	Mugwort	Artemisia vulgaris
Annes	Anise, Aniseed	Pimpinella anisum
Archangel	Archangel, Dead Nettle	Lamium album
[Almondez]	Almond	Prunus communis
Borage, Borage flourez	BORAGE	Borago officinalis
Betes	Beet	Beta vulgaris
Beteyn, Betayn	BETONY	Stachys officinalis
Basil(l)ican, Basyle	Basil	Ocimum basilicum
Bugle	BUGLE	Ajuga reptans
Burnett	Burnet	Sanguisorba minor
[Baytrees]	(Sweet) Bay tree	Laurus nobilis
Cabage(z)	Cabbage	Brassica oleracea
Chervell	Chervil	Anthriscus cerefolium
Carewey, Carawey	Caraway	Carum carvi
Cyves, Syves	Chives	Allium schoenoprasum
Columbyn	Columbine	Aquilegia vulgaris
Clarey	CLARY	Salvia sclarea
Colyaundr', Coliaundr'	CORIANDER	Coriandrum sativum
Colewort(es)	COLEWORT, KALE	Brassica oleracea acephala
Cartabus	? Bastard Saffron	Carthamus tinctorius
	? Cardoon	Cynara cardunculus
Cressez	CRESS	Lepidium sativum
Cresse(z) of Boleyn (Boulogne)	? Watercress	Roripa nasturtium-aquaticum
Calamynt	CALAMINT	Calamintha ascendens
Camamyll	CHAMOMILE	Anthemis nobilis
Ceterwort	Setterwort	Helleborus foetidus
[Cost] (generally supposed to be identical with Costmary, below)		
[Costmary]	Costmary, Alecost	Chrysanthemum balsamita
[Chykynwede]	Chickweed	? Stellaria media
[Cowsloppus of Jerusalem]	see Longwortz	
[Columbyn gentyle]	Garden Columbine	Aquilegia vulgaris, garden varieties
Daysez, Daysys, -ses	Daisy	Bellis perennis
Dyteyn, Deteyn	DITTANY	Origanum dictamnus
Daundelyon	Dandelion	Taraxacum officinale
Dragaunce, Dragans	Dragons	Dracunculus vulgaris
Dylle, Dyll	Dill	Peucedanum graveolens
[Date trese]	'Date tree'	? Prunus domestica var.
Elena campana	ELECAMPANE	Inula helenium
Eufras, Ewfrace	Eyebright	Euphrasia officinalis
Egremoyn, Egrymon	AGRIMONY	Agrimonia eupatoria

[Endyve]	Endive	Cichorium endivia
[Ersesmart]	Water Pepper	Polygonum hydropiper
[Elabre]	Hellebore	? Helleborus viridis
		? Helleborus niger
Fenell	FENNEL	Foeniculum vulgare
Foothistell, -tyll	see Sowthistell	
Fenecreke	Fenugreek	Trigonella foenum-graecum
[Fenell, Red, Croppus (i.e. crops or tops) of]		
Gromell	GROMWELL	Lithospermum officinale
Goldez, Goldes	Marigold	Calendula officinalis
Gyllofr'	Gilliflower	Dianthus caryophyllus
Germaundr'	Germander	Teucrium chamaedrys
[Gyllofr' gentyle]	Garden Carnation	Dianthus caryophyllus
[Seynt Mar' Garlek]	? GARLICK	Allium sativum
[Galyngale]	Galingale	Cyperus longus
[Gourdes]	Gourd	Cucurbita ? pepo
Hertez tonge, Hertes tong	HART'S-TONGUE	Phyllitis scolopendrium
Horehound	HOREHOUND	Marrubium vulgare
Henbane	HENBANE	Hyoscyamus niger
Isope	HYSSOP	Hyssopus officinalis
Ierlin	'Jerusalem (? Cross)'	? Lychnis chalcedonica
Iryngez	Eryngo, Sea Holly	Eryngium maritimum
Herbe Ive	Herb-Ive	? Ajuga chamaepitys
		? Plantago coronopus
		? Coronopus squamatus
Kykombre, yt bereth apples	Cucumber	Cucumis sativus
[Karett]	Carrot	Daucus carota
Longdebeff, Langdebefe	Languedeboeuf, VIPER'S BUGLOSS	Echium vulgare
Lekez	LEEK	Allium ampeloprasum porrum
Letuse, Letyse	LETTUCE	Lactuca sativa
Loveache	Lovage	Ligusticum scoticum
Lympons	? Lupin	Lupinus albus
	? Limpwort, Brooklime	Veronica beccabunga
Lylle, Lyles	LILY	Lilium candidum
Longwortz, [Cowsloppus of Jerusalem]	Lungwort, Jerusalem Cowslip	Pulmonaria officinalis
Mercury, Marcury	Mercury	Mercurialis annua
Malowes	Mallow	Malva sylvestris
Mynt(es)	MINT	Mentha spicata, etc.
Mageron	Marjoram	Origanum vulgare
Mageron gentyle	Sweet Marjoram	Origanum majorana
Mandrake	Mandrake	Mandragora officinarum
Mylone, Meloncez	Melon	Cucumis melo
[Mynt, Red, Redmynt]	? 'Red Mint'	Mentha sp.
[Mogwede] see Artemisie Mogwede		
Nept, Nepte	NEPP, CATMINT	Nepeta cataria
Nettell rede, Rednettyll, Red nettell	Red Dead Nettle	Lamium purpureum
Nardus capiscola	? Spikenard	? Lavandula spica
	? Ploughman's Spikenard	? Inula conyza
Orage	ORACH	Atriplex hortensis
Oculus Christi	WILD CLARY	Salvia verbenaca
Oynons	ONION	Allium cepa
Persely, Percely	PARSLEY	Petroselinum crispum

Pelytore, Pelytory	PELLITORY	Parietaria officinalis
Pelytory, -ore of Spayn	Pellitory of Spain	Anthemis pyrethrum
Puliall royall	Pennyroyal	Mentha pulegium
Pyper white	? Pepperwort	Lepidium heterophyllum
Pacyence, Pacience	Herb Patience	Rumex patientia
Popy whit'	White Poppy	Papaver somniferum
Prymerose, Prime Rose buddus (buds)	PRIMROSE	Primula vulgaris
Purselane, Purselan	Purslane	Portulaca oleracea
Philipendula, philypp-	Dropwort	Filipendula hexapetala
[Palma Christi]	? Castor Oil Plant	Ricinus communis
	? perhaps	Orchis maculata
[Popyroyall]	Garden Poppy	Papaver somniferum var.
[Persenepez]	Parsnip	Peucedanum sativum
[Peche trese]	Peach tree	Prunus persica
[Pyany Roman]	PAEONY	Paeonia officinalis
[Pyne Appull]	Pine	Pinus sylvestris
Qvyncez	Quince	Cydonia oblonga
Rapes, Rapez	Rape	Brassica napus
Radyche, Radiche	RADISH	Raphanus sativus
Rampsons, Ramsons	Ramsons	Allium ursinum
Rapouncez, Rapounses	Rampion	Campanula rapunculus
Rokett, Rokette	Rocket	Hesperis matronalis
Rewe, Rue	RUE	Ruta graveolens
[Rosemary]	Rosemary	Rosmarinus officinalis
[Rose Red, Rosers]	RED ROSE	Rosa gallica
[Rose Campy]	ROSE CAMPION	? Melandrium dioicum
		? Lychnis coronaria
Sauge	SAGE	Salvia officinalis
Saverey	SAVORY	Satureia montana
Spynache	SPINACH	? Spinacia oleracea
Sede-wale, Sedewale	SETWALL	? Valeriana pyrenaica
		? Centranthus ruber
Scalaceli, Scalacely	'Ladder of Heaven'	? Polygonatum multiflorum
		? Polemonium coeruleum
Smalache	SMALLAGE	Apium graveolens
Sauce alone	Sauce Alone, Garlic Mustard	Alliaria petiolata
Selbestryue, Selbestryune	? Herb Trinity	Viola tricolor
Syves	See Cyves	
Sorell	Sorrel	Rumex acetosa
Sowthistell, 'Foothistell, -tyll'	Sow Thistle	Sonchus oleraceus
Sothernwode	SOUTHERNWOOD	Artemisia abrotanum
Skabiose	SCABIOUS	? Scabiosa columbaria
Selian, Selyan		
Stycadose	Stickadove	Lavandula stoechas
Stanmarch, Buddus (Buds) of Stanmarche	see Alysaundre	
[Saffron]	SAFFRON	Crocus sativus
Tyme	THYME	Thymus vulgaris
Tansey, Wylde Tansey	TANSY	Tanacetum vulgare
[Turnepez]	Turnip	Brassica campestris rapa
[Thewberies]	Dewberry	Rubus caesius
Vyolett(es), Vyolette flourez	VIOLET	Viola odorata
Wermode	WORMWOOD	Artemisia absinthium

Wormesede	Wormseed	? Artemisia santonica
		? Erysimum cheiranthoides
		? Peucedanum officinale
Verveyn	VERVAIN	Verbena officinalis
[Vynes]	GRAPE VINE	Vitis vinifera

It will be noticed that in one case, 'Selian', also appearing as 'Selyan' in the list of plants for an Arbour, no suggested identification is advanced. In another case, that of 'Selbestryue', the suggestion is based on the flimsiest evidence: the second occurrence of the word, in the list of herbs used for Salad, has a mark of abbreviation over the letter 'u' indicating an omitted 'n', apparently making the name 'Selbes-tryune', or 'triune of itself', implying the Trinity. Since Violet flowers were eaten in Salads, it is not by any means impossible that the closely related Viola Tricolor, known as Herb Trinity, should also have served; but the hypothesis is little better than a guess. Disregarding the mark of abbreviation (not necessarily intended), the name could be read as a misspelling of 'Self-strive' analogous to Selfheal; but no such plant-name has so far been discovered.

APPENDIX II.

THE CATALOGUE OF WILLIAM LUCAS c. 1677

THIS LIST WAS discovered by the Reverend Arthur L. Drinkwater, rector of Little Bookham, Surrey, in a small notebook preserved with the parish registers and records. The copy was evidently made as a private memorandum and has no real connection with the remaining contents of the book. The mention of a single price opposite to the first item, Onion seeds, may indicate that there were prices on the original throughout, but otherwise the copy appears to be complete. It includes every category of seeds to be expected at the period, and agrees closely with slightly later standard lists that have survived.

No earlier English list showing a complete stock of seeds and plants seems to have been published, though there are lists of desirable plants in books on gardening, notably that of Leonard Meager printed in *The English Gardener* of 1670 (see pp. 8 — 12). Probably the large specialised seedsman, as exemplified by Lucas, was a new phenomenon after the Restoration. Earlier trade-lists were probably of groups of seeds stocked as a side-line by corn-chandlers and merchants, though the framework of the lost treatise by John Rose the King's gardener, indexed in *The English Vineyard Vindicated* (see p. 8) implies a complete and classified list.

Essentially the same list as that of Lucas continued to be that of his successor in trade, Edward Fuller, and in 1688 it was printed by J. Woolridge (or Worlidge) as an appendix to his book, *Systema Horti-culturae* (3rd edition, pp. 271-78). Woolridge gives the list as sold by three different London seedsmen: Edward Fuller at the Three Crowns and Naked Boy at Strand Bridge near the May-Pole; Theophilus Stacy, at the Rose and Crown without Bishopsgate; and Charles Blackwell, at the King's Head near Fetter-Lane-end in Holborn. For plants, Woolridge gives 'A Catalogue of House Greens, etc. sold by Mr. George Rickets, Gardener, at the Hand in Hogsden (Hoxton) without Bishopsgate, London, the great Collector and Improver of the Beauties of a Garden.' (*Systema . . .*, pp. 268-70)

A long and detailed account for seeds 'bought of Edward Fuller at Strand Bridge' between 18 December 1697 and 28 March 1698 has been brought to light by the National Register of Archives. The order of kinds of seeds in the account agrees almost throughout with that of Lucas's list of twenty years before. Fortunately the amounts are stated in many instances, from which it is possible to work out the prices per ounce for seed. For example, Turnip seed cost only 1d., Radish 1½d., Parsley 2d., Red Carrott 3d., Angelico, White Beet, Bugloss, Burnett, Carduus, Corn Sallad, Garden Cresses, Hyssop, Marygold and French Sorrell were all 4d. an ounce; Red Beet, English and Dutch Cabbage and Dutch Savoy, Selleree, Cabbage Lettuce and Skerritt, as well as the herbs Clary, Sweet Marjoram, Purslane, Winter Savory and Thyme, were 6d.; Onion seed 9d.; Borrage, Hartshorn, Leek and Scorzonera 1s.;

Prickly Cucumber 1s. 6d.; Small Indian Cresses (Tropaeolum minus) 2s. 6d.; and Best Collyflower, as always the most costly of seeds, at 5s. the ounce. The only Flower seeds with specified prices are Canterbury Bells at 9d., Double Larkswheel 1s., and Rose Larkswheel at 3s. an ounce.

The later history of the Strand Bridge seed-shop is reflected in at least two more lists which have survived. One is called a Catalogue of Grass Seeds, but is really a pamphlet on improvement of land by the sowing of kinds of Clover and the like, issued by E. Clarke, successor to ———— Fuller, at the Three Crowns and Naked Boy. Clarke's name is in this case written in ink; but later he (as Edward Clarke, of The Naked Boy and Three Crowns) issued 'A Catalogue of Garden Seeds' etc., with cultural notes, in the form of a broadsheet now in the John Johnson Collection of Ephemera at the Bodleian Library. This probably dates from somewhere in the second quarter of the 18th century, and marks the transition towards book-form catalogues with full cultural hints, such as those which were issued by John Webb in c. 1754 and in 1760 (John Johnson Collection).

A CATALOGUE OF SEEDS, PLANTS, &c.

sold by Will: Lucas att the Naked Boy near Strand Bridg, London

Seeds of Roots

Strasburgh		
Red Spanish		
White Spanish	Onion	8 d. (Allium cepa)
French		
English		
London		
French	Leeke	(Allium ampeloprasum porrum)
Red		
Orang	Carrot	(Daucus carota)
Yellow		
Parsnep		(Peucedanum sativum)
Swelling Parsnep		
Long		
Round	Turnep	(Brassica campestris rapa)
Yellow		
Skirret		(Sium sisarum)
Scorzonera		(Scorzonera hispanica)
Sassify		(Tragopogon porrifolius)
Potato		(Solanum tuberosum)
Shallots		(Allium ascalonicum)
Rocumbole		(Allium scordoprasum)
Garlick		(Allium sativum)

Sallad Seeds

London		
Sandwick		
Black Spanish	Radish	(Raphanus sativus)
White Spanish		

Cabbage ⎫		
Humbar ⎪		
Roman ⎪		
Arabian ⎬	Lettuce	(Lactuca sativa)
Savoy ⎪		
Rose ⎪		
Red ⎪		
Curl'd ⎭		

Round ⎫		(Spinacia oleracea glabra)
Prickly ⎬	Spinage	(Spinacia oleracea spinosa)
Berry bearing Orach		(Atriplex hortensis var.)
White ⎫		
Red ⎬	Beet	(Beta vulgaris)
Roman ⎭		
Curl'd Endive		(Cichorium endivia var.)
Italian Selleree		(Apium graveolens var.)
Fenochio		(Foeniculum vulgare dulce)
Sampier		(Crithmum maritimum)
Rockett		(Hesperis matronalis ?)
Spanish Rockett		(Eruca sativa)
Rampion		(Campanula rapunculus)
Hartshorn		(Plantago coronopus)
Tarragon		(Artemisia dracunculus)
French ⎫		(Rumex scutatus)
Candy ⎬	Sorrell	(Rumex spinosus)
Cardoon		(Cynara cardunculus)
Indian ⎫		(Tropaeolum minus)
Garden ⎪		(Lepidium sativum)
Broadleaved ⎬	Cresse	(Roripa nasturtium-aquaticum ?)
Curled ⎭		
Chervill		(Anthriscus cerefolium)
Sweet Chervill		
Pur(s)lane		(Portulaca oleracea)
Golden Purslane		(Portulaca oleracea var.)
Parsley		(Petroselinum crispum)
Curld Parsley		
Alisander		(Smyrnium olusatrum)
Cornsallad		(Valerianella locusta)
Asparagus		(Asparagus officinalis)
Dutch Asparagus		
Colyflower		(Brassica oleracea cauliflora)
English ⎫		
Dutch ⎪		
Russia ⎬	Cabbage	(Brassica oleracea capitata)
Red ⎭		
Colewort		(Brassica oleracea acephala)
Curl'd Colewort		
Broculus		(Brassica oleracea cymosa)
French Choux		
English ⎫		
Dutch ⎬	Savoy	(Brassica oleracea bullata subauda)
Coli Rapi		(Brassica oleracea gongyloides)

English ⎤		
French ⎥	Melon	(Cucumis melo)
Spanish ⎦		

English ⎤
French ⎥   Melon   (Cucumis melo)
Spanish ⎦

Long ⎤
Short ⎥   Cucumber   (Cucumis sativus)
Prickly ⎦

Pompion   (Cucurbita pepo var.)
Gourd   (Cucurbita pepo var.)
Mekin

Potherb Seeds

Endive   (Cichorium endivia)
Succory   (Cichorium intybus)
Borage   (Borago officinalis)
Bugloss   (Lycopsis arvensis)
Burnett   (Sanguisorba minor)
Bloodwort   (Rumex sanguineus ?)
Clary   (Salvia sclarea)
Sorrell   (Rumex acetosa)
Marygold   (Calendula officinalis)
Pot Marjoram   (Origanum onites)
Langdebeefe   (Echium vulgare)
Summer Savory   (Satureia hortensis)
Columbine   (Aquilegia vulgaris)
Tansie   (Tanacetum vulgare)
Nepp   (Nepeta cataria)
French Mallow   (Malva sylvestris ?)
Orach   (Atriplex hortensis)

Sweet Herb Seeds

Thyme   (Thymus vulgaris)
Hyssop   (Hyssopus officinalis)
Winter Savory   (Satureia montana)
Sweet Marjerome   (Origanum majorana)
Sweet Basill   (Ocimum basilicum)
Sweet Maudeline   (Achillea ageratum)
Rosemary   (Rosmarinus officinalis)
Lavender   (Lavandula spica)
Bawme   (Melissa officinalis)

Physicall Seeds

Carduus Benedictus   (Cnicus benedictus)
Scurvy-grass   (Cochlearia officinalis)
Angelica   (Angelica archangelica)
Lovage   (Ligusticum scoticum)
Smallage   (Apium graveolens)
Tobacco   (Nicotiana tabacum)
Dill   (Peucedanum graveolens)

1 Tuberose flower	9 Camomile double	17 Long blowing Honeysuckle	25 Mush Scabious
2 Single Nasturtium	10 Semper-Augustus turcula	18 Spiked Aster	26 Double white Musk rose
3 Yellow peren: Poppy	11 Indian Tobacco	19 Belladona Lilly	27 Box leav'd Myrtle
4 Purple Polyanthos	12 Arbutus double	20 Ever green Honeysuckle	28 Michaelmas Daisie
5 Saffron flower	13 Best flowering Geranium	21 Laminus or Archanged tree	29 Yellow Passion flower
6 Stript: double Colchicum	14 Guernsey Lilly	22 Black Cranes bill	30 Hollyhock always double
7 Single blow: Perwinkle	15 Autumn Carnation	23 Scarlet Cranes bill	31 Virgina Shrub: Aster
8 Trumpet flower	16 Agnus Castus	24 Marigold tree	

OCTOBER

Engrav'd by H. Fletcher.   From the Collection of Rob. Furber gardiner at Kensington. 1730.   Engrav'd by H. Fletcher.

Painted by P. Casteels   From the Collection of Rob.t Furber Gardener at Kensington 1730   Engraved by H. Fletcher

1 Royal purple Auricula.
2 African white flower'd Heath.
3 Pansies or Heart's ease.
4 White Corn Marigold.
5 Strawberry daisie.
6 Cape Marigold.
7 Shining leav'd Laurustinus.
8 Marvel du Mond Auricula.
9 Red spring Cyclamen.

10 White Cyclamen.
11 Yellow Picotee.
12 Yellow round Eternal.
13 Christmas flower.
14 Winter white Primrose.
15 Gentianella.
16 Yellow Corn Marigold.
17 Scarlet Geranium.
18 Canary Pellitory.

DECEMBER

19 Valerianella.
20 Winter double Cronfoot.
21 Stript leav'd Geranium.
22 Cape Marigold white within.
23 Peters Shrub.
24 Mountain Avens.
25 Single purple Anemone.
26 Sage & Rosemary tree.
27 Winter wall flower.

28 Winter flowering Pear.
29 Lavend.r leav'd gravelwel tree.
30 Scarlet African Aloe, with
      Pineapple Leaves.
31 Spanish Virgin's bower.
32 Glastenbury thorne.
33 Humble plant.
34 Baselia.
35 Monthly rose bud.
36 Stript African golden knob.

Common Fennell	(Foeniculum vulgare)
Sweet Fennell	(Foeniculum vulgare dulce)
Caraway	(Carum carvi)
Cumin	(Cuminum cyminum)
Anise	(Pimpinella anisum)
Coriander	(Coriandrum sativum)
Gromill	(Lithospermum officinale)
Henbane	(Hyoscyamus niger)
Plantain	(Plantago major)
Nettle	(Urtica dioica)
Fenugreek	(Trigonella foenum-graecum)
Flea	(Plantago indica)
Rubarb	(Rheum rhaponticum)
Burdock	(Arctium pubens)
Elecampane	(Inula helenium)
Balsam	(Impatiens balsamina)
White Poppey	(Papaver somniferum)
Cardamum	
Gourd	(Cucurbita pepo)
Citrull	(Citrullus vulgaris)
Wormseed	(Artemisia santonica ?)
Wormwood	(Artemisia absinthium)
Rue	(Ruta graveolens)
Oculus Christi	(Salvia verbenaca)
Line	(Linum usitatissimum)
Marshmallow	(Althaea officinalis)

Flower Seeds

Double July Flower	(Dianthus caryophyllus)
Stockgilliflower	(Matthiola incana)
Queens Gilliflower	(Hesperis matronalis)
Wall Flower	(Cheiranthus cheiri)
White Wallflower	(? Arabis albida)
Matted Pink	(Dianthus plumarius)
Mountain Pink	(Dianthus gratianopolitanus)
Double Columbine	(Aquilegia vulgaris flore pleno)
Virginian Columbine	(Aquilegia canadensis)
Double Larksheel	(Delphinium consolida)
Vpright Larksheel	(Delphinium ajacis)
Rose Larksheel	
Affrican ⎤	(Tagetes erecta)
French ⎦ Marigold	(Tagetes patula)
Snapdragon	(Antirrhinum majus)
Candy Tuft	(Iberis umbellata)
Sweet Scabious	(Scabiosa atropurpurea)
Spanish Scabious	(Scabiosa ? stellata)
London Pride	(Saxifraga umbrosa)
Capsicum indicum	(Capsicum ? frutescens)
Venus Looking Glasse	(Specularia speculum)
White Venus Looking Glasse	(Specularia speculum var. alba)
Venus Navell Wort	(Omphalodes linifolia)
French Honysuckle	(Hedysarum coronarium)
White French Honysuckle	(Hedysarum coronarium var. album)

Scarlett Lychnis		(Lychnis chalcedonica)
Rose Campion		(Lychnis coronaria)
Noli me tangere		(Impatiens balsamina)
Marvell of Peru		(Mirabilis jalapa)
Narturtium (sic) indicum		(Tropaeolum minus)
Sweet Sultan		(Centaurea moschata)
Red		(Centranthus ruber)
White	Valerian	(Centranthus ruber var. albus)
Greeke		(Polemonium coeruleum)
Branch'd Sunflower		(Helianthus decapetalus var. multiflorus)
Canterbury Bell		(Campanula medium)
Flos Adonis		(Adonis autumnalis)
Fox Taill		(? Alopecurus pratensis)
Iron colour Fox glove		(Digitalis ferruginea)
Nigella Romana		(Nigella sativa)
Urtica Romana		(Urtica pilulifera)
Moth Mulleine		(Verbascum blattaria)
Primrose Tree		(OEnothera biennis)
	purpureus	(Amaranthus caudatus)
Amaranthus	coccineus	(A. hypochondriacus var. sanguineus)
	tricolor	(A. gangeticus var. melancholicus f. tricolor
Green Amaranthus		(A. hypochondriacus var. viridis)
Princes Feather		(Amaranthus hypochondriacus)
Love Apple		(Solanum lycopersicum)
Thorn Apple		(Datura stramonium)
Double Poppy striped		(Papaver somniferum flore pleno)
Double Holly hock		(Althea rosea)
Lobels'Catchflie		(Silene armeria)
Goats Rue		(Galega officinalis)
Monks Hood		(Aconitum napellus)
Convolvulus	major	(Pharbitis purpurea)
	minor	(Convolvulus tricolor)
Bottles of all colours		(Centaurea cyanus)
Globe Thistle		(Echinops ritro)
Great Blew		(Lupinus hirsutus)
Small Blew		(Lupinus varius)
Yellow	Lupines	(Lupinus luteus)
White		(Lupinus albus)
Scarlett Beans		(Phaseolus coccineus)
Everlasting Pease		(Lathyrus latifolius)
Snaills & Caterpillars		(Medicago scutellata)
Horns & Hedghoggs		(Medicago intertexta)
Tulip		(Tulipa Gesneriana)
Anemony		(Anemone coronaria)
Auriculas		(Primula auricula)
Polyanthus		(Primula x variabilis)
Primrose		(Primula vulgaris)
Sensible Plant		(Mimosa sensitiva)
Humble Plant		(Mimosa pudica)

Seeds of Evergreen & Flowering Trees

Cypresse	(Cupressus sempervirens)
Silver Fir	(Abies alba)

Norway Fir		(Picea abies)
Scotch Fir		(Pinus sylvestris)
Great Pine		(Pinus pinaster ?)
Pinaster		(Pinus pinea ?)
Phillyrea vera		(Phillyrea latifolia)
Alaternus		(Rhamnus alaternus)
Perecanthus		(Pyracantha coccinea)
Arbutus		(Arbutus unedo)
Laurus tinus		(Viburnum tinus)
Amomum Plinii		(Solanum pseudocapsicum)
Mezereon berries		(Daphne mezereum)
Cedar		(Juniperus bermudiana)
Holly		(Ilex aquifolium)
Laurell		(Prunus laurocerasus)
Bay	berries	(Laurus nobilis)
Juniper		(Juniperus communis)
Yew		(Taxus baccata)
Mirtle		(Myrtus communis)
Evergreen Oake acorns		(Quercus ilex)
Corktree acorns		(Quercus suber)
Limetree seed		(Tilia x europaea)
Sena seed		(Colutea arborescens)
Althea seed		(Hibiscus syriacus)
Laburnum	majus	(Laburnum anagyroides)
	minus	(Laburnum alpinum)
Spanish Broom seed		(Spartium junceum)
Chesnuts		(Castanea sativa)
Allmonds		(Prunus communis)

Sorts of Pease, Beans &(c)

Barns Hotspur		
Short Hotspur		
Long Hotspur	Pease	(Pisum sativum)
Sandwich		
Windsor Grey		
White		
Grey		
Green	Rouncivall Pease	
Blew		
Maple		
Larg White Sugar		
Small White Sugar	Pease	(Pisum sativum saccharatum)
Grey Sugar		
White Rose		
Grey Rose		
Egg	Pease	
Wing		
Sickle		
Windsor		
Sandwich	Beans	(Vicia faba)
White		
Speckled	Kidney Beans	(Phaseolus vulgaris)
Canterbury		

Lentills   (Lens esculenta)

Seeds to improve land

Claver Grasse   (Trifolium repens)
Hopclaver cleansed   (Trifolium campestre)
Hopclaver in the husk
Sainefoin   (Onobrychis viciifolia)
La Lucer   (Medicago sativa)
Rye Grasse   (Lolium perenne)
French Furs   (Ulex nanus ?)
Dantzick Flax   (Linum usitatissimum var.)

Flower Roots

Ranuncula's all sorts   (Ranunculus asiaticus)
Double Anemonies all sort   (Anemone coronaria)
French Anemonies
Tulips all sorts   (Tulipa Gesneriana)
Double Julyflowers all sort   (Dianthus caryophyllus)
Auricula's double, striped   (Primula auricula)
& plain
Polyanthus all sorts   (Primula x variabilis)
Primroses all sorts   (Primula vulgaris)
Iris
Persian   (Iris persica)
Calcedonian   (Iris susiana)
Dwarfe &c.   (Iris pumila)
Crown Imperiall yellow double
& single   (Fritillaria imperialis)
Fraxinella's Purple & White   (Dictamnus albus and var. purpureus)
Hepatica   (Hepatica triloba)
Double Blew, &
Double Peachcolour
White, Blew, & Peachcolour single
Crocus's all sorts
Narcissus all sorts
Hyacinthus
Tuberosus,   (Hyacinthus orientalis)
plumosius, &   (Muscari comosum var. monstrosum)
Peruanus   (Scilla peruviana)
Junquills double & single   (Narcissus jonquilla)
Pionies — Black, Red, Purple
& Striped   (Paeonia officinalis)
Fritillaria all sorts
Hellebore White, Black & Xmas
Colchicum chio Purple,
Striped &c   (Colchicum variegatum)
Gladiolus all sorts
Cyclamen Vernum
& Autumnum   (Cyclamen europaeum and C. neapolitanum)
Lillies all sorts

Sorts of choise Trees & Plants

Oranges Striped	
& Hermaphrodite	(Citrus sinensis)
Limons	(Citrus limonia)
Citrons	(Citrus medica)
Pomgranat	(Punica granatum)
Mirtles	(Myrtus communis vars.)
broad-leaved,	
orangleaved,	
boxleaved,	
birdsnest,	
upright &	
double-flower'd	
Oliander Red & White	(Nerium oleander)
Phillyrea	
serrato folio &	(Phillyrea latifolia)
angusto folio	(Phillyrea angustifolia)
Alaternus striped with yellow	
and white	(Rhamnus alaternus)
Cytisus lunatus & secundus	(Medicago arborea)
Clusii	(Cytisus sessilifolius)
Amomum Plinii	(Solanum pseudocapsicum)
Holly's,	(Ilex aquifolium vars.)
striped with yellow,	
with white, &	
yellow beries	
Arbutus	(Arbutus unedo)
Paliurus	(Paliurus spina-Christi)
Olive tree	(Olea europea)
Cedrus	
Libani	(Cedrus libani)
Barmudi	(Juniperus bermudiana)
semper vivens	
Agnus castus	(Vitex agnus-castus)
Arbor Judae	(Cercis siliquastrum)
Platinus Orientalis	(Platanus orientalis)
Occidentalis	(Platanus occidentalis)
Tragacantha	(Astragalus tragacantha)
Horschesnut	(Aesculus hippocastanum)
Jessamines:	
Spanish,	(Jasminum grandiflorum)
Yellow,	(Jasminum fruticans)
Persian,	(Syringa persica)
White, &c	(Jasminum officinale)
Cistus all sorts	
Marum Syriacum	(Origanum maru)
Geranium noctu (sic) olens	(Pelargonium triste)
Jucca Peruana	(Yucca gloriosa)
Nightshade varigated	(Solanum ? dulcamara variegatum)
Woodbine varigated	(Lonicera periclymenum variegatum)
Althea,	(Hibiscus syriacus)
Purple,	
White &c	
with many other sorts	

You be here accomodated wth spad's hoes, rakes, reeles, lines, sheers, bass-mats &c proper for the use of gardiners; as also with all sorts of fruit trees, & Evergreens; & with Artichokes, Liquorice, Collyflower, Cabbage & Tarragon plants.

PRICES OF VEGETABLE SEEDS AT YORK, 1729-1759

IN THE ABSENCE of any priced list of Vegetable seeds for the mid-18th century, some long accounts for seeds supplied by Telfords of York to the Studley Royal estate in 1729-33 are printed in full. Another good series of accounts of the same type, also from Telfords, supplied to Francis Cholmeley of Brandsby,[1] exists for a rather later period, and extracts are given here to fill gaps in the list of seeds supplied to Studley. Many prices remained more or less unchanged, but by 1759 there is some evidence of an upward tendency. Among common seeds, Onion moved from a standard price of 3s. a lb. up to 4s., the cheaper kinds of Lettuce from 6d. to 9d. per oz., the choicer sorts from 1s. 3d. to 1s. 6d. Curled Endive rose from 6d. to 8d. and even 1s. an ounce, Thyme from 4d. to 6d. and Sweet Marjoram from 2½d. to 10d. and then to 1s.

The Brandsby accounts of 1756-59 show several purchases of seed of Scotch Fir at 1s. an ounce, but no other tree seeds. In the class of Seeds to improve Land, both White Dutch Clover and Best White Clover started at 6d. a lb., Best Red Clover at 6s. a stone; but by 1759 both White and Red Clover had gone up to 7d. a lb. Best Feeding Turnip seed cost 1s. a lb. Peas cost 8d. a quart for Large or Dwarf Marrow, or Union Peas, only 6d. a quart for Hotspur Peas. White blossom'd Beans and Hotspur Beans were 4d. a quart, but Speckled Kidney Beans 9d. a pint. A rather different choice of some vegetables seems to have been available: both Welsh and Spanish Onion seeds were bought, as well as Strasbourg, all at 4s. a lb.

In the Cabbage tribe, Dutch Savoy stayed at 6d. an ounce, but both Green and White Savoy found a market at 1s. and must have been greatly improved varieties. Early and Red Cabbage were still at 1s. an ounce, and Battersea Cabbage seed was also sold at the same price. London Radish went up to 1s. 4d. a lb., and Scarlet and Salmon Collourd were also supplied at the same price, but the latter when bought by the ounce cost 1½d. as against 1d. for other Radish seed. Curld Brocoli cost only 6d. an ounce, but 1s. was charged for Collyflour Brocoli; but the true Cauliflower generally cost 4s. an ounce as in 1730, though this was one item that showed a slight fall by 1759, to 3s. 6d. A new plant being grown regularly was Chou De Millan, at 8d. an ounce.

In other sections of the imagined list, there are prices for White Beet as well as Red, at the same price of 2d. an ounce; Celeriac, at 6d. an ounce, was being sown regularly, and so was 'Carduus' at the same price — presumably Cardoon, but if so the price had dropped to half the 1730 level. Curld Parsley and Dill were both supplied at 2d. an ounce, which was also the price for Double Marygold, probably still grown as a pot herb, since the flower seeds were lumped together for 1s. 6d. or 2s. without being specified. Among

[1] Northallerton, North Riding Record Office, ZQG, Vouchers.

Requisites, Mats were 6d. or 7d. each, an iron Shovel 4s., Middle Siz'd Garden
Spades 3s. 6d. each, and 9-inch Turnip Hoes 1s. 3d. each. Trees too were
being planted: in 1744 a thousand Oaks at 5s. per hundred; in 1758 1174
Scotch Firs at 10s. per hundred, 500 Spruce 2 feet high for £5, 500 Larch 2½
and 3 feet high at 25s. a hundred.

ACCOUNTS FOR VEGETABLE SEEDS, &c., 1729-33

*Supplied to John Aislabie at Studley Royal, near Ripon, Yorkshire, on the
orders of his head gardener, William Fisher*

*janry ye 9th 1729/30   The Rt Honrble John Aislaby Esqr. Bt. of Jno.
Telford.*

Best Stras (burg) Onion	2lb	0	6	0
Orange Carrot	2lb	0	5	0
Swelling parsnep	1lb	0	1	6
Short Topt Radish	1lb	0	1	2
London Leek	2oz	0	0	8
Brown Dutch Lettice	1oz	0	0	6
Capuchin Lettice	1oz	0	0	6
Silesia Lettice	1oz	0	1	3
Imperiall Lettice	1oz	0	1	3
Wtt Coss Lettice	1oz	0	1	0
Green Coss Lettice	1oz	0	1	0
Cabbage Lettice	4oz	0	1	0
Best Colliflowr.	1oz	0	4	0
Early Cabbage	1oz	0	1	0
Dutch Savoy	1oz	0	0	6
Early Cucumber	1oz	0	0	6
Long Cucumbr.	1oz	0	0	6
Long Hottspr. peas	2pks	0	7	0
Dutch Marrow peas	1pk	0	6	0
Large Egg peas	4qts	0	3	0
Blue Sugar peas	4qts	0	3	0
Windsor beans	1pk	0	2	6
Wtt. Kid(ney) beans	2qts	0	2	0
Dwarf Kid(ney) beans	1qrt	0	1	0
Dwarf peas	1qrt	0	0	9
Yellow Turnep	2oz	0	0	4
Red beets	2oz	0	0	4
Red Cabbage	½oz	0	0	6
Curld. Endive	2oz	0	1	0
Sellery	½oz	0	0	3
Sassife	1oz	0	0	8
Corn Sallad	2oz	0	0	4
Swtt. Marjorum	2oz	0	0	5
Span(ish) Cardoon	1oz	0	1	0

Purslan	2oz	0	0	8
Hysop	1oz	0	0	4
Thyme	½oz	0	0	2
Clary	1oz	0	0	4
Annuall Flowrs.		0	2	0
2 Garden Spades		0	8	0
6 Garden Hoes		0	7	0
1 Dozn of Matts		0	7	0
3 baggs		0	1	0
	Caryed Over	4	3	11
Novembr. ye 7th 1730 Span beans	1pk	0	2	6
a bagg to send them in		0	0	4
10th of Feb. 1730-1 Windsor beans	1pk	0	2	6
Sandwich beans	1pk	0	2	6
Dutch Marrow peas	4qts	0	3	0
Large Egg peas	4qts	0	3	0
Large Sugar peas	4qts	0	3	0
Swelling parsnep	1lb	0	1	6
Orange Carrot	2lb	0	5	0
Stras. Onion	2lb	0	6	0
Early Turnep	2lb	0	0	9
Shallot & garlick	2lb	0	2	0
Bordeux Spinage	1lb	0	1	2
Short Topt Radish	1lb	0	1	3
London Leek	2oz	0	0	8
Best Colliflowr.	1oz	0	4	0
Dutch Savoy	1oz	0	0	6
Purslan	1oz	0	0	4
Early Cucumbr.	1oz	0	0	6
Long Cucumbr.	1oz	0	0	6
Curld Endive	1oz	0	0	8
Red Cabbage	½oz	0	0	6
Red beets	2oz	0	0	4
Brown Dutch Lettice	1oz	0	0	6
Imperiall Lettice	1oz	0	1	3
Silesia Lettice	1oz	0	1	3
Capuchin Lettice	1oz	0	0	6
Wtt. Coss Lettice	1oz	0	1	0
Green Coss Lettice	1oz	0	1	0
Annuall Flowrs		0	2	0
1 Dozn. of matts		0	7	0
2 baggs		0	0	8
28th March Thyme	1oz	0	0	6
Hysop	2oz	0	0	8
Dutch Savoy	1oz	0	0	6
		7	3	3

(The following entry has been cancelled):

			£	s	d
21st March 1732-3 2 Dozn. of matts			0	12	0
Scorzonera	1oz		0	0	6
29th Swtt. Marjorum	1oz		0	0	10
Winter Savery ½oz 3d. Thyme ½oz 3d.			0	0	6
Brocoli	1oz		0	1	0
			7	18	0

Only £7 3s. 3d. was claimed in the account finally submitted as 'a note for Seeds formerly deliverd per ordrs. of Fisher'.

THE TWO CATALOGUES of Trees and Shrubs offered by the great Yorkshire firms of Telford of York, 1775, and Perfect of Pontefract, immediately afterwards, have been described in some detail in the text (see Chapter IV, pp. 33-43). It remains only to emphasise the fact that identification of the precise species and varieties offered is in many cases uncertain. It is surprising that names, obviously well understood by a wide public, should not conform to the standards set by, for example, the *Gardener's Dictionary* of Philip Miller, reprinted in edition after edition throughout the relevant period. In some cases synonyms are given in the lists, but appear to be mutually contradictory: thus Black Poplar, not White, is equated with Abele. Though unquestionably wrong from the standpoint of etymology, the 1670 listing of Leonard Meager (see p. 9) which separates and contrasts the 'Abeal' and the White Poplars supports the view that in the age of planting it was the Black Poplar that was alternatively known as the Abele. Among the conifers it is hard to understand the separate categories of Cluster Pines (Pinus pinaster of most authorities) and Pinaster. The latter is distinct from the Scotch Fir, which was called the 'Pinaster' by Gerard in 1599. Probably it is simply a question of two distinct varieties or forms of a single species.

It is also worth drawing attention to the fact that Perfects, but not Telfords, sold young stocks for Cherry, Crab, Pear and Plum. It has been seen (p. 29) that in 1738 Perfects had also supplied Studley with Peach and Apricot stocks.

Since these priced catalogues mention, but do not include, Flower Roots and Bulbs, some contemporary priced lists have been added from *The Universal Botanist and Nurseryman* compiled by Richard Weston. Prices for flower seeds are seldom recorded, and the amounts supplied (as in modern packets) doubtless varied greatly. It is common to find a lump sum included in seedsmen's accounts to cover 'Flower Seeds', and these were probably annuals for the most part. We have seen (p. 28) that in 1694-5, a period of high prices (Strasbourg Onion seed at 5s. a lb.), unspecified amounts of Double African Marigold and French Marigold seed were supplied at 1s. and 1s. 6d. respectively. In 1764 Telfords included free of charge in an order going to Kirkby Overblows Rectory, Double Violet Roots (p. 31). The Brandsby accounts show that in 1757 some Carnation seed was bought for 3d., but there is no clue as to how much this was. All that can be said is that purchases of flower seeds formed a very small and generally even insignificant proportion of the annual bill for seeds supplied to the county estates. Among the very few cases where a definite amount of flower seed is specified is an item of 1s. for a half-ounce of 'Brumpton Stock Gilly Flower' supplied to Lord Monson at Burton by Lincoln in 1744, in a bill of only 7s. altogether for seeds from London. Brompton Stocks, quite exceptionally among the annuals and biennials of the time, must have been fashionable for bedding-out on a large scale. The kinds of seeds to be had from general seedsmen of the period, though not their prices, can be seen from Stephen Garraway's broadsheet catalogue appended, probably to be dated c. 1770.

In the margin of Telfords' Catalogue an asterisk has been placed against the kinds noted as heavily stocked in 1782 (see p. 41 – 42).

The 'great Variety of Bulbous Flowers' stocked by Telfords at York is not recorded, but that a fantastically large variety was obtainable at the period is shown by a series of lists, mostly with prices, printed by Richard Weston in *The Universal Botanist and Nurseryman.* The first three volumes, published in 1770-72, provide general catalogues, arranged alphabetically under the Latin names of genera, of Trees and Shrubs, and of Herbs, Flowers and Bulbous Roots. In volume IV, not published until 1777, is a catalogue of Ferns, Mosses, Algas and Mushrooms, followed by the priced lists which are almost unique at that period. The very long lists of named varieties of 'Florists' Flowers' are not reproduced here, but extracts showing the price-range are given. Weston appends a valuable note, which is here placed first by way of introduction:

'The above Catalogues of Flowers are selected from the most esteemed and curious Dutch Florists, and the Roots may be procured by applying to any of the Nurserymen and Seedsmen at the Prices mentioned. The Auriculas, Polyanthuses and Carnations may be seen when in Flower, and are sold by Mr. James Maddock, Florist at Walworth, near London. All new-raised Flowers decrease greatly in price, in a few years after they are raised, particularly Hyacinths; and according to the scarcity the prices frequently vary annually.'

A Catalogue of curious Ranunculusses, 1769, includes 1,110 (!) different sorts, with prices ranging upwards from 5d. each, many costing 9d. or 1s. Prices for 100 of different sorts range from 10s. up to £6, while a collection of 700 different sorts might be had for £12 10s. 0d.

Tulips are priced from 2d. upwards and are listed in several categories. Early Blooming Tulips could be bought by the hundred, mixed, for 5s., and 100 of 25 different sorts cost 10s. Breeders, Striped, cost 12s. for 100 of 50 sorts, £1 11s. 6d. for 200 different. Violet, Grey and Rose-coloured Breeders were £1 10s. 0d. per 100.

	£	s	d
Striped Tulips,			
100 different, with their names	7	7	0
100 in 50 sorts	3	3	0
100 in 25 sorts	1	11	6
100 mixed, 50 violet, 50 bizars	2	12	6
100 bizars, or striped ones	1	5	0

White Grounds, striped, 100 best, £2 12s. 6d.; second best £1 11s. 6d.

	£	s	d
Hyacinths cost from 3d. each up to £2 2s. 0d.			
100 Double, very curious, different sorts & colours	8	8	0
100 of 52 different sorts	4	4	0
100 of 26 different sorts	2	2	0

Anemones, listed in 208 sorts, were priced from 3d. to 1s. 4d.

100 of 100 different sorts	2	2	0
100 of 50 sorts	1	5	0
100 of 25 sorts	1	1	0
100 various sorts		8	0
Polyanthus-Narcissuses were from 2d. to 1s. 8d. each			
100 in 10 sorts 12s. 100 in 21 sorts	1	5	0

Weston then prints a Catalogue of Auriculas dated 1777, at prices from 1s. to £2 2s. 0d., a Catalogue of Polyanthuses of 1777, without prices, and a Catalogue of Carnations, also 1777, priced from 2s. to 10s. 6d. each. There follows A Catalogue of Hyacinths, raised in Holland, of the newest and most valuable sorts, to the Year 1777: prices run from 2s. up to £21 for 'Black Flora'.

COLCHICUMS	s	d
Agrippina	0	5
Indicum Major	0	7
Double purple	0	7
Double yellow	0	7

CROCUSES		
100 of 13 different sorts	1	3

(Silvery blue; Dark Cloth of Gold; Flamed; Gold yellow; Great blue; Great yellow; Isabella; Merlioen; Porcellain; Saffron; Viceroy; White; Cloth of Silver)

CROWN IMPERIALS		
Aurora	0	4
Cinentus (? Cruentus)	0	4
– – – Yellow	0	8
Double yellow	2	6
– – – Red	0	9
Ditto, with striped leaves	0	5
Double Crowned	0	3
King William	0	3

CYCLAMENS		
Autumnal, flesh colour	1	6
Red, sweet-scented	4	0
White Aleppo	3	0
Ditto with red	3	0
Winter, purple	3	0
White Autumnal	1	6

FRITILLARIES by the Hundred	£	s	d
Twenty sorts with names	1	10	0
Many sorts without names	0	16	0
Common sorts	0	10	0

ENGLISH BULBOUS IRISES White and Porcelain Ground streaked with purple — By the Hundred

First sort of 25 different sorts	3	3	0
Second sort, ditto	1	10	0
Many sorts mixed	0	12	0

SPANISH BULBOUS IRISES

First sort of 25 sorts	2	2	0
Second sort of 12 sorts	0	12	0
Florentine Iris, each	0	1	0
Persian Iris	0	0	4
Chalcedonian	0	0	8
Snake's-head Iris	0	0	5

JONQUILS By the Hundred

Double Jonquils	0	4	0
Large Roots	0	14	0
Single Jonquils	0	3	0
Large Roots	0	10	0

LILIES
White and Red, various sorts (no prices given)

NARCISSUSES By the Hundred

Double White	0	6	0

ORNITHOGALUM

Large White, each	0	0	6
Small White	0	0	6
Green	0	0	6
Blue Peruvian	0	2	0
White Peruvian	0	2	0

SNOWDROPS By the Hundred

Double Snowdrops	0	1	6

TUBEROSES

Single Tuberoses, each	0	0	2

Weston also produced another book, *Flora Anglicana . . . The English Flora*, or A Catalogue of Trees, Shrubs, Plants and Fruits, Natives as well as Exotics . . . Also a General Catalogue of Seeds, in 1775, but this does not include any prices. In *The Supplement to the English Flora*, 1780, however, Weston did include one unusual price-list, A Catalogue of Gooseberry Trees raised from seed in Lancashire to the Year 1780 and sold by James Maddox, Florist, at Walworth, London. There are in all 320 sorts listed, classified according to the colour of the fruit: Amber, Black, Green, Red, Yellow and White. The prices go from 6d. a plant up to 10s. 6d., with many kinds at 1s.

A

2

CATALOGUE

O F

FOREST-TREES, ‖ EVER-GREEN AND
FRUIT-TREES, ‖ FLOWERING-SHRUBS,

SOLD BY

JOHN and GEORGE TELFORD,

NURSERY-MEN AND SEEDS-MEN,

I N

TANNER-ROW, *YORK.*

———————————

Y O R K:

Printed by A. WARD, in Coney-Street, 1775.

A

CATALOGUE, &c.

	£.	s.	d.		
ASHES, one Year old Seedlings —		10		per thousand	(Fraxinus excelsior)
Ditto transplanted, 1 Foot ——	1	10		per thousand	
Ditto —— 2 Feet ——	2			per thousand	
Ditto —— 3 Feet ——		7	6	per hundred	
Ditto					
Ash, Virginian Flowering —		6		each	(Fraxinus americana)
Ashes, Mountain, 2 Feet and 3 —	1	5		per hundred	*(Sorbus aucuparia)
Ditto —— 4 Feet —	1	13	4	per hundred	
Ditto —— 6 Feet —	2			per hundred	
Ditto —— 8 Feet —	2	10		per hundred	
Ash, Carolina —	1			each	*(Fraxinus caroliniana)
Areatheophrasti, 2 Feet —	1	5		per hundred	(Sorbus aria)
Ditto —— 4 Feet —	1	13	4	per hundred	
Ditto —— 6 Feet —	2			per hundred	
Acerplatanoides, or Norway Maple, 3 Feet		6		each	(Acer platanoides)
BEECHES, one Year old Seedlings, 6 Inches		10		per thousand	(Fagus sylvatica)
Ditto, two Years old Seedlings —		15		per thousand	
Ditto, transplantedd, 1 Foot —	2			per thousand	
Ditto —— 1½ Foot —		6		per hundred	
Ditto —— 2 Feet —		7	6	per hundred	
Ditto —— 3 Feet —		15		per hundred	
Ditto —— 4 Feet —	1			per hundred	
Beech, Purple —		5		each	(Fagus sylvatica purpurea)
Birches, transplanted, 2 Feet —		7	6	per hundred	(Betula pendula)
Ditto —— 3 and 4 Feet —			3	each	

A

* *indicates plants particularly well stocked in 1782*

4   F O R E S T - T R E E S.

		£.	s.	d.	
(Cedrus libani)	CEDARS of Libanus, tranfplanted, 1 Foot	3			each
	Ditto ———— 1½ Foot ————	4			
	Ditto ————-2 Feet ————				
*(Juniperus virginiana)**	Cedar, Red Virginian, 1 Foot ————	?			each
	Ditto ———— 1½ Foot ————	1	6		
	Ditto ———— 2 Feet ————				
(Chamaecyparis thyoides)	Cedar, White Virginian ———— ————	1	6		each
(Cupressus lusitanica)	———— of Goa ———— ————	4			each
(Cupressus sempervirens)	Cyprefs, Common, tranfplanted, 1 Foot —		6		each
	Ditto ————————— 2 Feet —	1			each
(C.sempervirens horizontalis)	Cyprefs, Male fpreading ———— ————	4			each
(Taxodium distichum)	————- Deciduous ———— ————	2	6		each
(Aesculus hippocastanum)	Chefnut, Horfe, one Year old Seedlings —	3			per hundred
	Ditto, tranfplanted, 1 Foot ————	5			per hundred
	Ditto, ———— 2 Feet ————	10			per hundred
	Ditto, ———— 3 Feet ————	15			per hundred
	Ditto, ———— 4 Feet ————	1			per hundred
(A. hippocastanum vars.)	Chefnut, Horfe, ftrip'd-leav'd; two Sorts	1			each
(Aesculus pavia)	———— ———— fcarlet flowering	2	6		each
(Aesculus octandra)	———— ———— yellow flowering ————	5			each
(Castanea sativa)	Chefnut, Spanifh, one Year old Seedlings —	4			per hundred
	Ditto, tranfplanted, 1 Foot ————	6			per hundred
	Ditto, ———— 2 Feet ————	10			per hundred
	Ditto, ———— 3 Feet ————	15			per hundred
	Ditto, ———— 4 and 5 Feet —	1			per hundred
	Ditto				
(C.sativa albo-marginata)	Chefnut, ftrip'd-leav'd Spanifh ————	5			each
(Ulmus procera)	ELMS, Englifh, grafted, 2½ Feet ————	15			per hundred
	Ditto, ———— 4 Feet ————	1			per hundred
	Ditto, ———— 6 Feet ————	1	10		per hundred
	Ditto, ———— 8 Feet ————	2			per hundred
	Ditto, ———— 10 Feet ————	2	10		per hundred

G

F O R E S T - T R E E S.   5

	£.	s.	d.		
Elms, Englifh, from Layers, the fame Sizes and Prices as the grafted ones.					
Elms, Witch, one Year old Seedlings ———		10		per thoufand	*(Ulmus glabra)*
Ditto, two Years old, 1 Foot ———	1			per thoufand	
Ditto, tranfplanted, 2 Feet ———		5		per hundred	
Elms, Cornifh ———————		1		each	*(Ulmus stricta)*
——— ftrip'd-leav'd Dutch ———			6	each	*(Ulmus x hollandica)*
FIRS, Scotch, one Year old Seedlings ———		7	6	per thoufand	*(Pinus sylvestris)*
Ditto, two Years old ——— ———		15		per thoufand	
Ditto, two Years old, tranfplanted ———		15		per thoufand	
Ditto, tranfplanted, 6 Inches ———	1	10		per thoufand	
Ditto, ——— —— 1 Foot		7	6	per hundred	
Ditto, ——— —— 1½ Foot ———		10		per hundred	
Ditto, ——— —— 2 Feet ———		15		per hundred	
Firs, Spruce or Norway, 1 Year old Seedlings		15		per thoufand	*(Picea abies)
Ditto, tranfplanted, 6 Inches ———	2			per thoufand	
Ditto, ——— —— 9 Inches ———	3	15		per thoufand	
Ditto, ——— —— 1 Foot ———		10		per hundred	
Ditto, ——— —— 1½ Foot ———		15		per hundred	
Ditto, ——— —— 2 Feet ———					
Firs, Silver, one Year old Seedlings ———	1	10		per thoufand	*(Abies alba)*
Ditto, two Years old ———	2			per thoufand	
Ditto, three Years old, tranfplanted —		5		per hundred	
Ditto, tranfplanted, 6 and 7 Inches —		7	6	per hundred	
Ditto, ——— —— 1 Foot ———		10		per hundred	
Ditto, ——— —— 1½ Foot					
Firs, Balm of Gilead, 6 Inches ———	1	5		per hundred	*(Abies balsamea)
Ditto, ——— —— 1 Foot ———			6	each	
Ditto, ——— —— 2 Feet ———			9	each	
Ditto,					
Firs, White American Spruce, 1 Foot ———			9	each	*(Picea glauca)
Ditto, ——————— 2 Feet ———		1		each	
Firs, Black American Spruce, ———		1		each	*(Picea mariana)*
——— Hemlock Spruce ——— ———		2		each	*(Tsuga canadensis)*

A 2

6   F O R E S T - T R E E S.

		£.	s.	d.	
*(Ilex aquifolium)**	HOLLIES, Green, tranfplanted, 6 Inches	1			per thoufand
	Ditto, —————————— 1 Foot —		5		per hundred
*(I. aquifolium vars.)**	Hollies, ftrip'd, of many Sorts, 1 Foot —			6	each
	Ditto, ————————— 2 Feet —			9	each
(Carpinus betulus)	Hornbeam, one Year old Seedlings ———		10		per thoufand
	Ditto, two Years old ——— ———		15		per thoufand
	Ditto, tranfplanted, 1 Foot ———		4		per hundred
	Ditto, ————— 1½ Foot ———		6		per hundred
	Ditto, ————— 2 Feet ———		8		per hundred
	Ditto, ————— 3 Feet ———		10		per hundred
	Ditto, ————— 4 Feet ———		15		per hundred
	Ditto, ————— 5 Feet ———	1			per hundred
(Larix decidua)	LARCHES, one Year old Seedlings ———	1	10		per thoufand
	Ditto, two Years old ———		4		per hundred
	Ditto, tranfplanted, 1 Foot ———		7	6	per hundred
	Ditto, ————— 1½ Foot ———		10		per hundred
	Ditto, ————— 2 Feet ———		15		per hundred
	Ditto, ————— 3 Feet ———	1			per hundred
	Ditto,				
(Tilia x europea)	Limes, tranfplanted, 1 Foot — ———		6		per hundred
	Ditto, ——— 2 Feet — ———		10		per hundred
	Ditto, ——— 3 Feet — ———		15		per hundred
	Ditto, ——— 4 Feet — ———	1			per hundred
	Ditto, ——— 6 Feet — ———	1	10		per hundred
	Ditto, ——— 8 Feet — ———				
(Quercus robur)	OAKS, Englifh, 1 Year old Seedlings, 6 Inch.		10		per thoufand
	Ditto, two Years old, 1 Foot ———		15		per thoufand
	Ditto, tranfplanted, 1 Foot ———	1	10		per thoufand
	Ditto, ————— 1½ Foot ———	2			per thoufand
	Ditto, ————— 2 Feet ———		7	6	per hundred
	Ditto, ————— 3 Feet ———		10		per hundred
	Ditto,				
(Quercus coccinea)	Oaks, Scarlet, 2 Feet —— ———			6	each
	Ditto, —— 3 and 4 Feet —— ———			9	each

FOREST-TREES.   7

	£.	s.	d.		
Oak, Devonshire or Lucombe		2	6	each	(*Quercus x hispanica Lucombeana*)
—— Ragnal			1	each	(*Quercus cerris* var.)
—— Strip'd-leav'd		2	6	each	(*Quercus robur variegata*)
—— Ever-green, or Ilex			6	each	(*Quercus ilex*)
—— Turkey		2	6	each	(*Quercus cerris*)
PINES, Ld. Weymouth's or New-England, 6 Inches			3	each	*(*Pinus strobus*)
Ditto, 1 Foot			4		
Ditto, 2 Feet			6		
Ditto, 3 Feet					
Pines, Cluster, transplanted, 4 Inches			6	per hundred	*(*Pinus pinaster*)
Ditto, —— 9 Inches			15	per hundred	
Ditto, —— 1 Foot		1		per hundred	
Ditto, —— 1½ Foot		1	5	per hundred	
Ditto, —— 2 Feet					
Pinasters, transplanted, 4 Inches			6	per hundred	*(*Pinus cembra ?*)
Ditto, —— 9 Inches			15	per hundred	
Ditto, —— 1 Foot		1		per hundred	
Ditto, —— 1½ Foot		1	5	per hundred	
Pines, Stone, transplanted, 1 Foot			6	each	(*Pinus pinea*)
Platinus, Oriental and Occidental, 2 Feet			3	each	*(*Platanus orientalis*)
Ditto, —— 4 Feet			4	each	*(*Platanus occidentalis*)
Ditto, —— 6 and 7 Feet			6	each	
Poplars, White, 1½ Foot			5	per hundred	(*Populus alba*)
Ditto, —— 3 and 4 Feet			10	per hundred	
Poplar, Black or Abele, 1½ Foot			5	per hundred	(*Populus nigra*)
Ditto, —— 3 Feet			10	per hundred	
Poplar, Italian or Lombardy 3 feet			10	per hundred	(*Populus nigra italica*)
Ditto, —— 6 feet			15	per hundred	
Ditto,					
Poplar of Carolina			1	each	(*Populus angulata*)
—— Berry-bearing			2	6 each	*(*P. canadensis ?*)
—— Balsam			2	6 each	*(*Populus candicans*)

A 3

❧   F O R E S T - T R E E S.

		£.	s.	d.	
(Acer pseudoplatanus)	SYCAMORES, 1 Year old Seedlings, 1 Foot		15		*per thousand*
	Ditto, tranſplanted, 2 Feet ————		7	6	*per hundred*
	Ditto, ———— 6 Feet ————	1			*per hundred*
	Ditto, ———— 8 Feet ————				
(A. pseudoplatanus albo-variegatum)	Sycamores, ſtrip'd, 2 Feet ————			4	*each*
	Ditto, ———— 4 and 5 Feet ————			6	*each*
(Crataegus oxyacantha)	THORN Quickſets, White ————				
(Juglans regia)	WALNUTS, tranſplanted, 1 Foot ————			4	*per hundred*
	Ditto, ———— 2 Feet ————			10	*per hundred*
	Ditto, ———— 4 Feet ————	1			*per hundred*
	Ditto, ———— 8 and 9 Feet ————			9	*each*
	Ditto,				
(Salix alba)	Willow, Huntingdonſhire ——— ————			3	*each*
(Salix babylonica)	——— Weeping ——— ————			2	*each*
(Salix pentandra)	——— Sweet ——— ——— ————			2	*each*
(Taxus baccata)*	YEWS, tranſplanted, 6 Inches ————		10		*per hundred*
	Ditto, ———— 1 Foot ————	1			*per hundred*
	Ditto, ———— 1½ Foot ————	1	13	4	*per hundred*
	Ditto, ———— 2 Feet ————	2	10		*per hundred*
	Ditto, ———— 3 Feet ————			9	*each*

FRUIT-TREEES.

	each. s. d.	
APRICOT Trees, Standards	2	*(Prunus armeniaca)*
——— Dwarfs	1 6	
Apple Trees, Standards	1	*(Malus pumila vars.)*
————— Dwarfs, on Crab-Stocks	8	
————— Dwarfs, on Paradise-Stocks	1	*(M. pumila paradisiaca)*
Cherry Trees, Standards	1 ½	*(Prunus cerasus vars.)*
——— Dwarfs	1	
Fig Trees	9	*(Ficus carica)*
Vines	9	*(Vitis vinifera)*
Medlars, Dutch, Standards	1 ½	*(Mespilus germanica vars.)*
——— English, ditto	1 6	
——— Dwarfs,	1	
Mulberries, Standards	3	*(Morus nigra)*
——— Dwarfs	1	
Peach Trees, Standards	2 6	*(Prunus persica)*
——— Dwarfs	1 5	
——— of the best French Kinds for Hot-Walls	2 6	
Nectarine Trees, Standards	2 6	*(Prunus persica var.)*
——— Dwarfs	1 5	
——— of the French Kinds	2 6	
Pear Trees, Standards	1 ½	*(Pyrus communis vars.)*
——— Dwarfs	1	
Plumb Trees, Standards	1 ½	*(Prunus domestica)*
——— Dwarfs	1	
Quince Trees, Standards	1 ½	*(Cydonia oblonga)*
——— Dwarfs	1	
Filbert and Spanish Nuts	2	*(Corylus maxima; C. avellana)*
Gooseberry Trees	2	*(Ribes grossularia)*
Currant Trees	2	*(Ribes nigrum; R. sativum)*

EVER-GREEN

AND

FLOWERING-SHRUBS, &c.

		each. s. d.
(Arbutus unedo) *	ARBUTUS, or Strawberry Tree	2 6
(Cercis siliquastrum)	Arbor Jude	1
(Prunus communis) *	Almonds, Standards	1 6
	—— Dwarfs	1
(P. communis vars.)	Almond, white flowering	1
	—— Dwarf single flowering	6
	—— Dwarf double	6
(Robinia pseudacacia) *	Acacia, Virginian	1
(Gleditschia triacanthos)	—— Three-thorned	2
(Robinia hispida)	—— Rose, or Red Robinia	2 6
(Acacia farnesiana)	—— Yellow Egyptian	5
(Vitex agnus-castus)	Agnus Castus	6
(Aralia spinosa)	Angelica Tree	2
(Hibiscus syriacus) *	Althea Frutex, Scarlet	6
*	—— Purple	6
*	—— Painted Lady	6
*	—— White	6
	—— Strip'd-leav'd	2
(Rhamnus frangula)	Alder, Berry-bearing	3
(Thuja occidentalis) *	Arbor Vitæ, Common, 1½ Foot	9
	Ditto —— 2 Feet	1
(Thuja orientalis)	Arbor Vitæ of China, 1 Foot	2 6
	Ditto —— 2 Feet	3
(Aspalathus chenopoda) *	Asphalatus	6
(Calycanthus floridus)	Allspice, Catesby's	6
(Solanum pseudocapsicum)	* Ammomum Plinii	1 6
(Melia azedarach)	* Azederach, or Bead Tree	2 6
(Camellia japonica)	* Althea, Double-flowering, or Japan Rose	4
(Rhododendron viscosum?)	Azalea	
(Staphylea trifolia)	BLADDER-NUT, with three Leaves	6
(Staphylea pinnata)	—— with five Leaves	3

EVER-GREEN, &c.

each.

		s.	d.	
Barberry, Common			3	*(Berberis vulgaris)*
———— without Stone			6	*(B. vulgaris* var. *asperma)*
———— with yellow Fruit		1		*(B. vulgaris* var. *lutea)*
———— with white Fruit			4	*(B. vulgaris* var. *alba)*
Broom, Spanish			3	*(Spartium junceum)
——— Dwarf-branching			3	*(Genista germanica)*
——— Jointed		1		
——— Dwarf-wing'd, or Genista S gitalis		2		*(Genista sagittalis)*
——— Lucca		1		
——— Butcher's, rough-leav'd			3	*(Ruscus aculeatus)
——————— smooth-leav'd			3	
——————— white				*(Semele androgyna)*
Bay Tree			6	*(Laurus nobilis)*
Buckthorn, Common			3	*(Rhamnus cathartica)
Bramble, Double-flowering		1		*(Rubus fruticosus flore pleno)
Box, Common			3	*(Buxus sempervirens)
——— Curl'd-leav'd strip'd			6	
——— Narrow-leav'd			4	
——— Dwarf, per Yard			3	*(B. sempervirens suffruticosa)*
Benjamin Tree			3	*(Lindera benzoin)*
CATALPA		2		*(Catalpa bignonioides)
Cassioberry Bush, or South-Sea Tea Tree		1		*(Viburnum cassinoides)
Cherry, Cornish or Cluster		1		*(Prunus padus var.)
——— Common Bird			3	*(Prunus padus)
——— Carolina Bird			6	*(Prunus caroliniana)
——— Cornelian			6	*(Cornus mas)
——— Hottentot		5		*(Cassine maurocenia)*
——— Double-blossom'd, Standard		1		*(Prunus cerasus vars.)*
——— Ditto, Dwarf			9	
——— Mahaleb, or Perfum'd			9	*(Prunus mahaleb)
Creeper, Virginian			3	*(Parthenocissus quinquefolia)*
Cistus, Willow-leav'd, with spotted Flowers		1		*(Cistus ladaniferus)
——— Sage-leav'd, with Purple Flowers			9	*
——— Ditto, with white Flowers		1		*(Cistus salvifolius)*
——— Gum, or Rock Rose			9	*(Cistus monspeliensis ?)*
——— Purple, spotted with Crimson		2	6	
Cytisus, Siberian		1		*(Cytisus austriacus)
——— Neapolitan, or Ever-green		1		*(Cytisus hirsutus)*
——— Secundus			3	*(Cytisus sessilifolius)
——— Lunatus		1		*(Medicago arborea)*

12   E V E R - G R E E N *and*

		each.
		s. d.

				s	d
*(Ribes alpinum)**	Curran, Goofeberry-leav'd	——	——		3
*(R. rubrum variegatum)**	—— Strip'd-leav'd	——	——		6
(Clematis virginiana)	Clematis, Virginian, with white Flowers		——		6
(Clematis crispa ?)	—— Upright Blue	——	——		6
*(Potentilla fruticosa)**	Cinquefoil Shrub	——			3
(Caragana arborescens)	Caragana, or Yellow Robinia	——	——	1	6
(Clethra tomentosa)	Clethra ——	——	——	2	6
*(Cephalanthus occidentalis)**	Cephalanthus, or Button Wood	——	——	1	
(Chionanthus virginicus)	Chionanthus, or Fringe Tree		——	3	
(Malus coronaria)	Crab, Virginian fweet-fcented	——	/	1	
(Malus prunifolia)	—— Siberian ——	——	——	1	
(Ceanothus asiatica ?)	* Ceonothus, Ever-green	——	——	2	
(Ilex vomitoria)	* Caffine, ditto ——	——	——	2	6
(Cassine oppositifolia ?)	* —— or Hyfon Tea	——	——	2	6
(Coronilla glauca, etc.)	? Coronilla, of Sorts	——	——	1	
(Celastrus scandens)	Celaftrus, or Staff Tree	——	——	1	
*(Cornus sanguinea)**	DOGWOOD, Female	——	——		6
*(Cornus amomum)**	—— Carolina	——	——		6
(Cornus alba variegata)	—— Strip'd Female	——	/		
*(Diervilla lonicera)**	Dier Vella ——	——	——		3
*(Sambucus nigra aurea-variegata)**	ELDER, Gold-ftrip'd	——	——	1	6
*(S. nigra albo-variegata)**	—— Silver-ftrip'd	——	——	1	
*(S. nigra laciniata)**	—— Parfley-leav'd	——	——		3
*(Sambucus racemosa)**	—— Large Red-berried	——	——		6
*(Sambucus nigra viridis)**	—— White-berried	——	——		3
(Physocarpus opulifolius aureo-marginata)	GUELDEROSE, variegated		——	1	
*(Viburnum trilobum)**	—— of Carolina	——	——		6
*(Physocarpus opulifolius)**	—— of Virginia	——	——		3
*(Viburnum opulus)**	—— Common	——	——		3
(Myrica gale)	Gale Sweet	——	——		6
(Baccharis halimifolia)	Groundfell Tree	——	——		6
(Pelargonium spp.)	* Geraniums, of Sorts	~~fmall to~~	——	2	6
(Bosea yervamora)	* Golden-Rod Tree	——	——	1	

FLOWERING-SHRUBS.

13 each.

	s.	d.	
HICKARY-NUT of Virginia	1		(Carya ovata)
Honeyfuckle, Virginian Trumpet	1		*(Lonicera sempervirens)
—————— New-England Trumpet	1		*(L. sempervirens minor)
—————— Ever-green		6	(Lonicera x americana)
—————— Strip'd-leav'd		6	(L. periclymenum variegata)
—————— Late Italian		6	*(Lonicera etrusca)
—————— Upright Red-berried		6	(Lonicera alpigena)
—————— Blue-berried		6	(Lonicera coerulea)
—————— Fly		3	*(Lonicera xylosteum)
—————— Early-red		2	*(Lonicera periclymenum belgica)
—————— Early-white		2	(Lonicera caprifolium alba)
—————— Late-red		2	*(Lonicera periclymenum serotina)
—————— Late-white		2	*(L. periclymenum var. ?)
—————— Long-blowing		2	*(L. periclymenum var. ?)
—————— Oak-leav'd		2	(Lonicera periclymenum quercina)
Hypericum Frutex		·3	*(Spiraea hypericifolia)
Hydrangula		3	*(Hydrangea arborescens)
Hornbeam Hop	1		(Ostrya carpinifolia)
Hartwort of Ethiopia	/	-	(Bupleurum fruticosum)
JOHN's, St. Wort, Canary		3	*(Hypericum canariense)
·—————— Warted	1		(Hypericum balearicum)
Indigo, Baftard	1		(Amorpha fruticosa)
Ivy, ftrip'd		6	(Hedera helix marginata)
Juniper, Common		4	*(Juniperus communis)
—————— Swedifh		6	(J. communis suecica)
Jack, Supple	2	6	(Berchemia scandens)
Jafmine, White		3	*(Jasminum officinale)
—————— Yellow		3	*(Jasminum fruticans)
—————— Yellow Spanifh		6	(Jasminum humile ?)
—————— Strip'd-leav'd	1		(Jasminum officinale aureum)
—————— Cut-leav'd Perfian		6	(Syringa persica laciniata)
—————— Common Perfian		4	(Syringa persica)
—————— White Perfian		6	(S. persica alba)
·—————— Yellow Indian		2	(Jasminum odoratissimum)
·—————— Catalonian		2	(Jasminum grandiflorum)
·—————— Azorian		2	(Jasminum azoricum)
●—————— Arabian		·2	(Jasminum sambac)
●—————— Double Cape	7	6	(Gardenia jasminoides florida)
Itea		3	(Itea virginiana)

14   E V E R · G R E E N *and*

		each.
		s. d.
(Wisteria frutescens)	KIDNEY-BEAN Tree, Carolina	2
(Kalmia latifolia)	Kalmia, Broad-leav'd	5
(Kalmia angustifolia)	———— Olive-leav'd	7 6
*(Laburnum anagyroides)**	LABURNUMS, Standards	6
	———— Dwarfs	3
(Laburnum alpinum)	———— Scotch, or Caledonian	6
*(Prunus lusitanica)**	Laurel, Portugal	1
*(Daphne laureola)**	———— Spurge	3
*(Prunus laurocerasus)**	———— Common	3
(P. laurocerasus variegata)	———— Variegated	1
(Viburnum tinus hirtum)	Lauruſtinus, Rough-leav'd	4
(Viburnum tinus)	———— Smooth-leav'd	3
(V. tinus lucidum)	———— Shining-leav'd	4
(Viburnum cassinoides)	———— American Deciduous	1
(Viburnum tinus variegatum)	———— Strip'd	1
*(Syringa vulgaris alba)**	Lilac, White	3
*(Syringa vulgaris)**	———— Blue	3
*	———— Purple	3
(Citrus limonia)	* Lemon Trees *from 7 6 to*	10 6
(Acer pennsylvanicum)	MAPLE, Pennſylvanian	1
(Acer saccharum)	———— Sugar	6
(Acer negundo)	———— Virginian Aſh-leav'd	6
(Acer rubrum)	———— Scarlet-flowering	1
(Acer saccharinum)	———— Sir Charles Wager's flowering	1
*(Daphne mezereum)**	Mezereon, Purple	6
*	———— Peach-coloured	4
*	———— White	4
(Myrica cerifera)	Myrtle, Candleberry	1
(Amelanchier ovalis)	Medlar, Dwarf Baſtard	6
	Meſpilus, Early-flowering	2 6
(Crataegus pentagyna)	———— Dwarf	2 6
(Amelanchier canadensis)	———— Snowy	2 6
(Aronia arbutifolia ?)	———— Lady Hardwick's	2 6
(Polygala myrtifolia)	* Milkwort, African or Polygala	2 6
(Origanum maru?)	* Marum, of Sorts	1 6
(Magnolia tripetala)	Magnolia, Deciduous	1 6
(Magnolia grandiflora)	———— Large Laurel-lèav'd	7 6
(Magnolia virginiana)	———— Small or Swamp	5

FLOWERING-SHRUBS

		15 each.	
		s.	d.
• Malabar-Nut	——— *sorted to* ———	2		(Adhatoda vasica)
• Myrtles, of Sorts		2	6	(Myrtus communis vars.)
Mulberry, White	——— ———	1		*(Morus alba)

• OLIVE, True	——— ——— ———	2	6	(Olea europea)
• ——— Box-leav'd	——— ———	2	6	(O. europea buxifolia)
Oleaster	——— ———	1		(Elaeagnus angustifolia)
• Oleander, Red Single	——— ———	2		(Nerium oleander)
• ——— Single White	——— ———	2		(N. oleander album)
• ——— Double	———	5		(N. oleander flore pleno)
• Orange Tree	*from 7/6 to* ———	15	12	(Citrus sinensis)

PERIWINKLE, Large Green	——— ———	2		(Vinca major)
——— Gold-strip'd	———	2		(V. major reticulata)
——— Silver-strip'd	———	2		(V. major variegata)
——— Double-flowering	———	4		(V. major flore pleno)
Plumb, Myrabolan	———	9		(Prunus cerasifera)
——— Persimon, or Pishamin	———	1		(Diospyros virginiana)
——— Cherry, Standard	———	1	4	(Prunus cerasifera var.)
——— Dwarf	———	1		
Pepper-Bush	———	2		(Clethra alnifolia)
Philerea, Rosemary-leav'd	———	1	6	(Phillyrea angustifolia rosmarinifolia)
——— Olive-leav'd	———	1		(Phillyrea latifolia media)
——— True	———	1		*(Phillyrea latifolia)
——— Alaternus	———		6	(Rhamnus alaternus)
——— Serrated-leav'd	———		6	(Phillyrea latifolia ilicifolia)
• ——— Gold-strip'd	———	2	6	(Rhamnus alaternus
• ——— Silver-strip'd	———	2	6	variegata)
• ——— Cape	———	5	—	(Cassine capensis)
Pomgranate, Double	———	2		(Punica granatum flore pleno)
——— Single	———	1	6	(Punica granatum)
Ptelia, or Trefoil Shrub	———	1		(Ptelia trifoliata)
Peter's, St. Wort Shrub	———		3	*(Symphoricarpos orbiculatus)
Privet, Ever-green	———		2	(Ligustrum vulgare)
——— Strip'd-leav'd	———	1		(L. vulgare variegatum)
Periploca, or Virginian Silk	———		4	*(Periploca graeca)
Phlomis major and minor	———		6	(Phlomis fruticosa; P. herba-venti)
Purslain Tree	———		4	*(Portulacaria afra)
Pyracantha	———		3	(Pyracantha coccinea)

16   E V E R - G R E E N *and*

		each.	
		s.	*d.*
*(Prunus persica roseo-plena)**	Peach, Double-flowering	1	6
(Passiflora coerulea)	Passion Tree	1	
(Rosa centifolia pomponia)	ROSE, Mieux	5	
(R. centifolia parvifolia)	—— Dwarf Burgundy	5	
(R. palustris var.)	—— Double Dwarf Pennsylvanian	2	6
(Rosa centifolia muscosa)	—— Moss Provence	2	
(R. foetida bicolor)	—— Red Austrian	1	
(R. damascena var.)	—— Blush Belgick	1	
(R. centifolia var.)	—— Ditto hundred-leav'd	1	
(R. gallica var.)	—— Dutch ditto	1	
(Rosa x alba var.)	—— Maiden's Blush	1	
(R. spinosissima var. ?)	—— Marbled	1	
(Rosa moschata plena)	—— Late White Cluster, or Double Musk	1	
(Rosa centifolia)	—— Blush Provence	1	
(R. spinosissima var.)	—— Red Scotch	1	
(Rosa gallica var.)	—— Double Velvet	1	
(Rosa hemisphaerica)	—— Ditto Yellow	1	
(Rosa x alba var.)	—— without Thorns		6
(R. damascena var.)	—— Red Belgick		6
(Rosa villosa)	—— Apple-bearing		6
(R. damascena var.)	—— White Damask		6
(R. damascena var.)	—— Strip'd Monthly		6
(Rosa gallica var.)	—— Semi-double Velvet		6
(Rosa foetida)	—— Single Yellow		6
(Rosa sempervirens)	—— Ever-green		6
(Rosa palustris)	—— Pennsylvanian		6
(Rosa cinnamomea plena)	—— Double Cinnamon		4
(R. centifolia var.)	—— Childing, or Red Provence		4
(Rosa pimpinellifolia)	—— Burnet-leav'd		4
(Rosa damascena)	—— Damask		4
(Rosa gallica var.)	—— Frankfort		4
(R. damascena var.)	—— Monthly		4
(Rosa centifolia)	—— Provence		4
(R. damascena var.)	—— Great Royal		4
(Rosa gallica)	—— Red		4
(Rosa x alba var.)	—— Virgin		4
(Rosa x alba)	—— Double White		4
(Rosa damascena versicolor)	—— York and Lancaster		4
(Rosa spinosissima)	—— White Scotch		4
(Rosa gallica versicolor)	Rosa Mundi		4

FLOWERING-SHRUBS

17
each.
s. d.

True Double Sweet Briar,		I	*(Rosa eglanteria duplex)*
Semi-double ditto		6	
Single ditto		2	*(Rosa eglanteria)*
Rhododendron, or Rose-Bay		15	*(Rhododendron maximum)*
Rhammoides		6	*(Hippophae rhamnoides)*
Rasp, Flowering, of Virginia		3	**(Rubus odoratus)*
Rosemary		3	*(Rosmarinus officinalis)*
* Royena	4		*(Royena lucida)*
* Rhus, or African Sumach	2		*(Rhus coriaria)*
Ragwort		I	*(Senecio cineraria)*

SENNA-BLADDER, Ethiopian, Scarlet		I	*(Sutherlandia frutescens)*
———————— Eastern, blood-coloured		I	**(Colutea orientalis)*
———————— Pocock's		I	*(Colutea istria)*
———————— Scorpion		3	**(Coronilla emerus)*
———————— Common		3	**(Colutea arborescens)*
Spirea of Pennsylvania, Red		6	**(Spiraea tomentosa)*
——————— White		6	**(Spiraea carpinifolia ?)*
——————— Common		3	*(Spiraea salicifolia)*
Spindle Tree, Broad-leav'd, or Euonimus		I	*(Euonymus latifolius)*
——————— Long-leav'd		2	*(Euonymus americanus angustifolius)*
——————— Deep Red-berried		3	*(Euonymus europeus intermedius)*
——————— White-berried		3	*(Euonymus europeus albus)*
——————— Pale Red-berried		3	*(Euonymus europeus)*
Stone Crop Tree		6	**(Atriplex halimus)*
Savin, strip'd		I	*(Juniperus sabina variegata)*
—— Common		3	**(Juniperus sabina)*
Styrax, or Liquid Amber	2	6	*(Liquidambar styraciflua)*
Syringa, Common		3	**(Philadelphus coronarius)*
—— Dwarf		3	*(P. coronarius nanus)*
Sumach, Virginian, or Stag's Horn		I	*(Rhus typhina)*
—— Carolina		I	**(Rhus glabra)*
—— Myrtle-leav'd		4	*(Rhus coriaria var. ?)*
—— Beach		I	*(Rhus ?)*
—— Venice, or Coccigria		I	*(Rhus cotinus)*
Sallow, strip'd		3	**(Salix caprea variegata)*
Service, True		I 6	*(Sorbus domestica)*
		2 6	*(Euonymus americanus)*

18   E V E R - G R E E N &c.

					each.

		s.	d.
(Liriodendron tulipifera)	TULIP Tree, Virginian	2	6
(Hypericum androsaemum)	Tutfan, Upright		3
(Hypericum calycinum)*	——— Spreading		3
(Hypericum chinense)	——— China	1	2
(Populus balsamifera)*	Taccamahacca		/
(Rhus toxicodendron)*	Toxicodendron, Upright		
(Rhus radicans)*	——— Creeping		6
(Clematis vitalba)*	Traveller's Joy		3
(Campsis radicans)	Trumpet Flower, or Bignonia		3
(Tamarix gallica)*	Tamarifk, French	1	
(Myricaria germanica)*	——— German		4
(Paliurus spina-Christi)	Thorn, Chrift's, or Paliurus		4
(Crataegus monogyna praecox)	——— Glaftenbury	2	6
(Crataegus flava)*	——— Yellow American		6
(Crataegus crus-galli)*	——— Cockfpur		6
(Crataegus oxyacantha plena)*	——— Double-bloffom'd		6
	——— Neapolitan Azarole		6
(Crataegus azarolus)*	——— Yellow Azarole		6
(C. crus-galli pyracanthifolia)	——— Pyracantha-leav'd		6
(Crataegus prunifolia)	——— Plumb-leav'd		6
(Crataegus uniflora)	——— Lord Ifley's		6
	——— Black Virginian		6
	——— Dwarf American	2	6
(Viburnum lantana)	VIBURNUM, Plain		
(V. lantana variegatum)	——— Strip'd		3
(Viburnum dentatum)	——— Serrated-leav'd	1	
(Clematis viticella flore pleno)	Virgin's Bower, Double	1	
(Clematis viticella)*	——— Single	2	
		1	6
(Cneorum tricoccum)	* WIDOW-WAIL	1	
(Zanthoxylum americanum)	ZANTHOXYLUM, or Tooth-Ach Tree	2	6

Alfo all Sorts of S E E D s, with feveral curious P E R E N N I A L
F L O W E R-R O O T s, and a great Variety of B U L B O U S F L O W E R S.

N. B. Thofe mark'd thus * are tender, and fit only for the Green-
Houfe or Stove.

3

A

C A T A L O G U E

O F

FOREST-TREES, ‖ EVERGREEN AND
FRUIT-TREES, ‖ FLOWERING-SHRUBS,

S O L D B Y

WILLIAM and JOHN PERFECT,

P O N T E F R A C T,

Y O R K S H I R E.

A

CATALOGUE

O F

FOREST-TREES,	EVER-GREEN AND
FRUIT-TREES,	FLOWERING-SHRUBS

SOLD BY

WILLIAM and JOHN PERFECT,

NURSERY-MEN AND SEEDS-MEN,

I N

PONTEFRACT, *YORKSHIRE.*

1777.

Y O R K:

Printed by C. ETHERINGTON.

N.B. John Rylands Library, Manchester, has a copy with date filled in as 1776, formerly in possession of family of Leigh of Adlington.

H

A

CATALOGUE, &c.

	£.	s.	d.	
AREATHEOPHRASTI, 2 Feet	1	5	.	*per hundred*
Ditto ——————— 4 Feet	1	13	4	*per hundred*
Ditto ——————— 6 Feet	2	.	.	*per hundred*
Ditto ——————— 8 Feet	2	10	.	*per hundred*
Aſhes, one Year old Seedlings, 4 Inches	.	10	.	*per thouſand*
Ditto, two Years old Seedlings, 6 Inches	.	12	6	*per thouſand*
Ditto tranſplanted, 1 Foot ——	1	10	.	*per thouſand*
Ditto ——————— 2 Feet ——	2	.	.	*per thouſand*
Ditto ——————— 3 Feet ——	.	7	6	*per hundred*
Ditto —— ——				
Aſhes, Carolina —— ——	.	1	.	*each*
Flowering —— ——	.	.	6	*each*
Manna ——	.	.	6	*each*
Aſhes, Mountain, 2 and 3 Feet ——	1	5	.	*per hundred*
Ditto ——				
Ditto ——				
Ditto ——				
BEECHES, one Year old Seedlings, 6 Inches ——	.	10	.	*per thouſand*
Ditto, two Years old Seedlings 9 Inches ——	.	15	.	*per thouſand*
Ditto, tranſplanted, 1 Foot ——	2	.	.	*per thouſand*
Ditto ——————— 1 ½ Foot ——	.	6	.	*per hundred*
Ditto ——————— 2 Feet ——	.	7	6	*per hundred*
Ditto ——————— 3 Feet ——	.	15	.	*per hundred*
Ditto ——				
Ditto ——				
Ditto ——————— 8 Feet ——	.	.	6	*each*
Ditto ——————— 10 Feet ——	.	.	8	*each*
Beeches, Purple —— ——	.	5	.	*each*
Birches, tranſplanted, 2 Feet ——	.	7	6	*per hundred*
Ditto ——				
Ditto ——				
† CEDARS of Libanus, tranſplanted, 9 Inches	.	2	6	*each*
Ditto ——				

F O R E S T - T R E E S.   3

	£.	s.	d.	
† Cedars, Red Virginian, 1 Foot ———	·	1	·	each
Ditto ——————— 1¼ Foot ———	·	1	6	each
Ditto ——————— 2 Feet ———	·	2	·	each
Ditto ——————— 3 Feet ———	·	2	6	each
† Cedars, White Virginian ———	·	1	6	each
Chefnuts, Horfe, one Year old Seedlings, 6 Inches —	·	3	·	per hundred
Ditto, two Years old Seedlings, 9 Inches ———	·	4	·	per hundred
Ditto, tranfplanted, 1 Foot ———	·	5	·	per hundred
Ditto ——————— 2 Feet ———	·	10	·	per hundred
Ditto ——————— 3 Feet ———	·	15	·	per hundred
Ditto ——————— 4 Feet ———	1	·	·	per hundred
Ditto ———————				
Chefnuts, Horfe, gold ftrip'd-leav'd	·	1	·	each
——————— filver ftrip'd-leav'd	·	1	·	each
——————— fcarlet-flowering	·	2	6	each
——————— yellow-flowering	·	5	·	each
Chefnuts, Spanifh, one Year old Seedlings, 6 Inches —	·	4	·	per hundred
Ditto, two Years old Seedlings, 9 Inches ———	·	5	·	per hundred
Ditto tranfplanted, 1 Foot ———	·	6	·	per hundred
Ditto ——————— 2 Feet ———	·	10	·	per hundred
Ditto ——————— 3 Feet ———	·	15	·	per hundred
Ditto ——————— 4 and 5 Feet	1	·	·	per hundred
Ditto ——————— 6 Feet —	1	5	·	per hundred
Ditto ——————— 8 Feet —	1	13	4	per hundred
Chefnuts, ftrip'd-leav'd Spanifh —	·	5	·	each
† Cyprefs, common, two years old Seedlings ———	1	·	·	per hundred
Ditto tranfplanted, 1 Foot ———	·	·	6	each
Ditto ——————— 2 Feet ———	·	1	·	each
Ditto ———————				
Cyprefs, deciduous	·	2	6	each
ELMS, Englifh, grafted on the broad-leav'd Witch Elm, 2½ Feet	·	15	·	per hundred
Ditto ——————— 4 Feet ——	1	·	·	per hundred
Ditto ——————— 6 Feet —	1	10	·	per hundred
Ditto ——————— 8 Feet —	2	·	·	per hundred
Ditto ———————				
Elms, Englifh, one Year old Layers 2 Feet ———	·	7	6	per hundred
Ditto tranfplanted, 4 Feet ——	1	·	·	per hundred
Ditto ——————— 6 Feet —	1	10	·	per hundred
Ditto ——————— 8 Feet —	2	·	·	per hundred
Ditto ———————				
Elms, ftrip'd-leav'd Englifh ———	·	1	·	each

A 2

4 F O R E S T - T R E E S.

	£.	s.	d.	
Elms, ſtrip'd-leav'd Dutch, 3 Feet —	.	.	6	each
Ditto ——————— 6 Feet —	.	.	9	each
Elms, Witch, one Year old Seedlings, 5 Inches ———	.	10	.	per thouſand
Ditto, two Years old Seedlings, 8 Inches ———	.	15	.	per thouſand
Ditto, three Years old Seedlings, 1 Foot ———	1	.	.	per thouſand
Ditto tranſplanted, 2 Feet ———	.	5	.	per hundred
† FIRS, Balm of Gilead				
Ditto ———				
Ditto ——————— 2 Feet ———	.	.	9	each
Ditto ——————— 3 to 4 Feet —	.	1	.	each
Ditto ——————— 6 to 8 Feet —	.	1	6	each
† Firs, Scotch, one Year old Seedlings, 2 Inches ———	.	7	6	per thouſand
Ditto, two Years old Seedlings, 4 Inches ———	.	10	.	per thouſand
Ditto. two Years old, tranſplanted, 4 Inches —	.	15	.	per thouſand
Ditto, tranſplanted, 6 Inches	1	10	.	per thouſand
Ditto ——————— 1 Foot —	.	7	6	per hundred
Ditto ——————— 1½ Foot —	.	10	.	per hundred
Ditto ——————— 2 Feet —	.	15	.	per hundred
Ditto ——————— 2½ Feet —	.	17	6	per hundred
Ditto				
† Firs, Silver, one Year old Seedlings, 2 Inches —	1	10	.	per thouſand
Ditto, two Years old Seedlings, 3 Inches —	2	.	.	per thouſand
Ditto, three Years old, tranſplanted, 4 Inches —	.	5	.	per hundred
Ditto tranſplanted, 6 and 7 Inches	.	7	6	per hundred
Ditto ——————— — 1 Foot	.	10	.	per hundred
Ditto ———————				
Ditto ———————				
Ditto ——————— 4 Feet	1	10	.	per hundred
† Firs, Spruce or Norway, one Year old Seedlings, 2 Inches	.	15	.	per thouſand
Ditto, two Years old Seedlings, — 4 Inches	1	.	.	per thouſand
Ditto tranſplanted, — 6 Inches	2	.	.	per thouſand
Ditto ——————— — 9 Inches	3	15	.	per thouſand
Ditto ——————— — 1 Foot	.	10	.	per hundred
Ditto ———————				
Ditto ———————				
Ditto ———————				

FOREST-TREES.   5

	£.	s.	d.	
† Firs, Black American Spruce, 1 Foot	.	.	9	*each*
Ditto ——————— 2 Feet	.	1	.	*each*
† Firs, White American Spruce, 1 Foot	.	.	9	*each*
Ditto ——————— 2 Feet	.	1	.	*each*
† Firs, Hemlock Spruce — —	.	2	.	*each*
† HOLLIES, Green, two Years old Seedlings, 2 Inches —	.	7	6	*per thousand*
Ditto, three Years old Seedlings, 4 Inches —	.	10	.	*per thousand*
Ditto transplanted, 6 Inches	1	.	.	*per thousand*
Ditto ——————— 1 Foot	.	5	.	*per hundred*
‡ Hollies, Striped, of various Sorts, 1 Foot	.	.	6	*each*
Ditto. — — 2 Feet	.	.	9	*each*
Ditto				
Hornbeam, one Year old Seedlings	.	10	.	*per thousand*
Ditto, two Year old Seedlings	.	15	.	*per thousand*
Ditto transplanted, 9 Inches	1	10	.	*per thousand*
Ditto ——————— 1 Foot	.	4	.	*per hundred*
Ditto ——————— 1½ Foot	.	6	.	*per hundred*
Ditto ——————— 2 Feet	.	8	.	*per hundred*
Ditto ——————— 3 Feet	.	10	.	*per hundred*
Ditto ——————— 4 Feet		15	.	*per hundred*
Ditto ——————— 5 Feet	1	.	.	*per hundred*
Ditto ——————— 6 Feet	1	5	.	*per hundred*
Ditto ——————— 8 Feet	1	10	.	*per hundred*
LARCHES, one Year old Seedlings, 2 Inches —	1	10	.	*per thousand*
Ditto, two Years old Seedlings, 6 Inches —	2	.	.	*per thousand*
Ditto transplanted, 1 Foot —	.	7	6	*per hundred*
Ditto ——————— 1½ Foot —	.	10	.	*per hundred*
Ditto ——————— 2 Feet —	.	15	.	*per hundred*
Ditto ——————— 3 Feet —	1	.	.	*per hundred*
Ditto ——————— 4 Feet —	1	5	.	*per hundred*
Ditto ———————				
Ditto ———————				
Limes, transplanted, 1 Foot —	.	6	.	*per hundred*
Ditto ——————— 2 Feet —	.	10	.	*per hundred*
Ditto ——————				
Ditto ——————				
Ditto ——————— 6 Feet —	1	10	.	*per hundred*
Ditto ——————— 8 Feet —	2	.	.	*per hundred*
OAKS, English, one Year old Seedlings, 6 Inches —	.	10	.	*per thousand*
Ditto, two Years old Seedlings, 1 Foot —	.	15	.	*per thousand*

A 3

6   F O R E S T . T R E E S.

	£.	s.	d.	
Oaks, transplanted, 1 Foot —	1	10	.	*per thousand*
Ditto ———— 1 ½ Foot —	2	.	.	*per thousand*
Ditto ———				
Ditto ———				
Ditto ———				
Oaks, Scarlet, 2 Feet — —	.	.	6	each
Ditto ———— 3 and 4 Feet	.	.	9	each
† Oaks, Devonshire or Lucombe ——	.	2	6	each
† —— Ragnal ———	.	1	.	each
—— Spanish ———	.	1	.	each
—— Strip'd-leav'd ——	.	2	6	each
† —— Ever-green, or Ilex ——	.	.	6	each
† PINASTERS, Seedlings, 2 Inches —	1	.	.	*per thousand*
Ditto, transplanted, 4 Inches —		6	.	*per hundred*
Ditto ———— 9 Inches —	.	15	.	*per hundred*
Ditto ———— 1 Foot —	1	.	.	*per hundred*
Ditto, ———— 1 ½ Foot —	1	5	.	*per hundred*
Ditto ———— 2 Feet —	1	13	4	*per hundred*
Ditto ———— 4 Feet —	2	.	.	*per hundred*
† Pines, Cluster, Seedlings, 2 Inches —	1	.	.	*per thousand*
Ditto, transplanted, 4 Inches —	.	6	.	*per hundred*
Ditto ———— 9 Inches —	.	15	.	*per hundred*
Ditto ———— 1 Foot —	1	.	.	*per hundred*
Ditto ———— 1 ½ Foot —	1	5	.	*per hundred*
Ditto ———— 2 Feet —	1	13	4	*per hundred*
Ditto ———— 4 Feet —	2	.	.	*per hundred*
† Pines, Stone, Seedlings, 4 Inches —	.	5	.	*per hundred*
Ditto, transplanted, 1 Foot —	.	.	6	each
† Pines, Lord Weymouth's, or New- England, transplanted 4 Inches — —	1	.	.	*per hundred*
Ditto, transplanted, 6 Inches —	1	5	.	*per hundred*
Ditto ———— 1 Foot ——	1	13	4	*per hundred*
Ditto ———— 2 Feet ——	.	.	6	each
Ditto ———— 3 Feet ——	.	.	9	each
Ditto ———— 4 to 5 Feet	.	1	.	each
Ditto ———— 6 to 8 Feet	.	1	6	each
Platinus, Oriental and Occidental, 2 Feet —— ——	.	.	3	each
Ditto ———— 4 Feet ——	.	.	4	each
Ditto ———				
Ditto———				
Poplars, Black or Abele, 1 ½ Foot —	.	5	.	*per hundred*
Ditto ———— 3 Feet —	.	10	.	*per hundred*
Ditto ———				
Poplars, Lombardy or Italian, 2 Feet	.	6	.	*per hundred*
Ditto ———— 3 Feet	.	10	.	*per hundred*
Ditto ———				
Ditto ———				

F O R E S T . T R E E S. 7

	£.	s.	d.	
Poplars, White, 1¼ Foot	.	5	.	per hundred
Ditto ——— 3 Feet	.	10	.	per hundred
Ditto ——— 6 Feet	1	.	.	per hundred
Ditto ——— 8 Feet	1	5	.	per hundred
Ditto ———				
Poplars, of Carolina	.	1	.	each
——— Berry-bearing	.	2	6	each
——— Balfam	.	2	6	each
SYCAMORES, one Year old Seedlings, 1 Foot	.	15	.	per thoufand
Ditto, tranfplanted, 2 Feet	.	7	6	per hundred
Ditto ——— 3 Feet	.	10	.	per hundred
Ditto ——— 6 Feet	1	.	.	per hundred
Ditto ——— 8 Feet	.	13	4	per hundred
Ditto ——— 10 Feet	2	.	.	per hundred
Sycamores, Strip'd, 2 Feet	.	.	4	each
Ditto ——— 4 to 5 Feet	.	.	6	each
Ditto ———				
THORN QUICKSETS, White	.	*5*	.	*per Thousand*
Ditto				
Ditto				
WALNUTS, tranfplanted, 1 Foot	.	4	.	per hundred
Ditto ——— 1¼ Foot	.	5	.	per hundred
Ditto ——— 2 Feet	.	10	.	per hundred
Ditto ——— 4 Feet	1	.	.	per hundred
Ditto ——— 8 Feet	.	.	9	each
Ditto ——— 10 Feet	.	1	.	each
Willows, Huntingdonfhire	.	.	3	each
——— Weeping	.	.	2	each
——— Sweet	.	.	2	each
† YEWS, tranfplanted, 6 Inches	.	10	.	per hundred
Ditto ——— 1 Foot	1	.	.	per hundred
Ditto ——— 1¼ Foot	1	13	4	per hundred
Ditto ——— 2 Feet	2	10	.	per hundred
Ditto ——— 3 Feet	.	.	9	each
Ditto ——— 4 Feet	.	1	.	each

Alfo young Cherry, Crab, Pear, and Plum Stocks,

(8)

FRUIT-TREES.

	each.	
	s.	d.
APPLE Trees, Standards	1	.
Ditto, Dwarfs upon Crab Stocks	.	8
Ditto, Dwarfs upon Paradife Stocks	1	.
Apricot Trees, Standards	2	.
Ditto, Dwarfs	1	6
Cherry Trees. Standards	1	4
Ditto, Dwarfs	1	.
Fig Trees	.	9
Vines	.	9
Dutch Medlar Trees, Standards	1	4
Ditto, Dwarfs	1	.
Mulberry Trees, Standards	3	.
Ditto. Dwarfs	1	.
Peach Trees. Standards	2	6
Ditto, Dwarfs	1	6
Ditto, Dwarfs of the beft French kinds	2	6
Nectarine Trees, Standards	2	6
Ditto, Dwarfs	1	6
Ditto, Dwarfs of the beft French kinds	2	6
Pear Trees, Standards	1	4
Ditto, Dwarfs	1	.
Plum Trees. Standards	1	4
Ditto, Dwarfs	1	.
Portugal Quince Trees. Standards	1	4
Ditto, Dwarfs	1	.
Filbert and Spanifh Nut Trees	.	2
Goofeberry Trees	.	2
Curran Trees	.	2

N. B. On Application, written Catalogues will be delivered, containing the particular Sorts of the Fruit-Trees propagated in thefe Nurferies.

(9)

E V E R-G R E E N

A N D

FLOWERING-SHRUBS, &c.

A

		each.	
		s.	d.
*	**A** CACIA, Scarlet-flowering, or Red Robinia	2	6
	———— Yellow Egyptian	2	6
	———— Three-thorn'd	2	.
	———— Virginian, or Two-thorn'd	1	.
	Agnus Castus, or Chaste Tree	.	6
* †	Alaternoides	1	.
* †	———— Heath leav'd	1	.
	Alder, Black Berry bearing, or Frangula	.	3
	Almond, Fruit-bearing, Standard	1	6
	———— Fruit-bearing, Dwarf	1	.
	———— White-flowering thin-shell'd	1	.
	———— Double-flowering, Dwarf	.	6
	———— Single-flowering, Dwarf	.	6
	Allspice, Catesby's	7	6
* †	Althea, Double-flowering, or Japan Rose	4	.
	Althea Frutex, White	.	6
	———— Red	.	6
	———— Purple	.	6
	———— Painted Lady	.	6
	———— Strip'd-leav'd	2	6
* †	Amomum Plinii	1	6
*	Angelica Tree	2	.
	Apricot, Bloch'd-leav'd	1	6
	Arbor Judæ	1	.
†	Arbor Vitæ, Common, 1½ Foot high	.	9
	———— 2 Feet high	1	.
†	Arbor Vitæ, Chinese, 8 Inches high	1	6
	———— 1 Foot	2	6
†	Arbutus, or Strawberry Tree	2	6
	Asphalatus	.	6
	Azalia	7	6
*	Azederach, or Bead Tree	2	6

B

		s.	d.
* †	Barba Jovis	2	6
	Barberry, with Red Fruit	.	3
	———— with Red Fruit, without Stone	.	6
	———— with White Fruit	.	4
†	Bay Tree	.	6
	Benjamin Tree	3	.

(Prunus armeniaca variegata)

EVER-GREEN   AND

	each.
	s. d.
Bladder Nut, five-leav'd	· 3
——— three-leav'd	· 6
——— American three-leav'd	1 ·
† Box Tree, Common	· 3
† ——— with Gold edg'd Leaves	· 4
† ——— with Strip'd curl'd Leaves	· 6
† ——— with narrow Leaves	· 3
† ——— with bloch'd Leaves	· 6
† ——— Dwarf —— *per Yard*	· 3
Bramble, with double Flowers	1 ·
† Broom, Butcher's, with prickly Leaves	· 3
† ——— with smooth Leaves	· 3
Broom, Dwarf branching	· 3
——— English	· 3
——— Lucca	1 ·
——— Spanish	· 3
Buckthorn, Common	· 3
——— Sea, or Rhamnoides	· 6

C

CARAGANA, or Yellow Robinia	1	6
Candleberry Bush, or South Sea Thea Tree	1	·
Catalpa	2	·
Celastrus, or Staff-Tree	1	·
Cephalanthus, or Buttonwood Tree	1	·
Cherry, Common Bird	·	3
——— New England Bird	·	6
——— Cornish Cluster	1	·
——— Cornelian	·	6
——— Double-flowering Standard	1	4
——— Double-flowering Dwarf	1	·
——— Perfumed, or Mahaleb	1	·
Chionanthus, or Fringe Tree	3	·
Cinquefoil Shrub	·	3
† Cistus, Male, or Rock Rose of Mountpelier	·	9
† ——— with Sage Leaves and Purple Flowers	·	9
† ——— with Willow Leaves and White Flowers	1	·
† ——— with Willow Leaves and White Flowers Spotted with Purple	1	·
† ——— with Purple Flowers Spotted with Crimson	2	6
Clematis, or upright Blue Climber	·	6
Clethra	2	6
❋ † Coronella Maritima, with broad Leaves	1	·
❋ † ——— with narrow Leaves	1	·
Cornus, with White Berries, or New England Amomum	1	·
Crab, Virginian, sweet-scented	1	·
——— Syberian	1	·
Creeper, Virginian	·	3
Curran, with Gooseberry Leaves	·	3

FLOWERING-SHRUBS.   11

	each.
	s. d.
Curran with ftrip'd Leaves	. 6
⚹ † Cytifius Lunatus, or Moon Trefoil	2 .
† —— Neapolitan, or Evergreen	1 .
—— Secundus	. 3
D	
DIERVILLA	. 3
Dogwood, Carolina	. 6
—— Female	. 6
—— Strip'd-leav'd	. .
E	
Elder, Parfley-leav'd	. 3
- —— Green-berried	. 3
—— White-berried	. 3
—— Mountain Red-berried	. 6
—— Silver-ftrip'd	1 .
G	
⚹ † GERANIUMS, in Sorts, from 1s. to	2 6
Groundfel Tree	. 6
Guelder Rofe, Common	. 3
—— Strip'd-leav'd	1 .
—— Virginian	. 3
—— Carolina	. 6
H	
† HARTWORT, Ethiopian	1 .
Hiccory Nut, of Virginia	1 .
Honeyfuckle, long-blowing	. 2
—— Red Dutch	. 2
—— Early Red	. 2
—— Early White	. 2
—— Late Red	. 2
—— Late White	. 2
—— Virginian Trumpet	1 .
—— Carolina Trumpet	1 .
—— Red Roman, or Italian	. 6
† —— Evergreen	. 6
—— Oak-leav'd	. 4
—— Strip'd-leav'd	. 6
—— Upright Red-berried	. 6
—— Upright Blue-berried	. 6
—— Fly	. 3
Hop Hornbeam	1 .
Hydrangula	. 4
Hypericum Frutex	. 3
I	
INDICO, Baftard	1 .
Itea	2 6
† Ivy, ftrip'd	. 6

		each.
		s. d.

J

	s.	d.
JASMINE, White	·	3
—————— Silver-ſtrip'd White	1	·
—————— Gold-ſtrip'd White	1	·
—————— Yellow	·	3
—————— Gold-ſtrip'd Yellow	1	·
—————— Large Spaniſh Yellow	·	6
❋ —————— Arabian	2	·
❋ —————— Catalonian	2	·
❋ † —————— White Indian	2	·
❋ † —————— Yellow Indian	2	·
❋ † —————— Cape, from 7 s. 6 d. to	10	6
—————— Perſian, with Privet Leaves and White Flowers	·	6
—————— Perſian, with Privet Leaves, and Blue Flowers	·	4
—————— Perſian, with cut Leaves, and Blue Flowers	·	6
Johnſwort, Shrubby St. the common	·	3
—————— Canary St.	·	6
❋ † —————— Dwarf warted St.	1	·
† Juniper, Engliſh	·	4
† —— Swediſh	·	6

L

	s.	d.
LABURNUM, Common, Standard	·	6
—————— Ditto, Dwarf	·	3
—————— Scotch, or Caledonian	·	6
† Laurel, Common	·	3
† —— Strip'd-leav'd	1	·
† —— Dwarf Portugal	1	·
† —— Spurge	·	3
† Lauruſtinus, Common, or ſmooth-leav'd	·	3
† —— Rough-leav'd	·	4
—— Deciduous	1	·
† —— Shining-leav'd	·	6
❋ † Lemon Trees, from 7 s. 6 d. to	10	6
Lilac, Blue	·	3
—— Purple	·	3
—— White	·	3

M

	s.	d.
❋ MALABAR Nut	2	·
Maple, Sugar	·	6
—— Virginian Aſh-leav'd	·	6
—— Scarlet-flowering	1	·
—— Dwarf Mountain	1	·
—— Norway, or Acerplatanoides	·	6
❋ † Marum, Upright	1	·
❋ † —— Spreading	1	·

FLOWERING-SHRUBS. 13

		each. s. d.	
Medlar, Dwarf Baftard	——	. 6	
* Melianthus ——	——	1 .	*(Melianthus major)*
Mefpilus, early-flowering	——	2 6	
——— Snowy ——	——	2 6	
Mezereon, Purple	——	. 6	
——— Red ——	——	. 4	
——— White ——	——	. 4	
* † Milkwort, African, or Polygala	——	2 6	
Mulberry, White	——	1 .	
* † Myrtles, in feveral Sorts	——	2 6	
† ——— Candleberry ——	——	1 .	
——— Dutch, or Sweet Gale	——	. 6	

N

NIGHTSHADE, ftrip'd-leav'd	——	. 3	

O

* † OLEANDER, Single	——	2 .	
* † ——— Double ——	——	2 6	
Oleafter ——	——	1 .	
* † Olive, True ——	——	2 6	
* † Orange Trees, in Pots, from 7s. 6d. to	——	10 6	

P

PASSION Flower Tree, Common	——	1 .	
——————— Fruit-bearing	——	1 .	*(Passiflora quadrangularis ?)*
* ——————— Purple-flowering	——	1 .	*(P. incarnata)*
Peach, Double-flowering	——	1 6	
Pear, Double-flowering, Standard	——	1 4	
—— Ditto, ——— Dwarf	——	1 .	
——— Strip'd-leav'd ——	——	1 6	
Periploca, or Virginian Silk	——	. 4	
† Periwinkle, Large Green	——	. 2	
† ——— Gold-ftrip'd ——	——	. 2	
† ——— Silver ftrip'd ——	——	. 2	
† ——— Double-flowering	——	. 4	
Peterfwort, Shrub St. ——	——	. 3	
† Phillyrea, True ——	——	1 .	
† ——— Olive-leav'd ——	——	1 .	
† ——— Plain and bloch'd Alaternus	——	. 6	
* † ——— Gold-ftrip'd Alaternus	——	2 6	
* † ——— Silver-ftrip'd Alaternus	——	2 6	
† ——— Serrated-leav'd Alaternus	——	1 .	
† ——— Strip'd Serrated-leav'd Alaternus	——	2 6	
Plum, Cherry, or Mirabilon, Standard	——	1 4	
—— Ditto, ——— Dwarf	——	1 .	
Plum, Perfimon ——	——	1 6	
Pomegranate, Double ——	——	2 .	
——————— Single ——	——	1 6	

14   E V E R-G R E E N   AND

		each.
		s. d.
† Privet, Italian Evergreen		. 2
Ptelia, or Trefoil Shrub		. .
† Purſlain Tree		. 4
† Pyracantha, or Evergreen Thorn		. 3

R

† * RAGWORT, Sea		1 .
Raſp, Virginian-flowering		. 3
Roſe, Apple-bearing		. 6
—— Red and Yellow Auſtrian		1 .
—— Dwarf Burgundy		5 .
—— Tall Burgundy		5 .
—— Burnet leav'd		. 4
—— Bluſh Belgic		1 .
—— Red Belgic		. 6
—— Bluſh Cluſter		1 .
—— Late White Cluſter, or Double Muſk		1 .
—— Double Cinnamon		. 4
—— Single Cinnamon		. 6
—— Childing, or Red Provence		. 4
—— Crimſon		. 6
—— Damaſk		. 4
—— White Damaſk		. 6
—— Dutch Hundred-leav'd		1 .
—— Bluſh Hundred-leav'd		1 .
† —— Evergreen		. 6
—— Thornleſs		. 6
—— Francfort		. 4
—— Maiden's Bluſh		1 .
—— Double Marbled		1 .
—— Semi-double Marbled		. 6
—— Monthly		. 4
—— Strip'd Monthly		. 6
—— White Monthly		. 5
—— Penſilvanian		. 6
—— Provence		. 4
—— Bluſh Provence		1 .
—— Moſs Provence		2 .
—— Roſa-mundi		. 4
—— Double Red		. 4
—— Great Royal		. 4
—— York and Lancaſter		. 4
—— Double Velvet		1 .
—— Semi double Velvet		1 .
—— Virgin		. 4
—— Double White		. 4
—— Double Yellow		1 .
—— Single Yellow		. 6
—— Red Scotch		1 .

FLOWERING-SHRUBS. 15

each.
s. d.

Rofe, White Scotch ——— ——— ———	. 4
—— Marbled Scotch ———	1 .
—— Single Sweet Briar ——— ——	. 2
—— Full double Sweet Briar ——— ———	1 .
—— Semi double Sweet Briar ——— ——	. 6
† —— Maiden's Blufh, or Evergreen Sweet Briar ——	1 .
† Rofemary ——— ——— ———	. 3

S

† SAGE, Silver ftrip'd ——— ———	. 6	*(Salvia officinalis sturnina)*
† —— Gold ftrip'd ——— ———	. 6	*(S. officinalis icterina)*
† Sage Tree, with broad Leaves, or Phlomis Major .	. 6	
† —— with narrow Leaves, or Phlomis Minor	. 6	
Sallow, with ftrip'd Leaves ——— ———	. 3	
† Savin, Common ——— ———	. 3	
† —— with ftrip'd Leaves ——— ———	1 .	
Senna, Bladder, with Yellow Flowers —— ——	. 3	
—— with Blood-colour'd Flowers ——	1 .	
† —— Ethiopian, with Scarlet Flowers ——	1 .	
—— Scorpion —— ——	. 3	
Service, Maple-leav'd ——— ———	1 .	
Spindle Tree, American broad-leav'd —— ——	1 .	
—— long-leav'd ——	2 .	
—— with deep red Berries —— ——	. 3	
—— with pale red Berries —— ——	. 3	
—— with white Berries — ——	. 3	
Spirea Frutex, Common —— — ——	. 3	
—— with Purple Flowers — ——	. 6	
—— with Gooíeberry Leaves — ——	1 .	
—— Dwarf White —— ——	. 6	
—— long-leav'd White —— ——	. 6	
† Stonecrop Tree —— —— ——	. 6	
Styrax, or Liquid Amber —— —— ——	2 6	
Sumach, Virginian Staghorn, with a Red Tuft ——	1 .	
—— Virginian Staghorn, with a Yellow Tuft	1 .	
—— Beech ——— ——— ——	1 .	
—— Myrtle-leav'd ——— ——	. 4	
—— Venetian, or Coccigria ——— ——	1 .	
Syringa, Common ——— ———	. 3	
—— Dwarf —— ——— ——	. 3	

T

TACCAMAHACCA —— —— ——	1 .	
Tamarifk, French ——— ——— ——	. 4	
—— German ——— —— ——	. 4	
Thorn, Chrift's, or Paliurus ——— ——	2 6	
—— Pear-leav'd, or common Azarole ——	. 6	*(Crataegus tomentosa)*
—— Plum-leav'd —— ——	. 6	
—— Willow-leav'd —— —— ——	. 6	*(Crataegus crus-galli salicifolia)*

16   E V E R - G R E E N,   &c.

		each. s. d.
Thorn, Neapolitan Azarole		1 .
——— Black Virginian		. 6
——— Long fpined B ack Virginian, or Lord Ifles's		. 6
——— Cockfpur		. 6
——— Double-flowering		. 6
——— Glaftoibury		. 6
——— Yellow-berried		. 6
(Crataegus uniflora) ——— Goofeberry-leav'd		. 6
Toxicodendron, American		1 .
————— Upright fmooth-leav'd		. 6
————— Creeping		. 3
————— Climbing		. 3
Traveller's Joy		. 3
Trumpet Flower, or Bignonia		1 .
Tulip Tree, Virginian, 1½ Foot high		2 .
——— 4 and 5 Feet		3 .
Tutfan, Upright		. 3
+ ——— Spreading		. 2
* + ——— Chinefe		1 .

V

(Rhus vernix) VARNISH Tree		2 6
Viburnum, Plain		. 3
——— Strip'd		1 .
——— Serrated-leav'd		1 .
Virgin's Bower, Double		2 .
——— Single		1 6

W

(Juglans cinerea) WALNUT, Virginian, long Black		. 6
(Juglans nigra) ——— Virginian, round Black		. 6
Widow Wail		1 .

Z

ZANTHOXYLUM, or Tooth-Ach Tree		2 6

Alfo, all Sorts of Seeds, with a great Variety of Perennial and Bulbous Rooted Flowers.

N B. Thofe marked thus * are tender, and require the Protection of a Greenhoufe or Stove. Thofe marked thus + are Ever-greens.

HERE WE HAVE the standard lists of seeds and bulbs obtainable from one of the principal London seedsmen in the year that Queen Victoria came to the throne. The general list is dated 1835, but was in all probability still current when the 1837 Autumn List of Bulbs ('Flower-Roots imported') came out within a month or so of the Queen's accession. The seeds are not priced, but it is possible to get a fairly definite idea of the cost of gardening from the prices for bulbs. This is not by any means to say that a standard factor of inflation can be deduced. Countering inflation between 1837 and 1970 has been the enormous increase in the numbers of some sorts bred, bringing prices down to a popular level. Thus in 1837 one hundred mixed Ranunculus (not named varieties) could be had in four grades at 5s., 10s., 15s. and £1 1s.; in 1970 a leading firm offered one mixture only at £1 a hundred – in this case on average the rise in price has been to rather less than double. Doubling the price is correct for mixed English Iris, 2s. 6d. a dozen in 1837, 5s. in 1970; and for Cyclamen coum, then 1s. 6d. each, now 3s. On the other hand, Large Yellow Dutch Crocus could be had by the hundred at 1s. 6d., 2s. and 2s. 6d., but have risen to 28s., 35s. or even 37s.; in this case the average factor is a rise of 14 to 18½ times, in spite of the bulk in which Crocus corms are now sold. The answer to this discrepancy is that, by 1837, the Crocus had already become cheapened to a mass-produced level of price.

Bulbs then rare such as Ixias, cost 3s. 6d. a dozen upwards, and have actually dropped to 2s. 6d.; Crown Imperials, then 6s.-9s., have gone up only to 7s. 6d.-10s. 6d. Various other bulbs take an intermediate position: Hyacinths, mixed, then at 4s. a dozen, are up to 20s. or 25s., Jonquils have moved from 2s.-4s. up to 4s. 6d.-10s. 6d.; Early Tulips from 10s. a hundred as the basic price up to 55s., and mixed Parrot Tulips from 1s. 6d. a dozen to 8s. 6d. In a good many examples a rise of five or six times is found, and the higher and lower extremes balance out. It has to be kept in mind that in 1837 the market in London and the South was still largely a specialist market for named varieties at high prices, as is shown by the long numbered list of named Hyacinths, and the prices quoted for the more expensive named Tulips.

Apart from the fashionable flowers, among which the Hyacinth was in the lead, followed by Narcissus, Tulips, Gladiolus, Ixias, Anemones and Ranunculus, there was a good variety available in the concluding miscellaneous section. There were some ten species or varieties of Lilium as well as the Guernsey Lily (Nerine sarniensis), the Bella Donna Lily (Amaryllis belladonna) and the Jacobea Lily (Sprekelia formosissima). Alstroemeria seed might be had in several sorts at 3s. 6d. a packet (in 1971 at 1s. 6d. or 2s. 6d. a packet, but we have no means of comparison). The Mediterranean Lily or Sea Daffodil (Pancratium maritimum) cost 12s. a dozen bulbs though they are now 3s. 6d. each. The general picture of bulbs grown had not changed much since 1777, apart from the increased availability of Lilies and Amaryllids; but this had been counter-balanced by a decided falling-off in Crown Imperials and in other Fritillaries. In 60 years the choice of Crown Imperials had dropped from eight kinds to two, though it may be that there were colour varieties obtainable but not listed in 1837. Fritillaries, which in 1777 had boasted over 20 named varieties (even though the names were not actually stated), and were listed at three prices per hundred, 10s., 16s. and £1 10s., were now undifferentiated 1s. 6d. a dozen, a price closely related to that for 'Common sorts' in the earlier list. This disappearance of any vogue for the genus Fritillaria between the heyday of George III and the death of William IV is one of the most curious incidents in English gardening.

The general list of seeds for both Vegetable and Flower gardens proves to be very closely comparable with that of William Lucas of 160 years before. The total number of species and varieties listed is far larger: over 1100 against rather less than 300. In the field of vegetable seeds the disproportion is less, some 270 to 170 in the 17th century, but agricultural seeds had risen from 8 sorts to 65, of which no fewer than 17 were different kinds of grass. Seeds of trees and shrubs had gone up from 30 to 140; flowers from 74 to over 650. Some of Lucas's old classes have coalesced, Sweet and Potherbs together taking the place of the two separate sections; physical seeds have gone. But in most respects the seeds of practical use are still listed on the old basis, and though the numbers of varieties have in some cases risen very greatly, it is noticeable that only half a dozen kinds of Potato were offered.

The enormous list of flower seeds is perhaps slightly exaggerated, for it looks as though a few traditional items have become duplicated for reasons of nomenclature. For example, Belvidere still appears with the synonym 'or Summer Cypress'; but as a separate entry there is also the scientific name, Chenopodium scoparium (now Kochia s.), without any indication that it is the same plant. It is in this case possible that the green and red forms, respectively, were supplied. But there are now the four entries 'Caterpillars', 'Hedgehogs', 'Horns' and 'Snails' instead of the two combined entries of Lucas. There may have been further differentiation of varieties of Medicago, or names may have changed. 'Caterpillars' may have meant Scorpiurus vermiculata by 1837, and 'Snails', the Snail Flower (Phaseolus caracalla). Even so, some duplication appears certain, since 'Lychnis fulgens' is in both the list of Hardy Annuals and in that of Hardy Biennials and Perennials, and it seems probable that the Campanula 'percissiflora' of the latter list is really the same plant as the C. persicifolia placed among the annuals. Similarly Echium violaceum and E. plantaginium appear in both lists.

Though slightly diminished by such critical appraisal, the long lists are none the less a splendid witness to the amazing floral riches already brought home from the four quarters of the globe by merchants and plant-hunters. Perhaps one-third of the typical seedsman's list of today had not yet arrived, but in 1837 there were a great many things not commonly to be found now. In many ways Flanagan & Nutting's catalogue looked back in that it still included the tried favourites of the previous two centuries of English gardening, but on the other hand it had incorporated much that was of very recent introduction. Traditional names like Flos Adonis (which incidentally still survives in the lists for 1971), Lobel's Catchfly, Roman Nigella and French Honeysuckle stand ranked with Clarkia, Nolana, Zinnia, Gloxinia,

Cobaea, Eccremocarpus, Maurandia and Penstemons in great variety.

It is natural that Flanagan & Nutting should, after some eight years, be able to stock seed of a great many of the famous crop of introductions by David Douglas of 1825-27. These included two Collinsias, two Clarkias, two Gilias, Eschscholzia, several Mimulus including Musk and a good deal else. But it is remarkable that the catalogue also offers seed of several plants whose dates of introduction were within the previous four years: Clarkia elegans, said to have arrived in 1832; Gilia tricolor (1833); Schizanthus humilis (1831); Mimulus roseus (1831) and 'Nierembergia phoenicia' (Petunia violacea), also of 1831. Finally there come a couple of plants that had 'got there the previous night': 'Lophospermum scandens' (Maurandia lophospermum), introduced in 1834, and Oenothera bifrons of D. Don, stated by Loudon to have come from Texas actually in 1835. The first of these surprises is probably a mistake owing to confusion with Maurandia erubescens, which had reached England in 1830, but it is evident that Messrs. Flanagan & Nutting were in any case truly enterprising in the choice they put before the gardeners of 1835.

A CATALOGUE

OF

SEEDS,

SOLD BY

FLANAGAN & NUTTING,

Seedsmen and Florists,

9,

MANSION HOUSE STREET,

OPPOSITE THE MANSION HOUSE,

LONDON.

METCALFE, PRINTER, 3, GROCERS' HALL COURT, POULTRY.

1835.

STRAWBERRY, RASPBERRY, AND FRUIT TREE SEEDS,

Of the best varieties,

ASSORTED AND PACKED FOR EXPORTATION.

GARDEN SEEDS FOR EXPORTATION,

SELECTED AND CAREFULLY PACKED FOR ALL CLIMATES.

Bird Seeds, Garden Mats, Split Peas, and Mustard Flour.

AN EXTENSIVE

ASSORTMENT OF BULBOUS FLOWER ROOTS

Annually imported, and a separate Catalogue printed.

FLOWERING SHRUBS, FRUIT TREES,

GREEN-HOUSE AND HERBACEOUS PLANTS,

American and other Foreign Tree, Shrub, and Flower Seeds imported.

A large Assortment of Grass Seeds.

BUDDING AND PRUNING KNIVES, GARDEN TOOLS, &c.

DAHLIAS.

FROM THE BEST COLLECTIONS,

Of which a separate Catalogue is printed.

GARDEN SEEDS.

PEAS.

Early Warwick
Early Single Blossom Frame
Early Double Blossom do.
Bishop's Early Dwarf
Early Charlton
Golden Hotspur
New Early Green Marrow
Dwarf Marrow
Large tall do.
New Matchless
Dwarf Sugar
Tall ditto
Blue Prussian
White Prussian
Royal Dwarf
Flanagan's New Royal Dwarf
Spanish Dwarf or Fan
Dwarf Blue Imp^d. Imperial
Scimitar
Waterloo Blue
Woodford Marrow
Knight's Tall Marrow
Knight's Dwarf ditto
New sort Knight's Dwarf
  Green
Do. Tall do.   do.
Superb branching Dwarf
  Blue

BEANS.

Early Mazagan
Early Long Pod
Turkey or Sword ditto
Hangdown ditto
Green ditto
Windsor
Taylor's Large Windsor
Green Windsor
Mumford
Toker
Scarlet Blossom Long Pod
White   ditto   ditto
Fan, Bog, or Cluster

KIDNEY BEANS.

Pale Dun Forcing
Dark Dun ditto
Negro
Canterbury
Large White ditto
Chinese
Yellow
Black Speckled
Red Speckled
Purple Speckled
Dutch Dwarf
Scarlet Runners
Dutch ditto

4

Artichoke
Asparagus
Beet, Red
    White
    Green
    Turnip-rooted
    Silver, or Sea Kail
Borecole, Tall Green, or
    Scotch Kail
        Dwarf Green
        Red
        Variegated
        Dwarf Canadian
        Jerusalem Kail
        Asparagus ditto
Brocoli, Early Sprouting
    ditto Purple, close
    headed
    Early Green
    Late Sprouting
    Large Purple
    Dwarf ditto
    Dwarf Danish
    Early White
    Late White
    Late Dwarf Hardy
        White, new sort
    Knight's superb,late
    Flanagan's Invisible
        White
    Brimstone, or
        Portsmouth
    White Cape, or
        Cauliflower

Brocoli, Early Purple Cape
    Late Dwarf Cape
Brussels Sprouts
Cabbage, Early York
    Early Dwarf
    Sup. Early Dwarf
    Large York
    Early heart shaped
    Early Emperor
    London Early
        Battersea
    East Ham
    Early Sugar-loaf
    Early flat Battersea
    Late flat Battersea
    Early Imperial
    Paington
    Large Drum-head
        or Scotch
    Red
    Drum-head, red
    Turnip-rooted,
        above ground
    Turnip-rooted,
        under ground
    Braganza, or
        Chouxtrochado
    Choux de Milan,
        or 1000-headed
Carrot, Long Orange
    Fine Surrey
    Altringham
    Short Orange
    New Sort Large do.

5

Carrot, Early Horn
    Scarlet ditto
Cauliflower, Early
    Late
Celery, Italian
    Solid White
    Solid Red
    Giant
    New Striped
Celeriac, or Turnip-rooted do
Cardoon, Spanish
Chervil, curled
Corn Salad
Cress, common
    fine curled
    broad-leaved
    American
Cucumber, early frame
    Flanagan's long
    frame
    fine Southgate
    fine Ridge
    long Prickly
    short Prickly
    Cluster
    White Turkey
    White Spine
    Hedgehog
    Green Turkey
Capsicum, of sorts
Endive, green curled
    white curled
    broad-leaved
    do. new variety

Endive, white, Batavian
Gourds, various
Leek, London Flag
    Common
Lettuce, White Coss
    Hardy ditto
    Green ditto
    Hardy Green ditto
    Egyptian ditto
    Brown or Bath
    Coss
    Paris ditto
    Florence ditto
    Brighton ditto
    Spotted ditto
    Kensington Coss
    Common Cabbage
    Grand Admiral
    Brown Dutch
    Hammersmith,
    Hardy Green
    Royal Cabbage
    Tennis Ball
    Asiatic
    Mogul
    Brown Silesia
    White Silesia
    Drum-head, or
    Malta
    Imperial
    Marseilles
Love Apple, large red
    Yellow
    Pear-shaped

6

Love Apple, Cherry
Melon, Early Cantaleupe
    Large Cantaleupe
    Netted Romana
    Large Black Rock
    Silver Rock
    Scarlet-fleshed
    Green-fleshed
    Snake
    Musk
Mustard, White
    Brown
Nasturtium, tall
    dwarf
Orach, White
    Red
Onion, White Spanish or
    Portugal
    Brown Spanish
    Reading or White
    Deptford
    Strasburg
    James' long keeping
    Globe
    Large Tripoli
    Blood-red
    Silver skin'd pickling
    Welch
    Lisbon or Spring
    Two-bladed
    Straw-coloured
Parsley, plain
    curled
    Flanagan's extra fine

Parsley, Hamburgh or long
    rooted
Parsnip, hollow-crowned
Radish, early frame
    scarlet
    salmon
    purple or salad
    white Turnip
    red Turnip
    black Spanish
    long White
Rampion
Rape
Rhubarb, Turkey
    Red or Tart
    New Early Red
Salsafy
Savoy, green-curled
    Drum-head
    Globe
    Yellow
Scorzonera
Skirret
Sorrel
Spinach, round
    prickly
    New Flanders
    New Zealand, or Tetra-
    gona Expansa
Sea Kail
Squash
Turnip, early Dutch
    fine early Stone
    Six Weeks

7

Turnip, Yellow Garden
   Maltese
   Scarisbrook
Zea, Maize, or Indian Corn,
  in varieties

SWEET & POT HERBS
Angelica
Anise
Balm
Borage
Burnet
Basil, large or sweet
   Bush or Dwarf
Carraway.
Clary
Coriander
Cummin
Dill
Fennel
Finochia
Hyssop
Lavender
Marjorum, sweet
    Pot or Perennial
Marygold, Pot
Purslane, green and golden
Rosemary
Savory, Summer
   Winter
Scurvy Grass
Sage
Thyme

ROOTS, &c.
Artichoke
Asparagus
  Grayson's new Giant
Garlic
Rocambole
Mushroom Spawn
Potatoes, early Forcing
   Kidney, early do.
   Ash-leaf, ditto
   Champion
   Ox Noble
   Early, Shaw's
Shallots
Tarragon
Rhubarb

GRASS,
AND OTHER
AGRICULTURAL SEEDS.
Barley, Common
   Winter
   Spring
Beans, Small Horse
   Large or Tick
   Early Mazagan
Broom
Burnet
Buck-Wheat
Cabbage, Drum-head
    Turnip-rooted
Canary
Clover, Red
   White Dutch
   Yellow or Trefoil

8

Chicory
Furze
Grass, Sweet Vernal
 Meadow Fox-tail
 Smooth Meadow
 Rough-stalked
 Crested Dog's-tail
 Meadow Fescue
 Sheep's Fescue
 Fine or Heath
 Rough Cock's foot or
  Orchard
 Timothy
 Rib or Plantain
 Brome or Soft
 Lucerne
 Ray or Bents
 St. Foin
 Yarrow
 mixed, for Lawns
Linseed, or Riga flax
 English
Mangle Würzel
 Yellow
Mustard, White
 Brown

Oats, Black
 Pollard
 Dutch Brew
 Tartarian
 Potato
Peas, Grey Rouncival
 White Boiling
Rape or Cole Seed
Tares, Winter
 Spring
Turnip, Green Round
 White Round
 Red Round
 Globe
 Large Scotch Yellow
 White Tankard
 Red Tankard
 Green Tankard
 Stubble
 Yellow Swedish
 Red-topped Swedish
Wheat, White
 Red
 Spring
 Talavera

FLOWER SEEDS.

HARDY ANNUALS,

Which may be sown, in open Borders, from the middle of February to the end of April.

Adonis, Flos, vernalis
 æstivalis
Agrostemma, Cœli rosa

Alyssum, maritimum, or
 sweet
Alkekengi

9

Amethystea cœrulea
Ambrosia, Species
Anthericum annuum
Anagallis Indica
　　　cœrulea
　　　new blush
Antirhinum bipunctatum
　　　　medium
　　　　speciosum
　　　　spartium
　　　　latifolium
　　　　triphyllum
　　　　viscosum
　　　　versicolor
Arctotis tristis
　　　anthemoides
Aster tenella
Athanasia annua
Balm, Moldavian, White
　　　Blue
Belvidere, or Summer
　　Cypress
Bidens diversifolia
Bladder, Ketmia
Briza maxima
Calendula hybrida
　　　stellata
Calliopsis bicolor
Calochortus venustus
　　　splendens
Campanula pentagonia
　　　persicifolia
Candytuft, Normandy
　　　purple

Candytuft, white rocket
　　　small white
　　　sweet scented
　　　dark purple, new
　　　　variety
Catananche lutea
Caterpillars
Catchfly, Lobel's, red
　　　white
　　　New Siberian
Centaurea cyanus, minor
　　　do. double dwarf
　　　Crupina, major
　　　Crocodilia
　　　Elongata
Cerinthe aspera major
　　　minor
Chenopodium scoparium
Chrysanthemum carinatum
　　(tricolor)
　　　coronarium, white
　　　　　yellow
　　do. quilled
　　　aureum
Clary, red top
　　　purple top
Claytonia perfoliata
Collinsia grándiflora
　　　verna
Convolvolus minor (tricolor)
　　　　(bicolor)
　　　　major purpurea
　　　　Michauxii
　　　　fine-striped

10

Convolvolus, colors, separate
Clarkia pulchella
        alba
     elegans
Coreopsis tinctoria
     diversifolia
     Atkinsonia
Coronilla Securidaca
Corydalis sempervirens
Dracocephalum canescens
Elsholtzia cristata
Echium violaceum
     plantaginium
Eutoca multiflora
Gilia capitata
     pulchella
     tricolor
Glaucium Phœnicium
     Violaceum
Gypsophila elegans
     viscosa
Hawkweed, yellow
     purple
     new straw
Hedgehogs
Horns
Hyoscyamus agrestis
     pictus
Iberis umbellata
     odorata
Impatiens
Isotoma axillaris
Knautea orientalis
Larkspur, Dwarf Rocket

Larkspur, tall Rocket
     fine Rose
     Branching
     Neapolitan
     Unique
     in distinct colours
Lavatera, Red
     White
Love lies Bleeding
Lobelia, Annual
Lupins, Yellow
     White
     large Blue
     do. Rose
     small Blue
     Straw-coloured
     Dutch Blue
Lupinus mutabilis
     micranthus
     Cruikshankii
Lusania calycina
Lychnis læta
     dwarf
     fulgens
Mallow, Scarlet
     curled
     Venetian
Malope trifida
     grandiflora
Malcomia Africana
Madia elegans
Melilotus cœrulea
Mignonette, Sweet
     Upright or Reseda

11

Nasturtium, tall
      dwarf
      new dark
Nigella, Roman
      Double Dwarf
      Orientalis
      Spanish
Nolana paradoxa
      prostata
Œnothera grandiflora
      Lindleyana
      purpurea
      rosea
      sinuata
      tetraptera
      tenuifolia
      tenella
      viminea
      molissima
      nocturna
      decumbens
      odorata
      Romanzovii
      rosea-alba
      bifrons
      taraxifolia
Peas, Sweet Purple
      do. Scarlet
      sweet Striped
      do. White
      do. Yellow
      do. Black
      do. Painted Lady
      do. Top-knot

Peas, large Scarlet Tangier
      small do. do.
      Painted Lady do.
      Yellow-winged
      Red do.
      Lord Anson's
Persicaria, Red
      White
Poppy, Carnation
      Picotée
      New Fringed
      Double White
      Ranunculus or Dwarf
      Dwarf, Chinese
      Do. French
      in separate Colours
Prince's Feather, Red
      White
Roman Nettle
Rudbeckia amplexifolia
Scabious, Starry
Scabiosa prolifera
Snails
Sun-flower, tall
      dwarf
      extra double
Snap-dragon
Stock, Virginia, Red
      White
Strawberry Spinach
Silene Atocion
      colorata
      disticha
      major

12

Silene picta
    pendula
    rubella
    vespertina
Trifolium incarnatum
    cœruleum
Veronica, Species

Venus's Looking-glass
    do. White
    do. large Blue
    do. new Lilac
    do. Navel-wort
Vicia atropurpurea
Ximinesia encelioides

HALF HARDY,

Which should be sown in March, under Hand Glasses, or on a very moderate Hot-Bed, and transplanted into the Border in the middle of April or beginning of May.

Ageratum Mexicanum
    Odoratum
Anthemis Arabica
Argemone albiflora
    Mexicana
    Ochroleuca
Aster, Chinese, red
    ditto, purple
    ditto, white
    ditto, bonnet
    ditto, new early Dwf.
    superb red
    ditto, white
    ditto, blue
    fine quilled blue
    ditto, white
    ditto, red
    striped red
    ditto, purple
    new German varieties
    new Turkey red
Balm of Gilead
Blumenbachia insignis

Cacalia coccinea
Campanula gracilis
Cardiospermum Halicaca-
    bum
Carthamus tinctoria
Calceolaria pinnata
Calendrina speciosa
    grandiflora
Centaurea Americana
Cistus guttatus
Claytonia alsinoides
Clintonia elegans
Cyclobothria pulchella
    alba
Coix lachryma
Colutea, scarlet
Cuphea viscosissima
Datura ceratocaula
    Metel
    Tatula
Dendromecon rigidum
Dolichos Lablab
    purpureus

13

Galinsogea trilobata
Hollyhock, Chinese
Hibiscus Africanus
Hornemannia bicolor
Ipomœa Michauxii
    barbigera
    discolor
    hederacea
    hepaticæfolia
Jacobea, purple
    white
    fine double
Kaulfussia amelloides
Leonurus heterophyllus
    Nepalensis
Lopezia coronata
    racemosa
Marvel of Peru, red
    white
    yellow
    lg. tube or sweet scented
    gold-striped
    silver-striped
    red-striped
Marygold, orange African
    lemon ditto
    fine quilled
    dwarf French
    tall ditto
    striped ditto
    new early dwarf
    unique
Molucella lævis

Mesembryanthemum
    glabrum
Nicotiana angustifolia
    glutinosa
    alata
    quadrivalvis
    odorata
    new, scarlet
    rustica, or Mary-
        land Tobacco
    Tabacum, or Vir-
        ginia Tobacco
    undulata
Palma Christi major
    minor
Petunia Nyctaginiflora
Pink, Indian double
    ditto, broad-leaved
Salpiglossis picta
    straminea
    atropurpurea
  and others
Schizanthus pinnatus
    porrigens
    Hookeri
    Humilis
Stock, new Russian, in forty
  colours
    Prussian
    giant, ten week
    fine scarlet
    ditto purple
    ditto white

14

Stock, wall-leaved white
  ditto purple
  ditto scarlet
Sultan, sweet purple
  white
  yellow
Sycios angulata
Tagetes corymbosa
  tenuifolia
Trachymene coerulea
Triteleia laxa
Xeranthemum, ann. white
    purple

Xeranthemum, lucidum
  (Elychrysum)
Zinnia elegans
    coccinea
    purpurea
  grandiflora
  fl. alba
  multiflora, red
     yellow
  revoluta
  tenuiflora
  verticillata
  grandiflora

TENDER ANNUALS,

Which require more than one Hot Bed to bring them to perfection, should be sown during the months of February and March.

Amaranthus, purple globe
  white ditto
  striped ditto
  bicolor
  tricolor
Balsam, fine double
  French varieties
Browallia elata, blue
  ditto, white
  demissa
Canna angustifolia
  coccinea
  indica
  lutea
Capsicum, long red
  yellow
  oxheart
  giant

Capsicum, cherry
  cayenne
  tomatoe
  bird pepper
Cleome spinosa
  pentaphylla
  rosea
Cockscomb, tall red
  fine dwarf
  branching
  pyramidal
  beautiful Chinese
   yellow and buff
Colutea, scarlet
Egg Plant, purple
  white
Hedysarum gyrans
Heliotropium Indicum

K

15

Heliotropium Peruvianum
Ice Plant
Ipomœa coccinea
    nil
      Quamoclit
Martynia annua

Martynia proboscidea
Mesembryanthemum cordi-
    folium, or purple Ice Plant
Sensitive Plant
Stramonium, double purple
      ditto white

BIENNIALS & PERENNIALS, NOT HARDY.

Alstrœmeria peligrina
    ditto alba
    pulchella
    Simsii
    aurea, and others
Calceolaria suberecta

Calceolaria pendula
    mixed varieties
Gloxinia formosa
    speciosa
Thunbergia alata
and many others

HARDY BIENNIAL & PERENNIAL FLOWER SEEDS,

To be sown from the beginning of April to the middle of June.

Acanthus spinosa
Aconitum album
    Lycoctonum
    Napellus
    rubrum
    variegatum
Agrostemma Flos Jovis
Ammobium alatum
Anchusa sempervirens
    incarnata
Anemone coronaria
    narcissiflora
Anagallis grandiflora
    Monelli
Antirhinum bicolor
    pictum
    majus
    new scarlet
    new yellow
Alyssum saxatile

Aquilegia Canadensis
    alpina
Argemone grandiflora
Astragalus alopecuroides
    bœticus
    galegiformis
Astrantia, species
Auricula
Betonica grandiflora
Calceolaria corymbosa
    many varieties
Campion, Rose
Catananche cœrulea
Campanula azurea
    glomerata
    latifolia
    ditto alba
    percissiflora
    pyramidalis
    urticifolia

16

Campanula versicolor
Canterbury Bells, blue
   white
Carnation, fine double
  seedling various
Celsia cretica
  urticifolia
Chelone in varieties
Commelina cœlestis
   tuberosa
Cobæa scandens
Columbine
Cowslip, in colours
Convolvolus ciliatus
   Scammonia
Cynoglossum pictum
Cyclamen
Dahlia, fine double
Delphinium azureum
   elatum
   grandiflorum
   intermedium
Dianthus alpinus
  superbus
  latifolius
  velutinus
Digitalis alba
 aurea
 ferruginea
 grandiflora
 lutea
 ochroleuca
 orientalis
 rubra
Dracocephalum altaicum
  canescens
  peregrinum

Eccremocarpus scaber
Echium rubrum
  Sibericum
  plantaginium
  violaceum
Epilobium spicatum
Eryngium alpinum
  amethystinum
  planum
Eschscholtzia californica
  crocea
Francoa appendiculata
Ferula tingitana
Flax, perennial
 Siberian
Fraxinella, red
  white
Galardia aristata
  bicolor
Galega officinalis, white
   blue
Gaura mutabilis
Geranium, from choice sorts
  Wallachianum
Gentiana acaulis
  asclepiadea
  cruciata
  saponaria
Geum album
 coccineum
 Quellion
Glaucium fulvum
 luteum
Hesperis matronalis
Heart's-ease
Hemerocallis cœrulea
Hieracium aureum

17

Hieracium maculatum
Hollyhock, double mixed
    in separate colours
       Antwerp
Honesty, or Lunaria
Honeysuckle, red French
       white ditto
Horn Poppy
Iris Florentina
   Siberica
   Susiana
   Xiphium
   Xiphioides
Ketmia versicaria
Lophospermum scandens
Larkspur, perennial
Lespedezia capitata
Liatris spicata
     scariosa
     elegans
Linaria alpina
    genistifolio
    purpurea
Lobelia cardinalis
    syphilitica
    bignonifolia
Lupinus lepidus
    mexicanus
    ornatus
    perennis
    plumosus
    polyphillus
    ditto albus
    tomentosus
    nanus
Lychnis fulgens
    scarlet
    white

Lythrum erubescens
Lathyrus latifolius
    heterophyllus
Linum, large new
Malva arborea
    moschata
Maurandia Barclayana
Mimulus guttatus
   luteus
   moschatus
   pictus
   rivularis
   roseus
Monkshood, various
Monarda punctata
    oblongata
Myagrum, species
Medicago arborea
Nierembergia, Phœnicia
    rosea
Oenothera biennis
    grandiflora
    fruticosa
    pumila
    spectabilis
Ononis hircina
    rotundifolia
Orobus niger
   vernus
   coccinea
   angustifolius
Papaver, bracteatum
    orientale
Peas, Everlasting
Penstemon atrorubens
    atropurpureum
    angustifolium
    Richardsonii

18

Penstemon diffusum
 digitale
 hybridum
 Lyoni
 ovatum
 pulchellum
Peony, in sorts
Phytollacca decandra
Pink, pheasant-eyed
 mountain
 Spanish
Polemonium, white
  blue
Polyanthus
Prunella grandiflora
Potentilla atrosanguinea
 formosa
 hirta
Primula prænitens
 prænitens alba
Psoralea grandiflora
Pulsatilla alpina
 vulgaris
Pulmonaria Siberica
Ranunculus
 aconitifolius
Rhodiola rosea
Rocket, sweet
Ruellia australis
Rudbeckia hirta
 laciniata
 purpurea
Scabiosa alpina
 caucasica
 moschata or sweet
 nana
Serratula alata
Spiræa Aruncus

Sisyrinchium Nuttalli
Statice latifolia
 tartarica
Stevia purpurea
Stipa pinnata
Stock, scarlet Brompton
 white Brompton
 purple ditto
 Twickenham
 scarlet Queen
 white ditto
 purple ditto
Tagetes lucida
Thistle, Globe
Trollius asiaticus
 europeus
 giganteus
Valerian, scarlet
 white garden
 Greek, white & blue
Veratrum nigrum
 viride
Verbena aubletia
 Lambertii
Verbascum Blattaria
 biennis
 formosum
 Ibericum
 Myconi
 pyramidatum
Veronica spicata
Vesicaria utriculata
Viola odorata
Wallflower, blood red
 yellow
William, Sweet. scarlet
 do. auricula-flowered

19

HARDY TREE AND SHRUB SEEDS.

Alder
Andromeda mariana
        paniculata
        racemosa
Arbutus
Ash, English
    mountain
Arbor Vitæ, of sorts
Acacia, of sorts
Bay, sweet
Broom, English
    Spanish
    white Portugal
    striated
    Lucca
Bladder, Senna
Betula excelsa
    lenta
    nigra
    populifolia
Bignonia radicans
Birch, common
    weeping
Briar, sweet
Catalpa cordifolia
Cedar, red Virginian
    white ditto
    of Lebanon
Cytisus purpurea
    capitata
Chesnuts, Spanish
    horse
    Chinquapin
Cypress, upright
    spreading
    deciduous

Chionanthus virginicus
Cercis, or Judas Tree
Cistus, of sorts
Ceanothus Americanus, or
    Button Wood
Clethra alnifolia
Clematis, sweet scented
Candleberry Myrtle
    evergreen do.
Colutea, Oriental
    common
Elder red berried
Elm, English
    Scotch
    American
    White
Euonymus, common
    evergreen
Fir, Norway Spruce
    red American
    white ditto
    black ditto
    Hemlock ditto
    Silver
    Balm of Gilead
    Scotch
Filberts
Furze
Gleditschia Triacanthos
Gerardia quercifolia
    flava
Halesia tetraptera
Hawthorn, English white
    American scarlet do.
Holly
Hornbeam, English

20

Hypericum Kalmianum
Hibiscus, **of sorts**
Hazel Nuts
      Spanish do.
Ilex opaca
   Dahoon
Juniper
    Swedish
Juniperus Virginiana
Kalmia, of sorts
Laburnum, English
    Scotch
Laurel, common
    Portugal
Laurus sassafras
Lime
Liriodendron Tulipefera
Maple, common
    Norway
    scarlet
    American
Magnolia glauca
    grandiflora
    umbellata
    tripetala
    macrophylla
Mezereon
Mulberry, red
    white
    black
Oak, common
    evergreen ditto
    American common
    cork ditto

Oak, swamp
    quercitron
    scarlet
    chesnut-leaved
Ostrya virginica
Pine, Weymouth
    cluster
    aster
    stone
    Siberian
    Jersey
    blue and white
    frankincense
Platanus orientalis
    occidentalis
Privet
Prunus virginiana
Pyracantha
Rhododendron maximum
        ponticum
        punctatum
Robinia, pseudo **Acacia**
    American
    European
Spiræa
Sumach
Tulip Tree
Viburnum
Walnut, black American
    white do.
    English or common
    thin shell'd hickory do.
    thick-shell'd do
Yew

DUTCH BULBS AND OTHER FLOWER ROOTS
Annually imported,
OF WHICH A SEPARATE CATALOGUE IS PRINTED

Metcalfe, Printer and Stereotype Founder, 3, Grocers' Hall Court, Poultry.

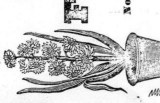

CATALOGUE OF FLOWER-ROOTS,

IMPORTED BY

FLANAGAN & NUTTING,

SEEDSMEN & FLORISTS,

No. 9, MANSION HOUSE STREET, opposite the MANSION HOUSE, LONDON.

1837.

Those marked * are earliest, and most proper for glasses.

HYACINTHS.

DOUBLE RED, OF DIFFERENT SHADES.

	£	s.	d.
*1 Acteur	1	2	6
2 Agatha Catherine	0	1	3
3 Amelia Galothy	0	0	9
4 Augustus Rex	0	3	0
5 Beauté Brillante	0	3	0
*6 Bouquet Royale, *fine*	0	2	6
*7 Bouquet Tendre	0	1	0
*8 Bruiksleed	0	1	0
9 Catharine la Victorieuse	0	4	0
10 Comte de la Coste	0	2	3
11 Comtesse de la Coste	0	2	0
12 Euterpe	0	1	0
*13 Flos Sanguineus	0	1	6
14 General Moore	0	3	0
15 General Ziethen	0	3	0
16 Gloriosa Superba	0	3	0
*17 Groot Vorst, *fine*	0	0	9
18 Hirsila	0	1	6
19 Hugo Grotius	0	0	6
*20 La Beauté Supreme	0	1	6
*21 La Tendresse	0	0	8
*22 Lavater	0	1	0
*23 L'Honneur d'Amsterdam	0	2	0
*65 Lord Wellington	0	1	6
66 Madame Marmont	0	4	0
67 Martinet	0	1	9
*68 Mignon Dryfhout	0	1	0
69 Mirabeau	0	2	6
70 Nigritienne	0	0	9
71 Noir Veritable	0	5	0
72 Orondates	0	2	0
73 Parmenio	0	1	6
*74 Pasquin	0	1	3
*75 Passe Tout	0	1	0
76 Pourpre Superbe	0	3	0
*77 Roi de Major	0	2	3
78 Rudolphus	0	1	6
79 Violet Foncé	0	1	0

DOUBLE WHITE, WITH VARIOUS COLORED EYES.

	£	s.	d.
*80 Anna Maria	0	1	0
*81 A la Mode	0	1	0
82 Cœur Noir	0	1	0
83 Couronne Blanche	0	0	9
*84 Don Gratuit	0	0	9
85 Francina	0	0	9
*86 Gloria Florum	0	1	3
87 Gloria Florum Suprema	0	3	0
*88 Grand Monarque de France	0	2	6

SINGLE BLUE.

	£	s.	d.
*127 Appius	0	1	0
*128 Buonaparte	0	1	0
*129 Emicus	0	0	9
*130 Emilius	0	1	6
131 Haller	0	1	6
*132 King's Mantle	0	2	6
133 La Crépuscule	0	1	3
*134 La Grande Vidette	0	1	6
135 La Plus Noir	0	1	3
*136 L'Ami duCœur	0	2	0
*137 Lord Nelson	0	0	6
138 Lyra	0	0	9
*139 Nimrod, *fine*	0	1	6
140 Orondates	0	1	0
141 Porcelaine Sceptre	0	0	9
142 Pronkjewel	0	1	0
*143 States General	0	0	9
144 Vulcan	0	1	9

SINGLE WHITE.

	£	s.	d.
*145 Grande Blanche Imperiale	0	1	3
*146 Hercules	0	1	3
*147 La Candeur	0	1	3
*148 Premier Noble	0	0	9

EARLY DOUBLE TULIPS.

	£	s.	d.
DucVan Thol, 10s.pr100, per doz.	0	1	6
Marriage Je ma Fille, ditto	0	1	0
Rex Rubrorum, ditto	0	3	6
Tournesol, ditto	0	2	6
Mixed, ditto	0	1	6
Yellow, ditto	0	2	0

LATE TULIPS.

	£	s.	d.
Named varieties, per 100, from £5 to	10	0	0
Norwich Black Baguet .. each	0	5	0
Extra fine Mixed, per 100, from named flowers	3	0	0
Fine Mixed .. ditto from 15s. to	1	10	0
Good Border .. ditto	0	12	0
Common ditto .. ditto	0	7	6

	£	s.	d.
Superfine Mixed ...... per 100	1	1	0
Fine ditto ...... ditto	0	15	0
Good ...... ditto 5s. to	0	10	0
Scarlet Turban ...... ditto	0	5	0
Yellow ditto ...... ditto	0	6	0
Black ditto ...... per doz.	0	3	0

AMARYLLISES.

	£	s.	d.
Formosissima ...... per doz.	0	6	0
Johnsonia ...... each	0	5	0
Longifolia Alba ...... ditto	0	3	0
Longifolia Rosea ...... ditto	0	3	0
Regina ...... ditto	0	5	0
Vittata ...... ditto	0	3	6
And others			

IRIS.

	£	s.	d.
Chalcedonian ...... per doz.	0	12	0
Pavonia Major ...... ditto	0	5	0
Persian ...... ditto	0	3	0
English Mixed ...... ditto	0	2	6
Spanish Mixed ...... ditto	0	1	0
English, by name ...... ditto	0	1	0
Spanish, by name ...... ditto	0	0	9

MISCELLANEOUS.

	£	s.	d.
Anomatheca cruenta .. per doz.	0	4	0
Arum Dracunculus .. ditto	0	9	0
Crocus, large Yell Dutch, per100	0	2	0
Large Yellow ...... ditto	0	2	0
Second size ...... ditto	0	1	6
Blue ...... ditto	0	1	6
Ditto Dutch ...... ditto	0	2	6
White ...... ditto	0	2	0

No.	Variety	£	s	d
*27	Pastor Fido	0	0	6
*28	Perruque Royale	0	1	9
*29	Rex Rubrorum	0	2	6
*30	Rose Mignon	0	0	6
*31	Rose Sceptre	0	1	6
32	Rose Surpassante	0	1	3
33	Rouge Bleuatre	0	1	3
*34	Rouge Charmante	0	0	9
35	Rouge Pourpre et Noir	0	3	0
*36	Superbe Royal	0	0	6
37	Velours Rouge	0	5	0
*38	Waterloo	0	1	0

DOUBLE BLUE OF VARIOUS SHADES.

No.	Variety	£	s	d
*39	Activité	0	0	9
*40	A la Mode	0	1	0
*41	Assingaris	0	1	0
*42	Bleu Foncé	0	0	9
43	Bouquet Constant, fine	0	5	0
44	Bouquet Pourpre, fine	0	3	6
*45	Bucentaurs	0	0	9
46	Buonaparte	0	3	6
*47	Commandant	0	2	0
*48	Comte de St. Priest	0	1	0
49	Comte de Very	0	1	3
*50	Duc d'Angoulême	0	1	9
*51	Duc de Normandie	0	1	0
52	Duc Louis de Brunswick	0	1	0
53	Envoyé	0	1	0
*54	Globe Celeste	0	3	6
55	Globe Terrestre	0	1	0
56	Grand Gradelin	0	1	6
*57	Helicon	0	5	0
58	Jupiter	0	2	3
*59	Kroon Van Indien	0	0	6
*60	La Bien Amie	0	0	6
61	La Majesteuse	0	2	0
62	L'Amitié	0	1	6
*63	La Renommée	0	3	0
*64	L'Illustre	0	1	6

No.	Variety	£	s	d
91	Heroine	0	2	6
92	Jeannette	0	1	0
93	La Cherie	0	1	0
*94	La Déesse	0	1	3
95	Miss Kitty	0	3	0
96	Montesquieu	0	1	0
*97	Nannette	0	0	6
98	Og Roi de Basan	0	1	6
*99	Passe Virgo	0	0	6
*100	Penelope	0	0	6
*101	Prince of Waterloo	0	0	6
*102	Prince William Frederick	0	1	3
103	Pyrene, fine	0	2	6
*104	Sphæra Mundi	0	1	3

DOUBLE YELLOW.

No.	Variety	£	s	d
*105	Sultan Achmet	0	1	3
106	Suprema Alba	0	3	0
*107	Triumph Blandina	0	1	3
108	Violet Superbe	0	0	9
*109	Bouquet d'Orange	0	1	0
110	Chrysolora	0	0	9
*111	Duc de Berri d'Or	0	3	0
112	L'Or Vegetable	0	0	9
*113	Louis d'Or	0	1	0
*114	Ophir	0	0	9

SINGLE RED.

No.	Variety	£	s	d
*115	Argus	0	1	0
*116	Charlotte Marianne	0	1	3
117	Felicitas	0	1	6
*118	Henriette Wilhelmina	0	1	3
*119	L'Amie du Cœur	0	2	6
120	La Belle Rose	0	1	9
121	L'Eclair	0	1	0
122	L'Eclatante Parfaite	0	1	0
123	Le Francq van Berkhey	0	4	0
*124	Lord Wellington	0	1	6
*125	Mars	0	3	0
*126	Paix d'Amiens	0	1	6

No.	Variety	£	s	d
*152	Vainqueur	0	1	3
*153	Volaire	0	2	0

MIXED HYACINTHS.

Variety		£	s	d
Double, red	pr.doz.	0	4	0
Ditto, blue	ditto	0	4	0
Ditto, white	ditto	0	4	0

NARCISSUS.

Variety		£	s	d
Bazelman Major	per doz.	0	12	0
Grand Monarque	ditto	0	3	0
Grand Primo Citronier.	ditto	0	4	0
Soleil d'Or	ditto	0	3	0
States General	ditto	0	3	6
Double Roman	ditto	0	4	0
Single Paper White	ditto	0	4	0
Double White Border, per 100		0	3	6
Poets' or Pleasant Eyed	ditto	0	3	6
Mixed Bordered	ditto	0	3	6

JONQUILS.

Variety		£	s	d
Largest Double Dutch, per doz.		0	4	0
Large double ditto	ditto	0	3	0
Single, sweet scented	ditto	0	2	6
Campernelle	ditto	0	2	0

EARLY TULIPS.

Variety		£	s	d
Bruid van Haarlem	per doz.	0	4	0
Charimond	ditto	0	1	6
Duc van Thol,13s.per 100, ditto		0	3	6
Florentine	ditto	0	1	9
Marquis de Weissenrode	ditto	0	12	0
Potterbakker, yellow	ditto	0	3	6
——— striped	ditto	0	4	0
Royal Standard	ditto	0	4	0
White and Red Border.	ditto	0	3	0
Mix'd Parrot	ditto	0	1	6

GLADIOLUS.

Variety		£	s	d
Flori-bundus	per doz.	0	18	0
Psitacinus	ditto	0	3	6
Cardinalis	ditto	0	5	0
Byzantinus	ditto	0	2	6
Communis, fl. alba	ditto	0	3	6
Ditto, ditto cerulea	ditto	0	2	6

IXIAS.

Variety		£	s	d
Bulbicodium	per doz.	0	3	6
Grandiflora	ditto	0	5	0
Tricolor	ditto	0	5	0
Viridiflora	ditto	0	5	0

ANEMONES.

Variety		£	s	d
A collection of 100 sorts, new varieties (never before imported)		7	10	0
Finest mixed double	per lb.	1	10	0
Fine ditto ditto ... ditto 15s. to		1	1	0
Good ditto ditto	ditto	0	10	6
Fen Superbe double Scarlet, per doz.		0	5	0
Josephine, large new scarlet, do.		0	12	0
High Admiral	ditto	0	6	0
Rose Surpassante	ditto	0	12	0
Early single	per lb.	0	6	0
New single	ditto	0	6	0
Single Scarlet	ditto	0	7	6

ANEMONE HORTENSIS.

Variety		£	s	d
Double Red	per doz.	0	5	0
Flore Violaceo	ditto	0	4	0
Single Red	ditto	0	4	0

RANUNCULUS.

Variety		£	s	d
By name, per 100	from	2	10	0
Extra fine Mixed, from named sorts	per 100	1	10	0

Variety		£	s	d
Ditto Cloth of Gold	ditto	0	2	6
Ditto Cloth of Silver	ditto	0	2	6
Saffron	ditto	0	3	0
Scotch	ditto	0	2	6
Mixed Dutch	ditto	0	2	0
Colchicums, double	per doz.	0	3	0
Crown Imperials ... ditto 6s.to		0	3	0
Ditto Crown upon Crown	ditto	0	12	0
Cyclamen Coum	each	0	1	6
Ditto Persicum	ditto	0	1	6
Ditto Europæum, Red	ditto	0	1	6
Ditto Ditto White	ditto	0	2	6
Ditto Hederæfolium	ditto	0	1	0
Dens Canis, White	per doz.	0	4	0
Ditto, Purple	per 100	0	10	0
Feathered Hyacinth	per doz.	0	3	6
Fritillarias	ditto	0	2	6
Grape Hyacinths	ditto	0	3	6
Lily, Guernsey	ditto	0	9	0
Ditto, Bella Donna	ditto	0	10	0
Ditto, Jacobea	ditto	0	6	0
Ditto Tiger	ditto	0	3	6
Ditto Orange	ditto	0	3	6
Ditto Martagon, scarlet	ditto	0	5	0
Ditto ditto white	ditto	0	5	0
Ditto ditto purple	ditto	0	5	0
Ditto ditto yellow	ditto	0	5	0
Ditto Fiery	ditto	0	6	0
Ditto White	ditto	0	6	0
Ditto Superb	each	0	2	0
Ditto Japan	ditto	0	12	0
Pancratium Maritimum, per doz.		0	2	6
Snowdrops, double	per 100	0	2	6
Ditto, single	ditto	0	2	6
Scilla Peruviana	per doz.	0	9	0
Summer Snow-flake	ditto	0	5	0
Tuberoses, double	ditto	0	5	0
Trigidia Pavonia	ditto	0	3	0
Ditto Conchiflora	each	0	1	0
Winter Aconites	per 100	0	6	0
Alstromeria seed, several sorts per packet		0	3	6

October and November are considered the most proper Months for Planting Hyacinths in Beds or Pots; or placing them in Glasses, to bloom in Water.

LADIES AND GENTLEMEN, IN GIVING ORDERS FOR HYACINTHS, ARE REQUESTED TO SPECIFY WHETHER THEY ARE INTENDED FOR EARTH OR WATER.

Garden Seeds carefully selected, and properly packed for all Climates.

DAHLIAS FOR EXPORTATION, &c. OF THE NEWEST AND BEST VARIETIES.

CARNATIONS, PINKS, &c.

A MOST INTERESTING provincial catalogue, fully priced, for trees and shrubs has been discovered by Mr. Francis W. Steer in the muniments of His Grace the Duke of Norfolk, who has kindly given permission for it to be reproduced here. It is important for two main reasons: firstly that it emanates from a leading firm, Mackie, of which a good deal is known; secondly, that its prices can be quite closely compared with those given for 1837-38 by J.C. Loudon as an appendix to his *Arboretum et Fruticetum Britannicum.* Loudon stresses the fact that the catalogues were prepared 'before the severe frost of January, 1838, which destroyed many thousands of ligneous plants in British nurseries . . .' The prices therefore remain comparable with those appearing in Mackie's Norwich catalogue of 1833. This is confirmed by the Norwich prices being sometimes higher, but frequently lower, than the London rates quoted by Loudon from the list of what was sold by Richard Forrest, successor to W. Malcolm & Co's Kensington Nursery.

Before proceeding to consideration of Mackie's list, it is worth mentioning that a number of lists and catalogues, mostly unpriced, have already been republished in this particular field. On account of the botanical interest of the introductions made by John Fraser (1750-1811), several of his lists were carefully preserved, covering both seeds and plants brought by him from America. Three of these have been reprinted, those of c. 1790 and 1796 in the *Journal of Botany* (XXXVII, 1899, 481-7; XLIII, 1905, 329-31), and a catalogue of 1813, issued by Fraser's sons after his death, in *Pittonia* (II, 1890, 116-19). Though they show what was becoming available in the way of new introductions around the turn of the century, these lists are much less relevant to the problem of what was actually being grown in normal gardens. In that respect much more can be gleaned from the surviving list of John Cree junior, covering what was sold by the Addlestone Nursery in 1829. (See *Gardener's Chronicle*, 14 July 1928, 30). This too, however, is untypical in that it is not only a metropolitan nursery within the London region, but one founded by the botanical and highly specialized nurseryman who, as has been seen, was supplying Kew Gardens with new rarities in 1768. (p. 49)

The firm of Mackie is fully representative of a substantial group of major provincial nurseries founded in the last third of the eighteenth century, about 100 years after Brompton Park and the great York Nursery. Such firms were Caldwell of Knutsford, Cheshire, and Pennell of Lincoln, already mentioned (pp. 50, 51), both founded in 1780; Joyce and Falla, both at Gateshead and founded by 1754 and 1734 respectively; and Littlewood of Handsworth by Sheffield, founded before 1779. The Norwich Nursery was formed about 1773 by John Mackie (died 1797), and had become significant within 15 or 20 years of the start. It was continued by the founder's two sons, William Aram Mackie (died 1817) and John Mackie junior (died 1818), then by Sarah

Mackie, William's widow, until her death in 1833, when their son Frederick Mackie took over. At the time of his mother's death Frederick, who had evidently begun to manage the business, had just acquired the unique collection of cacti and other succulents formed by Thomas Hitchen of Norwich (*The Gardener's Magazine*, IX, 1833, 751; Paxton's *Magazine of Botany*, I, 1834, 49; IV, 67-8, 89). This explains the concluding note in the catalogue here reprinted.

Mackies' Nursery was at Lakenham, south of the city, and reclaimed a large area that had been open waste land: it was in fact regarded as an outstanding example of the regeneration of virtually unprofitable land. Its large extent enabled a very wide variety of forest trees of all sizes, as well as Fruit Trees and Ornamental trees, shrubs and Evergreens, to be grown, and the list of 1833 is specifically only an abstract sheet catalogue, not an exhaustive one of all stock held. Even so, it includes 30 kinds of Forest Trees, besides 'all the most approved kinds' of each of a dozen sorts of Fruit Trees, as well as small fruit; some 50 varieties of Evergreens; and well over 200 Ornamental Trees and Shrubs, about 100 of which appear in the separate category of American Plants. Beyond this, a general note refers to an extensive collection of Geraniums, Dahlias, Camellias and Green-House plants, bulbs, and garden and agricultural seeds.

Nomenclature has not advanced much beyond the stage reached in the Telford and Perfect catalogues of two generations earlier. There is the same mixture of English names for common plants, Latin names for the more recent introductions and for most of the American plants, and here and there a time-honoured cognomen like Althaea Frutex or Alaternus. Some improvements had taken place: 'Persian Jasmine' has at last become Persian Lilac, and Taccamahacca has joined its congeners as the Tacamahac Poplar. There are still what seem to be trade names, now forgotten, such as the Chichester and Hertfordshire Elms, while the 'Caerulean' Willow is presumably what is now known as the Cricket-Bat Willow, whose varietal or hybrid status appears to be in doubt. On the whole the difficulties of identification have greatly diminished, as might be expected.

The prices are of interest both for their comparison with those of earlier and later dates, and because of their curious discrepancies when set against Loudon's reprints of 1837-38. A marked feature is the great drop in price of many Forest Trees as compared with the levels of 1775. For seedling Ash, one year old, Telfords had charged 10s. per thousand; these now cost only 4s.; transplanted Beech, 3 feet high, had come down from 15s. to 5s. per hundred; Wych Elm at 2 feet had been 5s. per hundred; at 2 − 3 feet were now only 30s. a thousand. Seedling Scotch Firs had fallen even more, at two years old being only 4s. per thousand against 15s. in 1775; transplanted trees, one foot high, had been 7s. 6d. a hundred; in the 9 to 12-inch range they could now be had for 15s. a thousand. This contrasts markedly with some prices of Ornamental Shrubs: whereas Mezereons had cost 4d. or 6d. each, according to colour, they were in 1833 up to 9s. a dozen. Even the common White Jasmine, formerly 3d. each, had gone to 4s. a dozen; on the other hand, Syringa had stayed the same price, 3d. each in 1775, 3s. a dozen in 1833.

Loudon gave reprints of the catalogues of Richard Forrest of London, and of Peter Lawson & Son of Edinburgh, as well as of two overseas nurseries: the

Brothers Baumann at Bollwyller (Haut Rhin), north-west of Mulhouse; and
James Booth & Sons at Flottbeck Nurseries, Hamburg. The list of Seeds of
Trees and Shrubs sold by George Charlwood, of 14 Tavistock Row, Covent
Garden, was also reprinted by Loudon. This last shows that seed of Silver Fir,
which had cost 2s. an ounce in 1695, was now only 3s. a lb. In 1758 Telfords
had supplied seed of Scotch Fir for Brandsby at 1s. an ounce; in 1837 it was
3s. a lb. Before leaving the subject of Charlwood's catalogue of seeds it may
be remarked that it stocked many kinds at 1s. a packet, many species Roses
at 6d. a packet, and some flowering shrubs by the ounce at prices such as 1s.
for Clethra alnifolia, 2s. for Catalpa, 2s. 6d. for Bignonia (Campsis radicans),
and varying by species for Andromedas (1s. 6d. to 2s. 6d. per ounce), Kalmias
(2s. to 2s. 6d.), Magnolias (1s. 6d. up to 5s.) and Rhododendrons (1s. to 3s.
6d.). Cheaper seeds were sold in some cases by the pound, e.g. Cupressus
sempervirens or C. stricta, Hibiscus syriacus, or Spanish Broom (Spartium
junceum) all at 6s.; Pinus pinaster or Thuja occidentalis at 4s.; or by dry
measure. Thus Common Maple (Acer campestre) was 5s. a bushel, and A.
pseudo-platanus only 4s., as were Betula alba and pendula; so was Common
Ash, while eight other species of Fraxinus were to be had at 4s. a quart.
Among the Oaks, acorns of Quercus pedunculata cost 5s. a bushel, but those
of Q. sessiliflora 7s. 6d.

In conclusion, a few comparisons may be made with the London and
Edinburgh prices of 1837 given by Loudon, to demonstrate the desirability of
shopping around at that period. As far as possible, precisely similar Seedlings
(S.) or Transplanted trees or shrubs (Tr.) have been chosen to illustrate this
variation.

Forest Trees		*Norwich* *Mackie*	*London* *Forrest*	*Edinburgh* *Lawson*
Acacia, S.	per 1000	15/-	15/-	15/-
Acacia, Tr.	100	7/6	10/-	50/-
Ash Tr.	1000	20/-	10/-	15/-
Beech Tr.	1000	20/-	40/-	20/-
Elm, Wych Tr.	1000	20/-	15/-	15/-
Fir, Scotch Tr.	1000	10/-	10/-	7/6
Hornbeam Tr.	1000	30/-	50/-	—
Larch Tr.	1000	14/-	10/-	6/-
Lime Tr.	100	15/-	20/-	5/- — 20/-
Oak, S. 2 year	1000	6/-	10/-	3/-
Oak, Tr. 1-1½ ft	1000	20/-	—	17/6
Sycamore Tr.	1000	15/-	15/-	12/6

Ornamental Trees and Shrubs				
Bay, Sweet	each	/6	/6	/6
Cotoneaster microphylla		1/-	1/6	1/6
Fothergilla alnifolia		2/-	1/- — 1/6	1/6
Gaultheria procumbens		1/-	1/-	/6
Gaultheria shallon		2/6	1/6 — 2/6	1/-
Holly, variegated		/9 — 1/-	1/6 — 2/6	1/- — 1/6
Hydrangea quercifolia		1/6	3/6	1/6
Kalmia latifolia		2/6 — 3/6	1/- — 5/-	2/6

Paeonia moutan	3/6 — 5/-	3/6 — 10/6	3/6 — 5/-
Rhododendron maximum	2/6	1/6 — 2/-	/9 — 2/-
Rhododendron ponticum	1/- — 1/6	1/- — 2/6	/6 — 2/-
Spiraea ariaefolia	1/6	2/6	1/6
Tulip Tree	1/3 — 1/6	/9 — 1/-	1/-

Fruit Trees		*Norwich* *Mackie*	*Edinburgh* *Lawson*
Apple, dwarf on Crab stock	each	1/-	/9
Apple, dwarf on Paradise stock		1/6	1/-
Apple, standard		1/6	1/-
Cherry, dwarf		1/6	1/-
Cherry, standard		2/-	1/- — 1/6
Medlar, dwarf		1/6	1/-
Medlar, standard		2/-	2/6
Mulberry, dwarf		3/6	—
Mulberry, standard		7/6 — 10/6	2/6 — 7/6
Peach, dwarf		2/-	1/6
Peach, standard, trained		9/- — 10/6	7/6 — 10/-
Pear or Plum, dwarf		1/6	1/-
Pear or Plum, standard		2/-	1/- — 1/6

The concluding note following Mackie's catalogue, remarking on the opening of the New Cut navigation channel from Norwich, is of particular interest. Mackie refers to regular vessels plying both to London and to the North of England, and was evidently hoping to reach new customers spread over a very wide area. Whereas in the late 17th century it was the difficulty of transport that led to the setting up of the first large nurseries in the provinces, improved transport now made it possible for provincial nurseries to compete on favourable terms for custom in all parts.

NORWICH NURSERY.

F. MACKIE'S

PRICES FOR AUTUMN, 1883.

SEEDLING FOREST TREES.

Tree	Per / Age	s.	d.
ACACIA	⅌ 1000, 1 year	12	0
	2 year	15	0
ALDER	2 year	5	0
ASH	1 year	4	0
BLACKTHORN	2 year	6	0
CHESNUT, Spanish	1 year	10	0
CRAB	1 year	5	0
ELM, Wych	2 year	6	0
FIR, Scotch	2 year	4	0
FIR, Norway Spruce, beded,	⅌ 1000,	5	0
—Larch	2 year	5	0
—Silver, beded		7	0
HAZEL	1 year	8	0
HOLLY	2 year	7	0
MAPLE	1 year	5	0
OAK	2 year	6	0
	1 year	5	0
	2 year	6	0
OAK, Levant	⅌ 1000, 2 year	15	0
PRIVET	2 year	7	6
SWEET BRIAR	1 year	6	6
	2 year	7	6
SYCAMORE	1 year	4	6
WHIN, Furze or Gorse	2 year	7	6
WHITETHORN	1 year	5	0
	2 year	5	0

TRANSPLANTED FOREST TREES.

Tree	Per / Size	s.	d.
ACACIA	⅌ 100, 2 to 3 ft.	7	6
	3 to 4 ft.	8	0
ALDER	4 to 5 ft.	10	0
	⅌ 1000, 1½ to 2 ft.	15	0
	2 to 3 ft.	20	0
	3 to 4 ft.	25	0
ASH	1 to 1½ ft.	15	0
	1½ to 2 ft.	20	0
	2½ to 3 ft.	25	0
BEECH	1½ to 2 ft.	20	0
	2½ to 3 ft.	30	0
	3 to 4 ft.	5	0
BIRCH	4 to 5 ft.	8	0
	⅌ 100, 1 to 2 ft.	25	0
	⅌ 1000, 2 to 3 ft.	30	0
	3 to 4 ft.	35	0
FIR, Larch	4 to 5 ft.	6	0
—Scotch	⅌ 1000, 6 to 9 in.	10	0
	9 to 12 in.	15	0
—Norway Spruce	1 to 1½ ft.	20	0
	1½ to 2 ft.	5	0
	⅌ 100, 2 to 3 ft.	5	0
—Silver	⅌ 1000, 1 to 1½ ft.	30	0
	⅌ 100, 2 ft.	5	0
HAZEL	⅌ 1000, 1 to 1½ ft.	15	0
	1½ to 2 ft.	20	0
	2 to 3 ft.	25	0
	⅌ 100, 3 to 4 ft.	5	0
HOLLY	⅌ 1000, 6 to 9 in.	20	0
	1 ft.	30	0
	⅌ 100, 1 to 2 ft.	7	6
HORNBEAM	⅌ 1000, 2 to 3 ft.	30	0
POPLAR, Black Italian }	⅌ 1000, 2 to 3 ft.	20	0
	3 to 4 ft.	25	0
	4 to 5 ft.	40	0
	⅌ 100, 5 to 6 ft.	10	0
Canada	⅌ 1000, 4 to 5 ft.	25	0
	⅌ 100, 5 to 6 ft.	45	0
	6 to 8 ft.	10	0
Black English,	⅌ 1000, 2 to 3 ft.	15	0
	3 to 4 ft.	25	0
Ontario	⅌ 100, 2 to 3 ft.	30	0
	3 to 4 ft.	5	0
	5 to 6 ft.	8	0
SYCAMORE	⅌ 1000, 1 to 2 ft.	15	0
	2 to 3 ft.	25	0

		s.	d.
.... Spanish	1½ to 2 ft.	25	0
....	1½ to 2 ft.	30	0
ELM, Wych	1½ to 2 ft.	20	0
....	2 to 3 ft.	30	0
FIR, Larch	1 to 1½ ft.	14	0
....	1½ to 2 ft.	14	0
....	2 to 3 ft.	25	0
.... ₱ 100,	3 to 4 ft.	4	0

		s.	d.
MAPLE	1½ to 2 ft.	25	0
....			
.... ₱ 100,			
OAK .... ₱ 1000,	1 to 1½ ft.	20	0
....			
....			
....			
.... ₱ 100,	3 to 4 ft.	4	0

		s.	d.
WILLOW, Cerulean	2 to 3 ft.	20	0
....	3 to 4 ft.	25	0
.... ₱ 100,	4 to 6 ft.	4	0
Bedford .... ₱ 1000,	2 to 3 ft.	20	0
....	3 to 4 ft.	25	0
.... ₱ 100,	4 to 6 ft.	4	0
WHITETHORN ...... ₱ 1000,		8	0
.... fine		10	6

ORNAMENTAL TREES AND SHRUBS.

		s.	d.
ACACIA, 3-thorned, ₱ 100,	2 to 3 ft.	30	0
—horrid thorned	4 to 5 ft.	40	0
AILANTHUS glandulosa	₱ doz.	18	0
ALMOND, double blossomed		18	0
—dwarf		18	0
—Siberian		18	0
—macrocarpa		24	0
ALDER, cut-leaved, ₱ 100,	3 to 4 ft.	30	0
....	4 to 5 ft.	50	0
—gooseberry-leaved	2 to 3 ft.	30	0
....	3 to 4 ft.	50	0
ARALIA spinosa	₱ doz.	24	0
ALLSPICE	₱ doz.	12	0
ALTHÆA Frutex	each	9	0
ASH, weeping	each	2	4
BARBERRY	₱ doz.	9	0
BEECH, purple	2 to 3 ft.	12	0
....	3 to 4 ft.	15	0
....	4 to 5 ft.	18	0
....	4 to 6 ft.	24	0
—fern leaved	2 to 3 ft.	24	0
BLADDER Nut	2 to 3 ft.		1
BIRD Cherry	1 to 5 ft.	6	9
—Virginian ...... ₱ 100,	3 to 4 ft.	3	3
BLADDER Senna	₱ 100,	12	0
BUCKTHORN	₱ doz.	4	0
—sea	6	18	0
CALYCA...	3 to 4 ft.	18	0
CYPRESS, deciduous		6	0
CANDLEBERRY Myrtle			

		s.	d.
ELM, Chichester .. ₱ 100,	4 to 5 ft.	15	0
—Dutch	7 to 8 ft.	30	0
EUONYMUS	₱ doz.	4	0
FILBERTS, of sorts, ₱ 100,	3 to 4 ft.	25	0
GALE, fern leaved	₱ doz.	9	0
GUELDER Roses	₱ 100	25	0
HYDRANGEA, Oak leaved	₱ doz.	18	0
—arborescens		9	0
HONEYSUCKLE, Tartarian		6	0
JUDAS Tree		9	0
JUGLANS nigra		4	0
JESSAMINE, white		4	0
—revolutum		9	0
LABURNUM ...... ₱ 100,	4 to 5 ft.	12	0
....	5 to 6 ft.	20	0
—Scotch	5 to 6 ft.	15	0
....	5 to 6 ft.	20	0
—Weeping	each	2	6
—Purple		2	6
—Oak leaved		2	6
LILACS ...... ₱ 100,		9	0
—Siberian		30	0
—White		9	0
—Persian	₱ doz.	9	0
LIMES ...... ₱ 100,	3 to 4 ft.	15	0
....	4 to 5 ft.	20	0
....	6 to 8 ft.	25	0
....	8 to 10 ft.	30	0
LAURUS, Benzoin		10	6
LIQUIDAMBER	₱ doz.	12	0
MAPLE, Ash leaved		6	0

		s.	d.
PLANES, Oriental, ₱ doz.	6 to 8 ft.	20	0
—Undulated	2 to 3 ft.	18	0
....	3 to 4 ft.	12	0
PEACH, double blossomed		18	0
PÆONY, Tree ...... each 3s. 6d. to		5	0
POPLAR, Carolina	₱ doz.	9	0
—Tacamahac		6	0
—Abele ...... ₱ 100,	4 to 5 ft.	10	0
....	5 to 6 ft.	15	0
—Lombardy	4 to 5 ft.	20	0
....	5 to 6 ft.	25	0
—Green	2 to 4 ft.	4	0
....	4 to 6 ft.	8	0
PTELIA, trifoliata	₱ doz.	6	0
PYRUS, japonica red		9	0
—white		12	0
—spectabilis		18	0
RHAMNUS, latifolius		6	0
—alnifolius		9	0
RIBES, aureum		9	0
—sanguineum ...... 18s. to		24	0
ROBINIA, inermis		18	0
—glutinosa		12	0
—tortuosa		18	0
ROBINIA, monstrosa		12	0
ROSE, acacia		12	0
SNOWBERRY ...... ₱ 100,		16	0
SNOWDROP TREE	₱ doz.	18	0
SPIRÆA, ariæfolia	each	1	6
—daurica		1	6
—crenata		1	6
—bella	₱ doz.	12	0

	s.	d.
Cherry, weeping, stands	18	0
—dwarfs	12	0
—double blossomed	18	0
—cornelian	4	0
Chestnut, Horse, ℔ 100, 3 to 4 ft.	12	6
—4 to 5 ft.	15	0
—℔ doz. 10 to 12 ft.	18	0
—scarlet	18	0
—yellow	24	0
—rose	4	0
Cytisus nigricans	3	0
—evergreen	6	0
Dogwood, of sorts ℔ 100,	25	0
Elm, Hertfordshire, 2 to 3 ft.	10	0
—3 to 4 ft.	12	6
—4 to 5 ft.	15	0
—5 to 6 ft.	25	0
—Chichester, 2 to 3 ft.	10	0
—3 to 4 ft.	12	6

	s.	d.
MEZERION	18	0
MOUNTAIN ASH .. ℔ 100, 2 to 3 ft.	9	0
—4 to 5 ft.	5	0
—6 to 7 ft.	7	6
—7 to 10 ft.	12	6
MULBERRY, White ℔ doz.	6	0
OAK, Scarlet American .. 2 to 3 ft.	6	0
—3 to 4 ft.	12	0
—Levant ℔ 100, 4 to 5 ft.	18	0
—1 to 2 ft.	6	0
—2 to 3 ft.	12	0
PLANES ℔ doz. 3 to 4 ft.	20	0
—4 to 5 ft.	35	0
—10 to 12 ft.	40	0
—Oriental 3 to 4 ft.	3	0
—4 to 5 ft.	5	0
—6 to 8 ft.	9	0
—3 to 4 ft.	12	0
—4 to 6 ft.	15	0

	s.	d.
—trilobata	9	0
—levigata	6	0
—sorbifolia	6	0
—salicifolia	4	0
SOPHORA, japonica	9	0
SUMACH, Stags Horn	6	0
—Venice	4	0
SYRINGA	3	0
THORNS, a choice variety, Dwarfs	12	0
—Stands	18	0
—New Scarlet	15	0
TULIP TREE 4 to 5 ft.	18	0
—5 to 6 ft.	46	0
WALNUTS, ℔ 100, 4 to 5 ft.	5	0
—6 to 8 ft.	15	0
—8 to 10 ft.	24	0
WEEPING WILLOW ℔ doz. 9s. to	12	0
—ring leaved	12	0

With many others too numerous for a sheet catalogue.

EVERGREENS.

	s.	d.
FIR, Pinaster in pots,	9	0
—Black American Spruce, ℔ 100 } 2 to 3 ft.	15	0
—3 to 4 ft.	20	0
—Weymouth	12	0
—Stone Pines ℔ doz. ℔ 100,	9	0
—Balm of Gilead ℔ 100,	8	0
—Siberian Stone Pine, ℔ doz. in pots,	24	0
—Hemlock Spruce	18	0
FURZE, double blossomed 9s. to	12	0
HOLLY, variegated 9s. to	12	0
IVY, Irish, ℔ 100,	25	0
JUNIPER 1 to 1½ ft.	15	0
—2 to 3 ft.	25	0
—Swedish ℔ doz.	6	0
LAUREL ℔ 100, 1 to 1½ ft.	16	0
—1½ to 2 ft.	20	0
—Portugal 1 to 1½ ft.	25	0
—1 to 1½ ft.	30	0
—1½ to 2 ft.	40	0
—Alexandrian ℔ doz.	9	0

	s.	d.
LAURUSTINES ℔ 100, 1 to 2 ft.	25	0
—shining leaved 2 to 3 ft.	30	0
LAVENDER ℔ doz.	6	0
—cotton	3	0
OAK, Luccombes 3 to 4 ft.	18	0
—Fulham 18s. to	24	0
—evergreen in pots, 12s. to	15	0
—holly leaved	18	0
PHILLYREAS from pots, 12s. to	15	0
PHOTINIA, serrulata 9s. to	12	0
PRIVET, Evergreen ℔ 100, 1½ to 2 ft.	8	0
—2 to 3 ft.	12	0
—Chinese ℔ doz.	12	0
PYRACANTHA	9	0
TAMARISK, German	3	0
—French	3	0
YEW 1 to 1½ ft.	12	0
—1½ to 2 ft.	18	0
YUCCA, filamentosa	18	0
—recurvifolia	18	0
—flaccida	18	0

	s.	d.
ALATERNUS ℔ doz.	12	0
—variegated	18	0
ARBOR VITÆ, American	4	0
—Chinese	9	0
ARBUTUS	12	0
ARISTOTELIA, Maqui	9	0
—variegata	12	0
AUCUBA, japonica	9	0
BAYS, sweet	9	0
BROOM, yellow Spanish	4	0
—white Portugal	6	0
BOX, Tree ℔ 100, 1½ to 2 ft.	15	0
—2 to 3 ft.	20	0
—℔ doz. 3 to 4 ft.	6	0
CEDAR, Red Virginian .. 1 to 1½ ft.	9	0
—2 to 3 ft.	40	0
CEDAR OF LEBANON, ℔ doz. 6in. in pots,	9	0
—1 to 1½ ft.	24	0
—1½ to 2 ft.	30	0
COTONEASTER, microphylla	12	0
CYPRESS 9s. to	12	0

AMERICAN PLANTS.

Plant	s.	d.
ANDROMEDA polifolia .... each	1	0
——paniculata	1	0
——racemosa	—	6
——pulverulenta	2	6
——catesbæi	2	6
——acuminata	2	6
——coriacea	3	0
——axillaris	2	6
——pilulifera	2	6
——serratifolia	2	6
——cassinefolia	1	6
——calyculata	—	6
——globosa, with many others .... ℔ doz.	12	0
AZALEA Pontica .... ℔ doz. .... each	3	6
.... alba .... each	3	6
.... glauca	1	5
.......;. tricolor	—	0
——viscosa	2	6
———— rubescens	1	6
———— grandiflora	2	6
——floribunda	1	6
——coccinea	—	6
——— major	5	0
——autumnalis rubra	2	6
——aurantia	5	0
——— maxima	3	0
——calendulacea	2	6
.... major	3	6
.... crocea	5	0
——tricolor	7	6
——bicolor	2	6
——new Salmon	2	6
——Bagshot, red	—	0
Thirty Choice Ghent Azaleas, with } many others	12	0
DAPHNE cneorum	2	0

Plant	s.	d.
DAPHNE Pontica .... each	1	0
——hybrida	2	6
——gnidium	2	6
——collina	2	0
ERICA arborea	2	0
——australis	1	6
——multiflora rubra ...... ℔ doz.	9	0
——alba	9	0
——herbacea	12	0
——mediterranea	12	0
——scoparia	9	0
——stricta	9	0
——Vagans pleno .... each	1	6
FOTHERGILLA alnifolia	2	0
FRINGE Tree	2	6
GAULTHERIA procumbens ... ℔ doz.	12	0
——Shallon, ... each	2	6
KALMIA latifolia ...... 2s. 6d. to	3	6
——angustifolia	1	6
.... rubra	1	6
.... nana	1	6
——glauca	1	6
LEDUM latifolium	1	6
——angustifolium	1	6
——buxifolium	2	0
——thymifolium	1	6
MAGNOLIA grandiflora ...... each	8	6
.... Exmouth ... 3s. 6d. to	5	6
——conspicua ...... 5s. 6d. to	7	6
——Thomsoniana	2	6
——purpurea	2	6
——tripetala	3	6
——acuminata	12	0
——glauca ...... 2s. 6d. to	1	6
MENZIESIA polifolia ...... ℔ doz.	5	0
——atropurpurea ...... each	2	6

Plant	s.	d.
MENZIESIA pumila .... each	2	6
——globularis	1	6
POLYGALA chamæbuxus	1	6
RHODODENDRON maximum	2	6
——Catawbiense	5	0
——dauricum atrovirens .. 3s. 6d. to	18	0
——ferrugineum ...... ℔ doz.	9	0
——hirsutum	18	0
——arboreum .... each 7s. 6d. to	10	6
——laurifolium	5	0
——magnoliæfolium	5	6
——Smithii, scarlet	7	6
——punctatum	2	6
——algarvense	3	6
——myrtifolitm	3	0
——azaleoides	2	0
——ponticum ...... ℔ doz.	12	0
.... fine	18	0
RHODORA canadensis	18	6
VACCINIUM Vitis Idæa ...... each	1	6
——uliginosum	1	6
——myrtillus	1	6
——amænum	1	6
——virgatum	1	0
——— Arctostaphylos	2	6
——resinosum	1	6
——frondosum	8	6
——sibiricum	5	6
——dumosum	7	6
——nitidun	2	6
——corymbosum	2	6
——fuscatum	3	6
——buxifolium	12	0
——erythrocarpum	2	6
——venustum	2	6

FRUIT TREES.

INCLUDING ALL THE MOST APPROVED KINDS FROM THE LONDON HORTICULTURAL SOCIETY.

		s.	d.
APPLES, dwarf, on Paradise Stocks, } each		1	6
—dwarf, on Crab ditto		1	0
—espaliers		2	6
—standards		1	6
APRICOTS, maiden, dwarfs		2	6
—dwarf, trained	6s. 0d. to	7	6
—standard, ditto	9s. 0d. to	10	0
CHERRIES, dwarfs		1	6
—standards		2	0
—espaliers		4	0
—standard, trained		5	0
CURRANTS, White, Red, & Black, ℔ doz.		4	0
FIGS, of sorts	each	2	0

		s.	d.
GOOSEBERRIES	℔ doz.	4	0
MEDLARS, dwarfs	each	1	6
—standards		2	6
MULBERRIES, dwarfs		3	6
—standards	7s. 6d. to	10	6
—espaliers		5	0
NECTARINES, maiden, dwarfs		2	6
—dwarf, trained	6s. 0d. to	7	6
—standard, ditto	9s. 0d. to	10	0
PEACHES, maiden, dwarfs		2	6
—dwarf, trained	6s. 0d. to	7	6
—standard, ditto	9s. 0d. to	10	0
PEARS, dwarfs		1	6
—standards		2	0

		s.	d.
PEARS, espaliers	each	4	0
—standard, trained		5	6
—dwarfs, on Quince Stocks		2	6
PLUMS, dwarfs		3	6
—standards		2	0
—espaliers		4	0
—standard, trained		5	6
QUINCE, dwarfs		2	0
—standards		2	6
RASPBERRIES, of sorts	℔ 100,	15	0
STRAWBERRIES, ditto	2s. 6d. to	5	0
VINES, in pots	each 1s. 6d. to	5	6
—very choice	3s. 6d. to	5	0

	£	s.	d.
Evergreen and Flowering Shrubs, in a large and beautiful collection, the sorts being left to my choice. ℔ 100, 1l. 0s. 0d. }	1	5	0

Roses of sorts ℔ 100, 1l. 0s. 0d.

	£	s.	d.
American Plants, in a numerous and beautiful variety, the selection being left to my choice. ℔ 100 }	5	0	0

Ditto, choice 1l. 10s. 0d.   Ditto, more choice 2l. 10s. 0d.

	£	s.	d.
Fine Perennial Plants for Borders, in a large and handsome assortment, the selection being left to my choice. ℔ 100) }	2	10	0

Ditto, fine and rare 5l. 0s. 0d.

Genuine Fruit Trees of every kind.

Russia Mats, Netting & Bunting for Fruit Trees, Fine Mushroom Spawn.

AN EXTENSIVE & CHOICE COLLECTION OF GERANIUMS, DAHLIAS, CAMELLIAS, & GREEN-HOUSE PLANTS IN GENERAL.

FINE DUTCH HYACINTHS, AND OTHER ROOTS, FOR GLASSES & FORCING.

BUDDING'S PATENT MOWING MACHINE. PRUNING KNIVES. FINE FORCING POTATOES.

GARDEN AND AGRICULTURAL SEEDS;

AND A COLLECTION OF THE MOST APPROVED KINDS OF GRASSES FOR LAWNS & PERMANENT PASTURES.

WITH EVERY OTHER ARTICLE IN THE NURSERY AND SEED TRADES.

A TABLE

SHEWING THE NUMBER OF PLANTS REQUIRED FOR AN ACRE OF LAND,

From One Foot to Twenty Feet Distance Plant from Plant.

DISTANCE. Ft. In.		DISTANCE. Ft. In.		DISTANCE. Ft. In.	
1 0	43,560	5 0	1,742	9 0	537
2 0	10,890	6 0	1,210	10 0	435
3 0	4,840	7 0	889	15 0	193
4 0	2,722	8 0	680	20 0	108

NORWICH NURSERY, OCTOBER 1st, 1833.

In handing the list of prices for the present year, F. Mackie thinks it necessary to inform his Friends at a distance, that from the present date there is the opportunity of a water communication from the city of Norwich to any Port in England; as the line of the new navigation is now completed and opened, regular vessels are appointed for London and the North of England, so that he thinks the friends of this Nursery will now be enabled to receive their plants as regularly and cheaply as can be desired, and that the great obstacles formerly operating against the conveyance of heavy goods, from the expence and delay attending it, will now be done away.

The stock of Forest and Fruit Trees is at this time ample and excellent in quality, the Herbaceous and Evergreen part is in great variety, and the curious in Succulent plants are informed that the stock of this kind, which has been thought by competent judges to be the most rare and valuable in the kingdom, is now added to this Nursery; of these plants, a separate catalogue is preparing for the inspection of the Public, which may be had on application at the Nursery, or at the Warehouse, at No. 10, Exchange Street, Norwich.

All orders left at No. 10, Exchange Street, directly opposite the Corn Exchange, will be immediately forwarded to the Nursery.

L*

CLASSIFICATION OF MODERN LISTS

NO ATTEMPT has been made in this book to carry the story of gardening catalogues beyond the accession of Queen Victoria in 1837. Nevertheless it is a matter of interest that lists of the present day continue to fall into different categories of classification. Firstly there is the division into firms that are primarily Seedsmen, and those mainly or exclusively Nurserymen. In each category examples taken from leading firms will be given, but it must be understood that many lists show special characteristics or single out individual products of the firm as classes by themselves, quite apart from the general method of classification; no attempt is made here to take account of such idiosyncracies. The catalogues examined are a chance collection of the last few years, but it is not to be inferred that the method of arrangement here discussed is necessarily that now adopted by the firm.

Seedsmen
The catalogues of Seedsmen can be divided into three main classes:

Class I The single Alphabetical List, in which seeds of Trees, Shrubs, Herbaceous and Bulbous plants all appear together. In fact I have not found an example of such a list in a 'pure' state, but until 1969 Messrs. Thompson & Morgan of Ipswich included in one alphabetical order everything (even Fern spore) except Ornamental Grasses and Vegetable seeds.

Class II This category includes a substantial majority of all seedsmen's lists, and is based on a main division into Flower and Vegetable Seeds, together with additional groups of e.g. Bulbs, Plants, Lawn Grass, and sometimes nurserymen's stock, culinary plants and the like. This class can be subdivided according to the treatment of the list of Vegetable seeds:

Class II A Single list of Vegetable Seeds, though normally including the heading 'Herbs' alphabetically under 'H. Examples: Messrs. Bees of Liverpool (Flowers subdivided: Greenhouse/Garden) Messrs. Ryders of St. Albans Messrs. Suttons of Reading (Potatoes classified separately) Messrs. Toogoods of Southampton (Culinary Plants and Roots, and Potatoes, as separate classifications)

Class II B Vegetable Seeds arranged in separate classes, with Herbs independently listed from the general alphabetical order and usually Peas and Beans also in separate categories. Examples: Messrs. Alexander & Brown of Perth (Sweet Peas separately) Messrs. J.W. Boyce of Soham (Uncommon Vegetables listed separately; additional list for commercial growers) Messrs.

Carters of Raynes Park (Sweet Peas separately) Messrs. Unwins of Histon
Sweet Peas separately; Potatoes)

Class III This class subdivides Flower Seeds culturally by status as Hardy
Annuals, Half-Hardy, Greenhouse, etc. The class may be further divided
according to whether the list of Vegetable Seeds is simple or subdivided.

Class III A Vegetable Seeds all in a single alphabetical list: Messrs. Thomas
Butcher of Croydon

Class III B Vegetable Seeds subdivided: Messrs. S. Dobie of Chester (Peas &
Beans; Herbs, separate) Messrs. Thompson & Morgan of Ipswich (from 1970)
(Herbs as an alphabetical section in general list; Peas & Beans separate) .

It will be seen that Class I is fundamentally derived from the type of Gerard's
1596 list of the plants growing in his garden. The other two classes represent
the classificatory tradition of the 'Fromond' list of c. 1500 and their direct
ancestor seems to be the Lucas list. The 'A' categories, Class II A and Class III
A, have become simplified by reducing the Vegetable Seeds to a single list,
except for the vestigial class of Herbs kept together under the letter 'H'. The
'B' categories retain to a greater or less degree the principle of subdivisions of
Vegetable Seeds. Class III has adopted the cultural classification of Flower
Seeds which was an innovation in the second half of the 18th century, found
in the works of Richard Weston and in the London catalogues of William
Malcolm, Luker & Smith and others.

Nurserymen
Classification is possible on much the same general principles as with the lists
of Seedsmen, but there are really only two classes:

Class I The single Alphabetical List, mainly adopted by nurseries specializing
in only one main aspect of the whole field. Examples: Bodnant Garden
Nursery of Tal-y-Cafn (Trees, Shrubs, Conifers etc.) Edrom Nursery of
Coldingham (Rock Garden Plants, Shrubs, etc.)

Class II This class includes all classified lists, but falls into three categories
according to the amount of subdivision. There are four main classes
represented in the lists of most general nurserymen: (a) Trees and Shrubs; (b)
Roses; (c) Fruit Trees; (d) Herbaceous and Alpine Plants. Sometimes a class is
omitted and in other cases additional classes appear.

Class II A Lists with main classes only: Slieve Donard Nursery of Newcastle,
Co. Down (Hedging and Screening plants form a separate class) Messrs.
Treseders of Truro (Hedging etc. plants, and Soft Fruit, form separate
subdivisions)

Class II B In these lists there is further classification, making Climbing and
Wall plants, Conifers, Hedging and Screening Plants, Bamboos, etc. into
separate alphabetical groups: Messrs. Hillier of Winchester (Individual
catalogues issued for several main classes; with separate price lists in some

cases) Messrs. Jackman of Woking (Clematis a separate subdivision) Messrs. Pennell of Lincoln (Clematis a separate subdivision)

Class II C Here classification is carried still further, separating, for example, trees from shrubs, sometimes Evergreens from Deciduous, or making special classes of individual genera, e.g. Rhododendrons, Camellias: Messrs. Laxton of Huntingdon (Trees, Evergreens, separated) Messrs. Notcutts of Woodbridge (Trees separately from Shrubs) Messrs. Rogers of Pickering (Trees separately from Shrubs) Messrs. Waterers of Twyford (Separate genera of plants, Trees, subdivided, separately from Shrubs; Border plants and Rock Garden plants separately, etc.)

As with Seedsmen, the Nurseryman's catalogue of Class I derives from lists like that of Gerard. Classification into woody and herbaceous plants goes back as far as Lucas; Fruit Trees seem always to have formed a separate category. The detailed subdivision of classes, as with Class III of Seedsmen, derives from the work of Richard Weston and others in the 18th century, though it has roots which stretch back to the lists of Leonard Meager, 1670.

One feature of very many Seedsmen's catalogues is a concluding section of Requisites, Horticultural Sundries, Insecticides, Fertilizers and the like. This has a continuous history from the days of Lucas and beyond, and has grown from a single sentence enumerating items 'proper for the use of gardiners' to, in some cases (e.g. Messrs. Carters), a separate catalogue on its own. One singular circumstance deserves mention: the apparently total disappearance of the Garden Bass-Mat, formerly used not only for wrapping plants in transit, but for the protection of tender wall plants, fruit trees etc. in winter. Gardeners now are put to all kinds of makeshifts if they wish to protect plants that, in given conditions, are less than absolutely hardy: it seems a pity.

BIBLIOGRAPHY

ALTHOUGH A FEW CATALOGUES, and extracts from gardening accounts, of different periods have been published, there does not seem to have been any study of such lists as a form. In the main their use has been in connection with dates of introduction and, more especially, the appearance of named varieties of fruits and roses. The list of works which follows is, therefore, mainly an acknowledgment of help received from standard histories and from a few books used in the identification of species grown. References to particular lists and catalogues will be found in the Notes.

Allan, Mea. *The Tradescants* (1964)
Amherst, A. *A History of Gardening in England* (1895/1910)
Coats, A.M. *Flowers and their Histories* (1956/1968) *Garden Shrubs and their Histories* (1963) *The Quest for Plants* (1969)
Gorer, R. *The Development of Garden Flowers* (1970)
Green, D. *Gardener to Queen Anne* (1956)
Hadfield, M. *A History of British Gardening* (1969)
Hanmer, Sir T. *The Garden Book of Sir Thomas Hanmer* (1659), ed. I. Elstob (1933)
Jackson, B.D., ed. *A Catalogue of Plants cultivated in the Garden of John Gerard* (1876)
Johnson, G.W. *A History of English Gardening* (1829)
Lemmon, K. *The Covered Garden* (1962) *The Golden Age of Plant Hunters* (1968)
Loudon, J.C. *Arboretum et Fruticetum Britannicum* (1838), 8 vols. *Encyclopaedia of Plants* (ed. J.W. Loudon, 1866)
Phillips, H. *Sylva Florifera: The Shrubbery* (1823), 2 vols.
Rohde, E.S. *The Story of the Garden* (1932)
Royal Horticultural Society *Dictionary of Gardening* (2nd ed., 1956), 5 vols.
Thomas, G.S. *The Old Shrub Roses* (4th ed., 1963)
Webber, R. *The Early Horticulturists* (1968)
Weston, R. *Flora Anglicana . . . The English Flora*, and Supplement (1775, 1780) *The Universal Botanist and Nurseryman* (1770-1777), 4 vols.

NOTES TO THE TEXT

References have not been inserted in the text, as they interrupt the narrative. Instead, each note appears under the relevant page and has a clue-word prefixed.

INTRODUCTION

p. 1   MODERN LISTS — see Appendix VII
p. 2   MEDIAEVAL   GARDENERS — see   Bibliography: Amherst, Hadfield, Rohde
        YORK — *Register of the Freemen of the City of York*, ed. F. Collins (Surtees Society, XCVI for 1896, 1897), 21, 29, 32
        MUSIC — see *The New Oxford History of Music*, especially II (1954), 274-5, 285, 313
p. 3   BRAY — British Museum, Sloane MS. 282, ff. 167v-173v
        CHARLEMAGNE — Capitulary *De Villis*, lxx
        ROSEMARY — B.M., Sloane MS. 3215, f. 24v; the date is confirmed by a manuscript formerly in the possession of Mr. Dickson Wright, a photocopy of which was kindly lent to me by Dr. C.H. Talbot
p. 4   JOHN GARDENER — edited by A. Amherst in *Archaeologia*, LIV, 157-72; for the highly probable view that the verse treatise is based on an earlier Latin original in prose, see A.G. Rigg in *Notes and Queries*, CCXI (1966), 326-7
        'FROMOND' LIST — B.M., Sloane MS. 1201; see Appendix I
        WOLSEY,— J.H. Harvey in *Journal of the British Archaeological Association*, 3 ser., VIII (1943), 53
p. 5   HAMPTON COURT — Amherst, *History;* M. Sands, *The Gardens of Hampton Court* (1950)
        GERARD — See Bibliography, Jackson

CHAPTER I

p. 7   HANMER — see Bibliography
        ROSE — John Rose, *The English Vineyard Vindicated* (1666), copy in British Museum, 969.a.43
p. 8   MEAGER — Leonard Meager, *The English Gardener* (1670), copy in British Museum, 41.a.5; Garrle's list at 82-8; general lists, 208-16, 242-50
        FITZSTEPHEN — H.E. Butler in F.M. Stenton, *Norman London* (Historical Association Leaflets, Nos. 93, 94, 1934), 27
p. 9   MEAGER — *op. cit.*, 81-2 CHAUCER — *The Romaunt of the Rose*, Lines 1349-1400; *The Parlement of Foules*, lines 172-82; *The Knightes Tale*, lines 2919-23
p. 10   HANMER — see Bibliography; Ricketts' lists at 166-71
        REA — see Bibliography, Hadfield, 145
        COOK — copy in British Museum, 234.e.7

BROMPTON — British Museum, Harleian MS. 6273, ff. 50-6

p. 11 LUCAS — see Appendix II

TITHES — W.E. Tate, *The Parish Chest* (1946), 134-37; MS. Survey of Great Bookham by Thomas Clay, 1614, in Surrey Record Office, f. 13

PRIVET — formerly called 'Prim' or 'Primwort', probably shortened in pronunciation to 'Prinet', mistakenly printed as 'Priuet' and thus reaching its modern spelling

p. 12 DATES — R.E. Latham, *Revised Medieval Latin Word-List* (1965), 129

p. 13 LAWSON — *A New Orchard & Garden*, etc., ed. E.S. Rohde (1927), 77

1639 LIST — British Museum, Sloane MS. 95, f. 153

CHAPTER II

p. 14 PHILLIPS — see Bibliography, also *Flora Historica* (1824/1829), *The Companion for the Orchard* (1822/1831)

WESTON, LOUDON, JOHNSON — see Bibliography

FURBER — 1727 catalogues, copies in British Museum, C.112.aa.18; also in Bodleian Library, Oxford, Sherard 127

MOSS ROSE — *Floricultural Cabinet*, VI (1838), 281

FURBER — W. Blunt, *The Art of Botanical Illustration* (1950/1955), 134; a complete copy of Furber's *A Short Introduction to Gardening* (1733) is in British Museum, B.151(3.)

p. 15 LONDON & WISE — *The Retir'd Gard'ner* (1706), 92-3

LUCAS — see Appendix II

p. 16 MORRIS — Hugh Phillips, *Mid-Georgian London* (1964), 180

ROCQUE — Miss E.J. Willson in *A History of Fulham*, ed. P.D. Whitting (1970), 238

GERARD — see Bibliography, Jackson, xiv-xv

p. 17 LOOKER — the repeated statement that Looker was gardener to the Queen Dowager, though possibly correct, is not supported by the main documentary evidence. Henrietta Maria had finally left England in 1665 and died in 1669; Looker himself states that he was 'Gardener to Her Matie' in 1681, which can refer only to Catherine of Braganza (British Museum, Harleian MS. 6273, f. 50)

p. 20 WOODMAN — Ellison Papers, Gateshead Public Library

BLITH — see Joan Thirsk, 'Seventeenth-Century Agriculture and Social Change' in *The Agricultural History Review*, XVIII (1970), Supplement, 159

p. 22 LUPIN — 'Faba lupina' is illustrated in the early 15th-century series of drawings of medicinal plants grown in England in British Museum, Additional MS. 29301, f. 52

POLYANTHUS — see Bibliography, Hanmer, 90

FLORISTS' FLOWERS — on this subject see, above all, Sacheverell Sitwell, *Old Fashioned Flowers* (1939)

CHAPTER III

CHAPTER IV

the John Rylands Library, Manchester, Portico Library pamphlets formerly in the possession of the family of Leigh of Adlington

p. 38   SPACING — elaborate tables showing the number of trees per acre at various spacings have been inserted in manuscript in a copy of E. Hoppus, *Practical Measuring* (1827) in the York Minster Library. I am obliged to Mr. Bernard Barr for bringing this to my notice. A simplified table in print is prefixed to the catalogue of Forest Trees etc. issued by William. Falla and Co. of Gateshead in the 1820's (facsimile issued by Samuel Finney & Co. Ltd., 1925 — copy in Lindley Library, Royal Horticultural Society, 83.E (box).)
NURSERIES — D. Lysons, *The Environs of London,* 2nd ed. (1811), II part ii, 839-42

p. 39   WATTS — Lincolnshire Archives Office, Nelthorpe IX/1/92-4
SEATON DELAVAL — Northumberland Record Office, 2 DE.34/6

p. 40   MALCOLM — copies of the 1771 catalogue (which was priced at 1s.) are in British Museum, 443.d.27(6.) and B.81(3.); a copy of the much enlarged and modernized edition of 1778 (price 2s.) is T.251(1.); also copies of both in Lindley Library, Royal Horticultural Society, 42.1 C.15 a; 43.2 B(back) 4a
GORDON, DERMER — a copy of their catalogue is in British Museum, 1489.t.42
LODDIGES — a copy of their catalogue of 1777 is in British Museum, B.67(4.)

p. 41   KILNWICK — Beverley, East Riding Record Office, DDGR.42/28, 38/163
PONTEY — ibid., 43/2

p. 42   GARRAWAY — ibid., 38/68
MIDDLEWOOD — copy in Library of University Botanic Garden, Cambridge
WEBB — copies in British Museum, B.66(1.); R.H.S., 43.2 B.3(back); Bodleian (Johnson Collection)
CLARKE — W. Roberts in *Gardeners Chronicle,* LXII (1917), 135-6

p. 43   BRUNTON — copies in British Museum, B.116(3.); Birmingham Reference Library, Cat. no. 57720, where the two later issues are Cat. nos. 243006, 72300
MACKIE — catalogue, Norwich Public Library
LAUDER — catalogue, Library of University Botanic Garden, Cambridge
THOMPSON, PERFECT, TELFORD — catalogues, ibid.; Perfect 1788, Durham Co. Record Office

p. 44   BACKHOUSE — catalogues, R.H.S., 83.E (box)

CHAPTER V

p. 46   BORTHWICK — catalogue printed in James Justice, *British Gardener's Calendar* (1759), 401-12. I am much indebted to Miss P. Minay for a copy of this

p. 47   FERGUSON — Tweeddale MSS. in National Library of Scotland
CLEPHANE — T. Donnelly, 'Arthur Clephane, Edinburgh Merchant

and Seedsman, 1706-30', in *Agricultural History Review,* XVIII part ii, (1970), 151-60

KENNEDY & LEE — copies of their catalogue of 1774 are in British Museum, B.67(3.); British Museum (Natural History), and Hammersmith Public Library

LUKER & SMITH — catalogue, British Museum, B.67(5.)

p. 48   LUKER — entries from Parish Registers of St. Luke Old Street in great card index, Society of Genealogists, London

CURTIS, catalogue, British Museum, 968.a.5

COLVILL — catalogue, British Museum, 07028.k.22

POCKET-BOOK — British Museum, Sloane MS. 2354

KEW — Windsor Castle, The Royal Archives, nos. 55512, 55517, 55544, 55546, 55557, 55584, 55624-25

p. 49   CLARKE — catalogue in Lindley Library, R.H.S., 43.2 B(back) 10.e

p. 50   FALLA — Durham County Record Office, D/Sa/E 747.4, 5, 17; also Northumberland Record Office, 2 DE.34/6/13, 14; catalogue among Baker-Baker papers, The Prior's Kitchen, The College, Durham. A later catalogue issued by William Falla & Co. in the 1820's was reprinted in facsimile in 1925 by Samuel Finney & Co. of Newcastle-upon-Tyne, Falla's successors in the business, to whom I am indebted for a copy

p. 51   PENNELL — Lincolnshire Archives Office, see *Archivists' Report* 20 (1968-69), 59-62; Messrs. Pennell retain their set of catalogues.

EPILOGUE

p. 53   SMITH — *York Courant,* 7 and 14 April 1730; the files of the paper are held at York City Library, which has indexed them in great detail

INTRODUCTIONS — for the dates of introductions of important species the best guides are those by Miss Alice Coats — see Bibliography

p. 55   CAMELLIA —— Coats, *Garden Shrubs,* 51

p. 57   HANMER — *op. cit.,* 115, 140

CORRIGENDUM

Evidence has come to light showing that the story of the Strand Bridge seed-shop (above, pp. 16, 66) can be corrected and amplified. Edward Fuller was still in charge in 1719 (J. Woolridge, *Systema Horti–Culturae,* 4th ed., 271); but must have died before 1726, when Mrs. Arabella Fuller was selling a slightly expanded list of seeds and plants (Benjamin Townsend, *The Complete Seedsman,* 1st ed., title–page and full list printed at pp. 78–82; copy in Lindley Library, R.H.S., 42. 1a. 7). Mrs. Fuller presumably remarried, for an engraved billhead shows Arabella Morris 'at the Naked Boy and Three Crowns' in 1748. The bill was receipted by E. Clarke, no doubt her manager and successor (British Museum, Department of Prints and Drawings, Heal Collection, large cards).

INDEX

This index includes all names and main subjects in the text and in the introductory notes to each appendix; the names of plants in the reprinted lists are not indexed. For biographical material see the collected entries Catalogues and Gardeners . . . For the Plates see separate index at end.

INDEX TO PLATES

The plants illustrated on Furber's plates provide a remarkable conspectus of some 400 species and varieties grown at Kensington by the leading nurseryman of 1730. Modern generic names have been supplied as far as possible. The abbreviations are: Fr — Frontispiece; and the Months Ja, Fe, Mr, Ap, My, Jn, Jl, Au, Se, Oc, No, De; the numbers are those on the plates.

Vinca — see Periwinkle
Viola — see Pansy, Violet
Violet, Double blue (Viola
  odorata), Ja 7
Virgin's Bower (Clematis),
  Double purple, Au 33
——— Spanish, De 31
Vitex — see Agnus Castus

Wallflower (Cheiranthus cheiri),
  Mr 24, Ap 7, De 27
Wisteria — see Kidney-bean Tree

Zisolo from Genoa (Zizyphus
  jujuba), Au 26
Zygophyllum — see Caper Bean